Michael B. Kennedy
W6962 Century Rd
Greenwood, WI 54437

THE FOUR PAGES
OF THE SERMON

THE FOUR PAGES
OF THE SERMON

A Guide to Biblical Preaching

Paul Scott Wilson

ABINGDON PRESS
Nashville

THE FOUR PAGES OF THE SERMON

Copyright © 1999 by Abingdon Press

This book is printed on recycled, acid-free paper.

Library of Congress Cataloging-in-Publication Data
Wilson, Paul Scott, 1949-
    The four pages of the sermon : a guide to biblical preaching /
Paul Scott Wilson.
        p. cm.
    ISBN 0-687-02395-5 (alk. paper)
    1. Bible—Homiletical use. 2. Preaching. I. Title.
    BS534.5.W55 1999
    251—dc21   98-52200
                                                                          CIP

Scripture quotations, unless otherwise indicated, are from the New Revised Standard Version Bible, copyright © 1989, by the Division of Christian Education of the National Council of the Churches of Christ in the United States of America.

Scripture quotations noted KJV are from the King James Version of the Bible.

Scripture quotations marked (NLT) are taken from the *Holy Bible,* New Living Translation, copyright © 1996. Used by permission of Tyndale House Publishers, Inc., Wheaton, Illinois 60189. All rights reserved.

Scripture quotations noted RSV are from the Revised Standard Version of the Bible, copyright 1946, 1952, 1971 by the Division of Christian Education of the National Council of Churches of Christ in the USA. Used by permission.

Excerpts taken from *The Library of Distinctive Sermons,* © 1996, by Questar Direct, are reprinted by permission of Multnomah Publishers, Inc.

00 01 02 03 04 05 06 07 08—10 9 8 7 6 5 4 3 2

MANUFACTURED IN THE UNITED STATES OF AMERICA

CONTENTS

ACKNOWLEDGMENTS

I dedicate this to John M. Rottman, a friend who faithfully pestered me to write more on what I teach, and to all my students in the Toronto School of Theology, in both basic degree and doctoral programs, from whom I receive so much. Thanks are also due to a number of other people, including students and faculty of Wesley Theological Seminary in Washington, D. C., of the D. Min. in Preaching Program at McCormick Seminary in Chicago, Illinois, and of The Eastern Baptist Theological Seminary in Philadelphia, Pennsylvania, for the privilege of delivering the Wilmer C. Swartley Lectures; to members of the Anglican Diocese of Calgary, Alberta; and to the staff and participants at the 1998 Preacher's Conference at The King's University College in Edmonton, Alberta, where I had the opportunity of testing many of these ideas. Principal Roger Hutchinson of Emmanuel College and the Board of Regents of Victoria University in the University of Toronto provided ongoing support and encouragement for which I am grateful. Special thanks are also owing to Stephen Farris, Marie Goodyear, Gyeong-Jin Kim, Hank Langknecht, Sarah Martin, Doug McKenzie, Mike Rattee, Kyung-Sik Ryoo, Todd Townsend, and Reinder Van Til. As usual, my greatest and deepest debt is to Deanna for her ongoing love, good humor, encouragement, and nurture; and for her willingness to share her preaching journey and life with me.

CHAPTER ONE

Movies, Pages, and God

My father is a minister so our family was always in church. After worship, the empty church presided over the long hour when everyone else had gone home, while I waited with my twin sister and older sister for Mom and Dad to drive us home for lunch—time I spent wandering through the building looking at the fresh drawings in the school rooms, or in the sanctuary trying out the pulpit microphone, or in the gymnasium. During the week the church was where we had choir practice or Scout meetings, and where we played hide and seek with friends while waiting for a ride home. Church came home with us and sat down in conversation with us at the dinner table, played hymns on Mom's piano during the week, and was often on the telephone making calls that I overheard from secret hiding places; and on Saturdays, church was clacking on my father's old Underwood typewriter as he prepared his sermon in the study. Church tucked us into bed at night and was usually up doing God's business by the time we had spread the brown sugar on our oatmeal at breakfast. Growing up with the church never far away: I moved from loving it to hating it; from leaving it as a late teenager to coming back to it as an adult. And for many years now I have been loving it once more, loving when it is at its best and aching when it is not. I love the preaching of the church when it is good, and I love trying to make it better.

Every age must find its own way to revitalize the preaching task. I first learned the importance of narrative for preaching at the dinner table, hearing about peoples' lives, and listening to my father preach on Sundays. Sometimes I learned more about the faith from the stories than from the sermon's well-crafted points. Narrative the-

9

ory influenced my own preaching and eventually informed my teaching. I have heard hundreds and hundreds of class and Sunday sermons, listening as often for what is missing as for what is present. Gradually I found that I moved beyond narrative, not leaving it behind, but being more attentive to those things like theology and the role of God that had taken a back seat while that new important paradigm made its mark. Yet telling stories was a helpful way for a generation of preachers to imagine how to avoid making the Word of God sound boring—a form of heresy worth avoiding.

I received an important insight when I heard several experienced oral storytellers tell stories that for me verged on boredom. These speakers did not make the common errors: plots too linear, characters too flat, or emotions too singular. Rather, their language had little sensory appeal; there was little to see or taste or touch.

Ever since childhood, when our family bought its first television set (with some discussion over whether it was proper to watch on Sundays), I have been fascinated by movies. Movies are a symbol of our audiovisual culture, and I am finding movie making to be better than telling stories as an analogy for preaching. Most of us preachers have never made a movie in the formal sense, but we have seen or held videocameras and the concept of movie making still holds mystery and intrigue, in spite of the excesses of Hollywood.

Movie making is a hobby easy to conceive. Yet movie making as a method of sermon preparation is not as easy to imagine. Instead, we unconsciously may invoke many of the hard-won lessons of essay writing and apply them to our sermon composition. Some of these lessons are good for sermons, like the rule that each paragraph should be about one idea and only one idea, and that an entire essay should have just one overarching theme. For the spoken word, however, we must discard or modify other essay rules: do not repeat yourself; use as many big words as possible; give only the facts and no extra detail; avoid descriptive material; eliminate conversations. As long as we prepare our sermons by conceiving of our task as equivalent to writing an essay, as typing, or perhaps even as speaking into a computer that turns our thoughts into words on a page, the essay concept will influence our preaching, often in negative ways, because we will unwittingly apply the rules of writing, which are not always effective for spoken presentations. We still need to use good grammar and sentence structure—thus writing a sermon manuscript can be an important discipline. However, the spoken word, not the essay, is the goal.

Given that many churches are in a period of declining membership, such a change may be important. Yet if we shift the mental image of sermon composition from essay writing to movie making, we will see a tremendous change in how we arrange our thoughts. If preaching is to reach youth and teenagers especially, it needs an approach like this movie making idea. We still need to be cautious and moderate, especially concerning descriptive passages and conversations. For instance, brief visual details that quickly paint a scene are better than long descriptions, and short snippets of conversation that allow a character to come to life are preferred to long monologues or dialogues. Thus, if we imagine that we are directing a film we allow ourselves to think and compose sermons in a visual manner—which is how most of us think in any case. More than simply telling plots, or becoming one character in a narrative, we will create entire worlds that address the senses, the mind, and the heart. When I speak of movie making to students in my classes and preachers around North America, I sense their own excitement at the possibilities. I hope that this book can communicate to readers some of the excitement that I feel.

Why then does the title of this book make no mention of movies? Why does it speak of pages instead? What do movies and pages have in common? I would have loved to stay with one metaphor or the other, in the same way that I teach that sermons should have just one dominant image. But a book is longer than a sermon and I found a single image impossible, given the complexity of the preacher's task in the current age. I resolved the dilemma by recognizing that even movies need scripts, and scripts have pages.

Moreover, web pages on the internet provide another model for combining movies and pages. Some web pages are so elaborate that they will run a movie clip to teach or demonstrate a particular subject or product when the viewer double-clicks on the relevant box. In other words, the webpage contains both words and pictures, information and movies, which is a good model for the sermon. Readers of this book do not need to be computer literate to understand the appeal of the web page as effective communication. Here, the web page concept offers a way of combining two essential metaphors for the preaching task, making movies and composing discrete pages of a sermon. Movies address the need for creative imagination and they model its movement. Pages address the need for theology to shape the sermon and describe how best this can be accomplished. Together they suggest a new model for preaching in this new millennium—instead of three points we may speak of four pages. Instead of a two-part structure we can use use a four-part structure.

Why four pages and not some other number? First, four pages corresponds to the number of basic theological stances found in most sermons. Second, as much as students and preachers become excited about making movies, they also become excited about the simplicity of having only four pages to write, and about the possibility of breaking sermon preparation into four manageable assignments for four days in the week. They like the practical implications of working on a metaphorical page, of knowing what the creative goals are for that page, and of having theological standards by which to measure it. They like the ease of being able to refer to what a preacher did on Page Two of his or her sermon; and of being able to talk about the flow of a sermon according to its pages, in whatever order they might appear.

Hopes and Dreams

I have some dreams for this writing project: First, I wish to encourage preachers to be biblical, grounding their sermons in the biblical text, and allowing the text to "speak" the sermon. Second, I want to encourage preachers to be more attentive to God, to foster hope in congregations. These goals are something to get excited about. It is as surprising as it is discouraging to discover how many sermons across denominational boundaries encourage trust in human resources and how few focus on God or encourage faith in God in more than minimal ways. This new vision of preaching promises renewal, a recovery of a profound sense of God's grace and of the joy of faith.

Third, I wish to present in the simplest possible way ideas that have kept me loving the teaching of preaching for over eighteen years. When I began this project I asked myself, what has worked best in my teaching? I have written this book for the church and laid out the preaching path as clearly as possible, without, I hope, oversimplifying the issues. I have kept footnotes to a minimum. Readers seeking greater detail, background, and range can turn to my *The Practice of Preaching* (Abingdon Press, 1995). There, and in sources by other authors, students may find, among other things, detailed explanation and exercises for the exegetical process.[1] I limit my focus here to actual sermon composition, spread over several days of the week—the best means I know of stewarding a preacher's precious resources of time and energy for faithful proclamation.

Fourth, I invite readers into a homiletics classroom to rethink the purpose and practice of sermon composition. Some of us preachers have had no formal homiletics training. Others have had instruction only in the theology of preaching or in biblical exegesis and exposition; or received lessons in sermon form and structure; or had guidance on how best to use our bodies and voices for preaching. However, no one has considered in detail how the sermon form we choose influences the theology we preach and so affects everything we say. Preachers have tended to think that sermon form is secondary to sermon content or even that form is largely irrelevant; yet, ineffective sermon form pervades and distorts the theological content like a computer virus that infects every file. Many preachers today use trusted sermon forms, unaware that the nature of the good news they preach is largely predetermined by the forms they follow. As a result, the gospel of Jesus Christ suffers. I have devised a manageable way of addressing the depth structure of sermons by dividing sermon preparation into four separate theological tasks. I offer readers a reliable way of reconceiving the task of proclamation by suggesting that the form of the sermon be conceived as four theological pages. The content of the four pages comes from the four kinds of material we can include in our sermons: basically, we are confined to talking about (1) sin and brokenness in the biblical world, (2) sin and brokenness in our world (3) grace in the biblical world, and (4) grace in our world. One could ask, of course, where history fits in, the period between the Bible and now. History, doctrine, and tradition are part of each of our four pages; only on a rare occasions should a sermon become heavily historical, thus to conceive of history as separate pages seems unwise.

The two-part structure many preachers have been taught, from exposition to application, like a deflated front tire on a car, tends to steer the entire sermon towards the shoulder of the road and a theology of human responsibility. A four-part structure that ventures an additional movement in exposition and application, keeps the sermon securely headed toward a theology of grace, highlighting the centrality of what God has actually accomplished in Jesus Christ on the cross.

Finally, I hope that students will learn to love preaching and that cynical preachers will fall in love with preaching again; that their efforts to grow will be richly rewarded with a renewed sense of the power of the Holy Spirit speaking through their labors; that their congregations will grow in faith and ministry. Creative communication can facilitate the hearing of God's Word. Untutored imagination is worth very little: as a product of free-association thinking, it lacks direction and purpose. It is also hit and miss: sometimes it works and sometimes it fails, and the preacher is not able to predict the result. However, given appropriate theological structures and guidelines for the sermon, we can use our imaginations in effective and reliable ways for the service of God.

The sermon's four pages represent distinct theological functions that the preacher can arrange in various orders, producing different models. Here, in order to present them for purposes of homiletical practice, I offer them first in one order that makes theological sense and fosters hope. Later I offer other ways to arrange the pages. I am convinced that beginning students do best to concentrate on one primary method that is theological and adaptable to many forms, rather than to learn many diverse methods of varying strengths, and learn none adequately.

I hope that experienced preachers will receive this book as an affirmation of some of the best practices they have been using and will also find here an invitation to improve other sermon practices.

Two Deep Dreams

What if people in the church pews on Sunday were to view the content of our sermons as movies that they are seeing in their minds as we speak? What if we were to evaluate our past sermons as biblical and theological films, if we were to play the videotapes in our homiletics classroom—not the videotapes of us standing in the pulpit actually preaching, but the videotapes of the pictures we are presenting through our words—what would we learn? I see two big recurring problems. The first problem is that preachers need help making pictures and appealing to a full range of the senses. At one extreme are text-centered preachers whose language is so far from being concrete that the only drama congregations experience is that of pages being read and turned—there is nothing for them to "see" besides the preacher in the pulpit. On the other extreme are preachers who equate creativity with focusing the videocamera from place to place or zooming from person to person—there is much to "see" but nothing connects. The Holy Spirit must work hard with both kinds of sermons to be able to speak to the hearts and minds of needy listeners and a needy world. Our question should always be, what can I do better to help the work of the Holy Spirit?

The second major problem in many of our sermonic films is the apparent absence of God. Appropriate theological emphasis is lacking, especially as seen in joyless sermons. Recent changes in sermon form help us to be better communicators but they do not reach the deeper theological problem: congregations need to be led to a reliance upon God. For this, the movie metaphor alone cannot be the solution. Lack of joy in preaching requires a solution that unites form and theology.

The Metaphor of Four Pages for Sermon Evaluation

Anyone who has read sermons from history knows how notoriously difficult they are to compare and evaluate; this is one reason that scholars in biblical studies, theology, and even history generally ignore them. Even sermons in our own time seem to operate by their own rules. When we seek to have a conversation about them, we observe whether a point form or narrative form is dominant, and we may have deeper discussion on how a text, doctrine, or story is used. However, we lack common language to move beyond these comments. When it comes time to make comparative evaluations from one sermon to another (something I discourage with class sermons) or to assess theologically the ability of sermons to encourage faith and empower action, it is as though a bell rings in the corridor to mark the end of class and the conversation is over.

The four pages I have devised identify four basic kinds of theological focus; this allows us to talk about any sermon theologically, which we have not always been able to do well in the past. Of course, I use *page* here not as a literal page but as a metaphor for theological function and appropriate creative endeavor. Four pages are four distinct moments of preaching. We can discuss and analyze each

15

of the four pages with clarity and thus describe with some accuracy what needs to happen on any page. We can use the pages to sharpen presentation of biblical and theological material in our sermons. Further, the pages can be a guide to greater creativity and imagination, for they provide specific focus for creative endeavor that helps prevent imagery from becoming excessive, stories from going astray, and doctrines from becoming mere turbid or turgid discourse.

We can also arrange these four pages in a sequence that ensures, as much as this is humanly possible, that preaching fosters faith in God and joyful lives of service and mission. The sequence in which I present them is somewhat arbitrary, given all of the possibilities. However, since I must present them in a sequence, I choose one that makes the best theological sense, given the purposes and objectives of preaching.

Content of the Four Pages

Page One I devote to trouble and conflict in the Bible—in other words, as preachers, we consider the Bible in its own time. On Page Two we look at similar sin or human brokenness in our time. Page Three returns to the Bible, this time to identify what God is doing in or behind the biblical text as it opens the story of good news. And on Page Four we point to God graciously at work in our world, particularly in relationship to those situations named on Page Two.

Visualizing the four pages in sequence can help us to compose our sermons and prepare a script for the movie we will make. To conceive of the four pages as having an organic or theological flow from one to four, is to conceive of a four-page sermon model. Not every sermon need follow this movement from trouble in the biblical text and our world to grace in the biblical text and our world. A colleague consistently follows this pattern: Page Two (trouble in our world), Page One (trouble in the biblical text), Page Three (grace in the Bible: what God did), Page Four (grace in our world: what God does). How we arrange the pages, and whether or not we use all of them in any one sermon, these four theological functions present the basic options available to preachers. Later, once each page is understood and demonstrated, we can reshuffle the pages and vary them in other ways. Though I favor one sequence as normative, I present not one option, but as many as the number of possible variations and arrangements.

What I am presenting is also to some extent beyond method: here are tools we can use to analyze, evaluate, and improve the theology and creativity of sermons, whatever method is followed. Well-meaning preachers often inadvertently communicate bad theology, or communicate theology badly; or they fail adequately to represent the Bible, our contemporary situation, or God. Often congregations encourage preachers to improve their preaching, assuming that they know how to make the necessary changes. Preachers may be told: preach more narrative, or preach more doctrine; yet these instructions do not necessarily result in sermons that provide what is missing. I hope that preachers will employ the functions of the four pages as a means to evaluate their own sermons and to determine how best to improve their labors.

Not every sermon corresponds to four physical pages. One sermon literally may be ten pages long and may never get beyond theological Page One; another may begin on Page Two; another might skip Page Three or Page Four. As preachers, we should be able to go back over recent sermons and determine quickly what page or pages need more attention. We need not discount our previous sermons as ineffective vehicles of God's Word if some of these functions or pages are missing. Still, if one or more of these pages is consistently absent, or is consistently not given adequate focus and development, at least from a biblical and theological perspective, there may be room for us to grow.

The Four Pages in sequence present a model and thus may seem like yet another misguided attempt to use form as a solution to deeper homiletical problems. Moreover, four pages may seem short to those who preach for thirty or forty minutes, and long to others who preach for less than ten. But whether the sermon is long or short is not the point, and form on its own is not the issue. I am not speaking of four literal pages. The four pages are four biblical and theological functions that I am proposing to divide the sermon, whatever its length, into four consecutive tasks of roughly equal duration that I claim are ideal for proclaiming good news. This approach is simple: the work of writing the four pages is spread over the days of the week. It is biblical: the Bible is our authority to preach and cannot be wisely by-passed. It is imaginative: it defines and assigns specific creative tasks for each page and day. It is theological: it recognizes that preaching must be rooted in and strengthened by dialogue with tradition and it provides a framework and methodology for accomplishing this. It is pastoral: it links local and global needs with the love of God who claims all people as beloved children. It is evangelical in the broadest sense: it embraces concerns in many churches for spiritual renewal and the joyful proclamation of the gospel. Here preachers may find opportunity for a renewal of preaching, whether they are ordained or lay, experienced pastors or students in an introductory preaching class in seminary.

Our culture is becoming increasingly reliant on oral and aural media and less on the written word. Thus, to advocate a page-centered approach to preaching may still seem odd. To speak of the sermon as four acts, or functions, or episodes, or moments might better reinforce the auditory nature of preaching. Still, the page is not about to die soon: as long as computer printouts are needed, and as long as preachers need to jot notes, the printed page will be present. More important, faithful preaching is never off the cuff, and the need for well-prepared sermons is more urgent now, in this period when too many churches are experiencing declining membership, than it ever has been.

The purpose here also is not to argue whether the sermon should be composed on paper and delivered from a manuscript. Four consecutive "pages" are an ideal norm for communication of good news, for the following reasons. Two initial pages identify the trouble in the Bible and our world. Two additional pages identify what God graciously has done and is doing in relationship to that trouble, again in the Bible and our world. Certain theological and imaginative functions are appropriate to each page. Such a model makes efficient use of preparation time because it provides a valuable structure for thought and for organizing material. One does not need to waste time wondering where various kinds of material belong. Once one has composed the sermon, its simple structure can be an aid to memory in delivery. Ironically, the four-page model facilitates getting the sermon off the page and into the lives of God's children as we prepare for the coming week.

Sociological Reasons for a New Approach to Preaching

Why do we need this four-page approach? Numerous factors in church and society have changed the nature of ordered ministry and put pressures on preachers. A number of important sociological shifts can be identified:

1. Great upheavals have taken place in society since earlier times when the Bible and the preacher had uncontested authority. Postmodern society has no shortage of information and poses challenges to most authority, including that of the church, Scripture, and the preacher. In this climate, truth is perceived as relative. What used to work in preaching is no longer necessarily effective.

2. Time pressures on individual and family life have increased, reducing the amount of time and energy people have available for the church. Volunteerism is down. Education programs of the church reach fewer people, increasing the burden on the worship service for both instruction and spiritual encounter.

3. The nature of ordered ministry has changed. The preacher faces increased pressures and is less often conceived as the central executive officer. Key decisions are often shared in time-consuming committees and there are important benefits to this. But more people expect to be involved in making decisions, in leading worship, and in leading other church events, all of which requires coordination of busy schedules. Administrative tasks at the level of the local and regional church have expanded to include difficult personnel issues and exhausting and costly legal disputes. On top of this, married clergy are expected to take more of a role in the rearing of their families than in previous eras.

4. Less time is available to preach the sermon in some denominations because the service involves more music, more Scripture readings, more frequent celebration of Communion or Eucharist, and the increased participation of laity and children.

5. Historical-critical and literary approaches to biblical texts, combined with increased use of the lectionary, have helped many denominations move away from preaching verses of Scripture taken out of context and recover more complete literary scriptural units. But in using these approaches and relying on the lectionary, preachers may have been lulled into a false complacency, as if the goal were to preach the biblical text as a literary unit, or develop a fascinating image or metaphor from that text, or preach the biblical plot, or introduce listeners to

some character in the text, when in fact these things are not goals but means to serve preaching God. Recovery of an historically reliable text, or a literary interpretation of it, is no substitute for discerning for yourself what the text says about God.

6. At the same time, theological approaches to the Bible have been in decline since the biblical theology movement came under criticism and only now are showing signs of recovery, for instance, in the work of Brevard Childs.[2] Preachers have lacked guidance in how to preach Jesus Christ. Some preachers sought to remove the offense of the gospel by becoming politically correct and avoiding the offense of Christ. Others avoided the authority of Scripture by pursuing the historical Jesus behind the text, as if the original form of the text were more central for preaching. Still others thought that in preaching the biblical text they had already preached Christ.

7. Important gains have been made in homiletics with narrative: biblical stories now stand on their own without being reduced to propositions; stories now communicate people's experience where previously generalized reflection on experience was common; and many individuals and groups who had been excluded from positions of privilege in society and were previously silenced are now being heard. But homiletics itself has given much less attention to explicit theological matters than is warranted.[3]

Theological Reasons for a Change

Preaching has been dominated by sermons constructed in three points; but I would argue that four pages rather than three points is a more appropriate structure for this new millennium. I propose the four pages as a worthy norm for sermons for one key reason: God is missing in many of our sermons. It may be that God is missing from the center of our own lives at times and we need to pay more attention to caring for our mind body and spirit in the midst of daily life. But I want to focus on the results for the church when God is absent from our sermons. Sermons are less joyful than they ought to be. Given the good news of the gospel and all that God has accomplished on our behalf in Jesus Christ, joy seems reasonable to expect. Why then are sermons often glum not only in the so-called liberal or mainline traditions, but also in the so-called conservative or evangelical traditions, where the emphasis ought to be on joy? Churches on opposing ends of the theological spectrum have real differences, yet they are distressingly alike in this regard.

The preacher who focuses mainly on improved individual relationships with Jesus Christ is little different from the one who preaches social justice week after week. Each puts the burden of responsibility on the congregation; each lists essential shoulds, musts, and have-tos, and appropriately indicates the trouble facing humanity for failing to meet God's will. So far so good, but sadly, both tend to stop there. Congregations have little problem getting to Good Friday and the cross with such preaching. They do not get as easily to Easter and the empty tomb, or to Pentecost. From a theological perspective, self-reliance is a sure recipe for disaster. God's grace alone is what saves us. Yet many preachers persist in preaching messages that proclaim our condemnation as humans, for they sentence us to the limitations of our own accomplishments. For preaching to change, preachers need to get God in the viewfinder of the videorecorder as they prepare their sermons.

While most of us have been taught about grace and speak about it, and all of us have experienced it, few of us have been taught how to preach it effectively.[4] Many preachers fear preaching grace lest they "let their people off the hook," so to speak. Others fear having less than the full sermon to discuss complex issues. Others fear talking about God's grace lest they take a risk and are wrong. Still others fear sounding sentimental, romantic, superficial, or sickly sweet; they fear that to preach good news will appear "to make everything all better" when that is not what we understand by our faith. As a result, preachers tend to convict their listeners, and they often preach as though the resurrection of Christ makes no difference to the world.

Not only is God missing in many of our sermons, there is a second problem. We have inherited forms of preaching that have served previous generations well. But they did not ask, any more than we generally do, whether good news must sound like good news. Yet how can the gospel not be good news? As a result they were little better than we are in proclaiming grace, yet we often continue to use their homiletical methods. But since society is now putting pressure on the church, and churchgoers have less time for church, many churches, regardless of theological position, are facing decline in membership. Many people decide against the church simply on the basis of what they see on television or in the news. Clearly something is wrong. However, before we put too much blame on society, perhaps we should set our own houses in order. In part this means that preaching needs to foster faith and hope and love. Preaching needs to identify what is wrong, but it cannot stop at guilt and responsibility. It needs to get back to God.

A third problem is that, because God is missing from many sermons, or makes only a cameo appearance, much of what God has done in the life, death, and resurrection of Jesus Christ becomes irrelevant to how many Christians view the world. Exactly what has God accomplished? This world-changing event should make all the difference for daily life. What was required has been supplied by God and is not just up to us. What was needed God has done. God places no demand on us humans that God does not enable us to meet.

True, we live under the consequences of our sin, our lack of forgiveness, and our failures to act in love. And the ongoing brokenness, sin, and suffering of the world continue; each day more children are born in crack houses and other desperate situations of abuse and poverty. But we also live under the unmerited and wondrous sufficiency of the grace of God, who meets us in our inability to do what is required and, having fulfilled all righteousness on the cross and in the resurrection, lavishly pours upon us the gift of the Holy Spirit. Men and women discover God's power beyond their own abilities, as God helps them change their lives or care for the sick and homeless.

Grace does not cancel the reality of human sin and the need for change. Easter does not obliterate Good Friday, although it puts it in a different perspective. Both are true—they exist in a tension, the final outcome of which has been determined. God alone is the final word. Here, between these two inescapable realities of merited trouble and unmerited yet fully sufficient grace, Paul tells Christ's followers to "work out your own salvation with fear and trembling, for it is God who is at work in you, enabling you both to will and to work for his good pleasure" (Philippians 2:12-13).

In the preaching of most churches, we could be excused for thinking that little was accomplished on the cross for it stands primarily as a memorial to underscore the depth of human sin and the necessity of human change. I call these sermons, 'sermons from

Golgotha,' for in them we view the empty tomb only in the distance, if we glimpse it at all. The emphasis remains merely on human action to rectify what is wrong, though God long ago determined we were inadequate to the task. As the Bible so clearly states, human actions on their own inevitably lead to Good Friday.

This human responsibility perspective is seductive because, of course, it is true. We are sinners; we are responsible for straying from God's purpose for us; we must change. Yet this is not quite good news, though we often confuse it with the gospel. How can it be good news if upon our own we will fail? As Paul said, "For I do not do the good I want, but the evil I do not want is what I do" (Romans 7:19). True, the drug addict must stop taking drugs, the tax cheat must be honest, the greedy must be generous, the promiscuous must be chaste, the powerful must be humble, the warmakers must be peacemakers, the sinners must repent. Each of these instructions contains a whiff of good news. Yet if, as preachers, we stop here, then we omit the good news, which is the power of God's love in Christ over all powers, even death. Something died with Christ on the cross, the power of our sin over us, that in his divinity Christ took upon himself. It was the sin of the old self and the power of oppression to have the last say. Good news is not just an idea for our intellectual contemplation. The Holy Spirit acts with power in people's lives not just to make them receptive to God's Word but to continue Christ's liberating ministry. Preaching and the sacraments serve as the effective gift of this power—God chooses to meet us humans right now while we are yet sinners (Romans 5:8). The sermon makes God's new reality present in the world. This is the good news we celebrate.

There is yet a fourth dimension of our problem. In most of our sermons, we allow few signs of God's work in the world. Our people may hear about God's will, and we may tell them that God cares and understands and knows their suffering. But where do listeners witness God stooping with a loaf of bread to feed the one who hungers, or picking up the child felled by a land mine, or bringing world leaders to a peace table? In faith we affirm that God does this. Where in the sermon do people see God acting, doing something that makes a difference in the problems of world, much less to the woman who has been abused, or neighbors who have just lost their jobs, or teenagers who have gone with the wrong crowd? Either God is active and the center of all life, working for the good of all people everywhere, or God is passive and irrelevant. Preachers should be prepared to make bold claims in faith about where God is acting in the world.

For most of us at times, God's presence is not as obvious as we might wish. When I was a child, on cold winter nights I used to be able to see the northern lights, or aurora borealis, in the sky to the north of the city. I used to wonder why God did not just write in the heavens for all to see, in big letters, I AM GOD. There are many adults, as well as children, who wonder why God does not make God's presence a little more evident. However, writing in the sky would not necessarily convince people. Some would think the letters were written by a plane as part of a hoax. Others would think a UFO was responsible; many people would sooner believe in aliens, with no evidence, than in God, whose signs are everywhere without being obvious to everyone.[5]

Throughout the history of Israel and continuing to our time, God acts on behalf of all people; the sun shines and the rain falls on the just and the unjust (Matthew 5:45). God's intervention in history in Jesus Christ is a unique act through which we, in faith, are able to discern God's lively concern for all people. For those who have eyes to see, God's vital acts of vulnerable love are to be found even in the midst of great suffering and evil. God does not remain aloof from the human dilemma, whatever our experience may be in this regard. We may encourage people to have a relationship with a God, who has already made a difference to their lives and is the source of all goodness. If we who are preachers are unable to point to God at work, who will? If God is not acting in the world, if Christ is not risen, we have nothing to proclaim.

A fifth problem remains: as preachers, we are not doing what we could to assist the work of the Holy Spirit in many sermons, and people could be relying more upon God in their lives because of our preaching. Good news is often missing. God is often missing. God could be dead. Preachers who regularly leave sermon preparation until the last moment, or who resist preparation, claiming instead to rely upon the Holy Spirit for inspiration in the pulpit, might keep in mind the example of Jesus. When the devil took him to the pinnacle of the temple, he refused the temptation to jump and to be upheld by the angels and said, "Do not put the Lord your God to the test" (Luke 4:12). Many preachers by contrast, take the leap, and call upon God for miraculous intervention, when common sense is required along with faithful reliance upon the Holy Spirit through adequate preparation during the week.

The bottom line is this: proclamation of the gospel is something that God does through the Holy Spirit. But that does not spare us from the need to help God as much as we can, to ensure that God's good news is communicated effectively. While in some ways the following statement may seem too simple, it is generally true: good news should be experienced as good news. To claim "this is good news even if it does not sound like it" is to invite disbelief and foster continued decline in some church memberships. A simple principle may guide preaching: the congregation should leave the worship service with more, not less, hope, faith, courage, love, and joy than they had when they entered. Christians are called to be a people of hope and every Sunday we are to celebrate the resurrection. Celebration of life before God is one of the great purposes of worship. Our goal can be for people to leave church with both a sense of corrected direction, of tasks to do, as well as with a sense of relieved burden and increased joy. In faith they may have confidence that God goes ahead of them and will work great things this week, in them, through them, in spite of them, and in the world at large.

Four Pages as Deep Structure

I propose the four-page approach to preaching, and the variations it allows, as a way to address many of the challenges we face today in composing God-centered sermons. These are not the only ways to preach, but they represent a wide range. The four pages can provide a solid methodology for beginning preachers, and can be added to the repertoire of experienced preachers. Still, we ought to be cautious in considering sermon structure: Genuine good news comes only from God. If the Holy Spirit does not choose to use our words, there is nothing we can do to make them into good news. We cannot fix lack of good news in a sermon by mere devices we might conceive. However, God chooses to be known in preaching and the sacraments and through other aspects of the worship service and daily life. God's nature of self-giving love and community-transforming power is imparted in the event of Christ speaking in preaching. The good news is an event that we cannot control or adequately communicate ourselves. Yet when people hunger for the Word, find their lives corrected and strengthened by it, and rejoice in celebration for all that God has accomplished and is accomplishing in the world, we have communicated good news.

Already the reader may be thinking that four pages will be restrictive. In response, I say the four pages already exist—they are not simply an invention. They are four theological functions that are easily identified and any sermon can be analyzed using them. Moreover, any sermon that preaches good news will contain most of them. They can be reordered in various ways to considerable effect, as we also will see. Again, this book is not about one model of sermon but about many models; and more than providing models, it provides theological tools that preachers can use to improve their preaching.

Other readers may resist the idea of a norm: the congregation will grow weary and, as preachers, we will grow bored with our own preaching. However, a norm is not a constant and, as with icebergs floating in the northern seas, much goes unseen. This approach says more about the deep theological structure of the sermon than about the surface level of which most of our listeners are aware. Normally they are engaged at a surface level of the spoken discourse: they are engaged by the voice and the speaker. They follow the train of thought, stories and images, connections with what went before, and the overall unifying purpose; they are engaged often at the intellectual or emotional level of the words. Most hearers become aware of the three points of a three-point sermon only when they are identified. Listeners to sermons that follow an exposition/application format do not say on the steps of the church, "Oh preacher, I do wish you would not always talk about the Bible and then about us." Few individuals are aware of other devices that have been used to structure sermons, nor will they be alert to a four-page format now.

When we choose among various sermon forms, we are usually making decisions about surface form, which affect the depth structure, but are not it per se. We do not need to reduce our options for the surface form of the sermon—e.g., the form of points, a letter, a lecture, an instruction, stories, drama, or a mixture—and we can still accomplish a range of sermon tasks, be they deductive, inductive, expository, doctrinal, ethical, or teaching, although some of these may have more merit than others. However, I am convinced that we should retain one of the deep theological structures that fosters hope, for hope is the nature of God's living Word. Furthermore, if we can minimize our own deliberations about form and structure, we can spend our best creative efforts each week doing what matters most, discerning and proclaiming God in the Bible text and the world. The four-page sermon is precisely about generating more hope, courage, and faith in the congregation.

The Advantages of Four Pages

The four pages in sequence promise efficient and effective use of time. They help us to know what we are doing and gently steer our creative efforts in directions that are most likely to be effective for proclamation. Once we are familiar with the pages, we do not have to waste time wondering where best to put an item in the sermon: we will know where it belongs by its theological function. If an item is biblical, it belongs either on Page One (if it represents human brokenness, sin, or suffering) or Page Three (if it represents God's grace). Alternatively, if an item is from our contemporary world it belongs on Page Two (if it deals with trouble) or Page Four (if it manifests God's grace). And once we are familiar with the pages, we can also consider when best to arrange them in a different order, the subject of a later chapter.

The four pages provide what has been lacking: a practical and effective way to do theology and to facilitate theological renewal in preaching. I have divided the pages over the days of the week. We cannot serve a fine meal of several courses with only an hour of preparation; by the same token, we cannot do strong imaginative and biblical preaching with a day of crammed effort at the end of a long week. With this method, each day is devoted to one page with one easily managed, well-defined task. Again, I use "page" here as a metaphor for work appropriate to one-quarter of the sermon, and "day" is a similar metaphor. A preacher might follow "day" literally (even as "page" might be followed literally), though preachers responsible for composing two sermons each week will want to work their own variation on this. The great Scottish preacher James S. Stewart (1896–1990) advocated finishing the Sunday morning sermon by Wednesday night and the Sunday evening sermon by Friday night; and he reserved every entire morning for uninterrupted study and preparation.

Although established preachers will have their own rhythms, we are all wise to spread the task of composition over several days, even if we do long-range advanced planning of the church year during the summers. The old rule is an hour in the study for each minute in the pulpit, but we need to modify that rule by rationing the time a couple of hours per day over several days. Each day has a separate theological thrust and hence a distinct emotional or spiritual "mood." All of us can be more creative if the writing assignment for each day is only one page because much of the creative activity of our minds happens at a subconscious level while we are working on other tasks or sleeping. Eight or ten hours spread over four or five days is worth double that time spent into the late night on Saturday. A cartoon says it well: a haggard preacher, with glasses askew and rumpled hair and clothes, is fighting exhaustion in the pulpit; two elders sit behind the pulpit, their passive expressions veiling their agony in trying to comprehend the sermon; and the caption beneath the picture reads, "Pastor Spitzwaller's philosophy: Why spend all week sweating over a sermon when you can rise at 3 A.M. on Sunday morning, crank it out, and deliver it while it's still fresh on your mind?"[6] If we do start early in the week we will have the added advantage of increased opportunities for revision and refinement.

The four pages promise more imaginative biblical sermons. We are surrounded in our culture by videocassette and digital recorders, satellite dishes and cable television, computers and the internet, and all of these have combined to make society more visual. I have already expressed my hope that preachers will think of these pages primarily as visual pages like scenes from movie scripts or like web pages geared for the eye and ear, with heavy use of video clips, rather than as written pages. Technology makes it possible for individuals now to download images from their videocameras directly into their computers, and preachers similarly might conceive of downloading their own biblical and relevant contemporary movie scenes directly into their sermons.

Revelation is not revelation until it is received. To capture listener attention and to communicate well, sermons need to be reconceived; we must still effectively teach the Bible, communicate the tradition, reflect on experience, invite people into the faith, and challenge them to action. But in order to do so effectively we are wise to pay attention to rhetoric, that is, to anticipate what listeners need and to help them to receive what is said. We can provide listeners things to see and people to meet. We can take them into homes to see parents caring for a child with a disability, or other parents struggling not to give up even though their children have nothing for breakfast—in addition to reflecting upon experience and Christian understandings. While sermons should be conceived more as movie making than as essay writing, a web page (or ordinary page) is a helpful metaphor for sermon composition.

As any musician knows, a fresh rendering of a musical score comes as a result of devotion and discipline, not apart from it. I hope that preachers treat this four-page approach, and variations on it, as a fresh invitation to preaching, and also as a spiritual exercise to be tried over a period of months, to see what a difference it can make in their own lives and that of congregations. In fact, the church has placed so little emphasis on grace in both preaching and in the life of the church that there is much to learn. So many church meetings with well-meaning members end up being merely critical and hurtful. With sermons, a structure needs to be in place for grace to be clearly proclaimed and heard; so, too, in meetings, we might provide intentional time for identifying the good things that have happened, the ways in which God has been perceived to be at work. No Christian is off-base in trying to practice grace, in communicating God's love and affirmation, and discerning God in the world, in others, and in daily life. When our preaching is better equipped to foster an awareness of God in everyday life, we will better equip communities to witness to Jesus Christ.

In the sections that follow, I demonstrate how to spread the task of sermon preparation across the week. Monday is used to make six decisions, some of which concern matters that are new for us to contemplate. The days from Tuesday to Friday are each assigned to one of the four pages. For each day, one chapter of theological reflection is combined with a second chapter of examples from published sermons, in the understanding that we often learn best from experiencing what others have done. In a final concluding section, I present two complete sermons and options for reshuffling and varying the pages.

SECTION I
GETTING STARTED: MONDAY

CHAPTER TWO

Ensuring Sermon Unity

One Text, One Theme, One Doctrine, One Need, One Image, and One Mission

Early in the week, the preacher needs to begin sermon preparation in earnest. Deferring sermon work until later in the week will preclude much of what the Holy Spirit has an opportunity to do with our creative labors. On Monday (or Tuesday at the latest) we should be at our study desk with a blank sheet of paper, an open Bible, a cup of coffee, newspapers, and a stack of books and journals, many open at marked pages. We should have in mind vivid images and stories from the morning national and international news broadcasts on television or radio.

Perhaps I am not unusual in having often hoped that God's Spirit will hover over my blank pages as over the waters at the beginning of creation, and that in the same seemingly effortless way my sermon will suddenly come into being and bring forth God's magnificent purpose for the congregation this week. Only on extremely rare occasions has a sermon come to me with such ease. Would that sermon composition were simply a matter of inspiration, with God speaking as we prayerfully listen and transcribe. Still, there are steps that we can follow to save time and provide sharper focus, making the task much easier.

By starting on Monday, preachers not only can move sermon composition forward in the week, they can break the sermon task into distinct theological assignments. Effective sermons result from preparing throughout the week, for a bare minimum of two hours per day—more, if one preaches twice on Sundays. This time should be regular, protected time when one's energy and concentration are at their peak.

Many of my students lament that their traditions do not have a practice of spirituality such as that developed by Ignatius, yet from the perspective of preaching, preparation of the sermon is the traditional spiritual discipline of preachers. It involves regular study, prayer, meditation, writing, and dedication. This study time seems like private time and many preachers feel selfish in protecting it. But it is not private time, it is congregational time of the highest order so protecting it is justified and not an act of selfishness. A preacher's devotional, spiritual and intellectual life needs to be strong, for every aspect of ministry depends on our relationship with and growing knowledge of God. Only in this relationship can we hope to be like the willow tree, supple and able to bend before harsh storms. Our study time finds its greatest expression in the ministry of Word and Sacrament on Sunday when we reach the largest number of people at one time in the week. Listeners hear the sermon as members of a crowd, conscious that others are also being addressed, yet also as individuals in some form of personal relationship with the preacher. Our offering should demonstrate appropriate care and stewardship of this privilege and opportunity. We should not allow other needs or opportunities regularly to violate that time.

Simply locking the door and using the telephone answering machine or service for a protected period of time each day is not enough, however. The study time should include the actual writing of one-quarter of the sermon, a quarter per day, however long this takes. One of the most common ways to delay putting pen to paper for sermon composition is to say, "I must complete my reading first." While this excuse works well—for we must read if we are going to write—reading should lead to writing on a daily basis. Sermon composition is not a daunting task if we need to compose only one page each day, each with its own clear requirements.

There is another reason preachers like to delay putting ink to paper. As long as the page is still clean and the sermon is not written, it is potentially a perfect sermon. Most sermons begin in the preacher's mind as potentially perfect. Even the desire for perfection in service of God is a sin, however. We do well to remember the following theological truths:

- God deserves more than the best we can offer. God can send the Spirit on whom God wants, and can raise children of Abraham and Sarah from stones. By our own resources, we do not have what God needs. We preach only by the grace of God who equips us for the task in calling us, setting us apart for a particular ministry, and upholding us in our ministry, graciously providing for our every need.
- God called us in the particularity of our being, with our abilities and limitations, gifts and experience. Yet we should not be like the preacher who said, "You really must hear my sermon on humility;" or like the person who was given an award for humility—and when she accepted it—had it taken away. As the psalmist says, "A broken and contrite heart, O God, you will not despise" (Psalm 51:17).
- A sermon is not our own but belongs to God. Concerns about how well we will do are appropriate only with regard to the faithfulness and worthiness of our offering. Glory for God is what we seek, not for ourselves.
- The only perfect sermon is the one Jesus Christ preaches through the Holy Spirit. He is the Word made flesh. While Jesus commands us to "be perfect, therefore, as your heavenly Father is perfect" (Matthew 5:48), the perfection of which he speaks is not something we obtain through our efforts. It is obtained through faith and utter reliance upon Christ. The sooner in the week we commence sermon preparation, the sooner we claim this reliance for our preaching.

Achieving Sermon Unity

To preach is to take a week-long journey that many seek to delay and compress into a tight time frame. Perhaps sensing they are late, many preachers then rush for the homiletical highway, making up for lost time. They go too fast and do not observe all the posted signs along the route. We will consider six signs that preachers should observe before proceeding to the highway of sermon composition. Preachers should stop six times to identify: one **text** from

35

the Bible to preach; one **theme** sentence arising from that text; one **doctrine** arising out of that theme statement; one **need** in the congregation that the doctrine or theme sentence addresses; one **image** to be wed to the theme sentence; and one **mission**. Attending to each of these signposts may seem to slow the journey but in fact they hasten it, for they ensure that we arrive safely and with all our luggage. These six signposts, text, them, doctrine, need, image and mission, may be memorized using the awkward acronym TTDNIM or, as I have done, one can recall the more easily remembered sentence, The Tiny Dog Now Is Mine.

One Bible Text (The Tiny Dog Now Is Mine.)

Choose one text from the Bible. The Scriptures as the Word of God provide our immediate authority to preach. Some churchgoers may question the authority of the church, of ordination, of the Bible, of preaching as God's Word. Some casual hearers may not even care if "the message" comes from the Bible.[1] But week by week, as people experience God encountering their lives through preaching, the authority to preach is renewed. God speaks through the reading and appropriate interpretation of Scripture.

The sermon is a journey and one needs to make preparations. Sermons need planning: we must choose the biblical real estate or terrain, determine textual boundaries, check translations, and consult biblical commentaries. This exegetical process requires many literary, historical, and other questions of the text to be answered, from plot and character to parallel passages and personal responses. Many other writers have provided detailed guidance on these issues and on 'executing' our own world situation.[2]

Preachers in some denominations and independent churches choose their own biblical texts according to the needs they perceive in the congregation. A preacher may also use a Sunday lectionary, such as the ecumenical *The Revised Common Lectionary* (published in book form by Abingdon Press, 1992); it eliminates searching for a fresh text each Sunday and has the advantage of linking to a wide body of biblical scholarship and to possible Sunday school programs. Based on the Roman Catholic lectionary that arose out of Vatican II, it has gone through three separate revisions to meet ecumenical and scholarly concerns. Each Sunday, in a three-year cycle that rotates through Matthew, Mark, and Luke (John is represented in a small portion of each year), the lectionary provides three lessons (Old Testament, Epistle, and Gospel) plus a psalm. Some preachers try to link these various readings in the sermon. The practice may be satisfying to a preacher, but unless the link is immediate, obvious, and easily conveyed, such attempts to link readings are wasted on congregational members. They have pressing legitimate concerns from daily life and world affairs that they want addressed more than how one reading relates to another.

Most preachers do not have enough time in the sermon to expound more than one text; to refer anywhere in the Bible is appropriate, but one main text is all that most listeners can manage. In other words, even with a lectionary, a choice of a text must be made. This may be made on the basis of congregational need (provided the preacher does not impose a desired meaning on the text); on the basis of location in the Bible—the norm is to preach the Gospel and frequently to preach the Old Testament or Epistle; or occasionally on the basis of the preacher's personal preference or interest that week.

There are strengths and weaknesses to any method of choosing texts to preach. We preach from the Bible to ensure that God's Word is proclaimed and the lectionary provides an excellent safeguard against preaching only one's favorite texts. Unless preachers are careful, however, lectionary preaching can lead to a diminished ability to speak prophetically on specific topics, current issues, or general doctrines. To counter this danger, preachers might address important topics as they arise, preach doctrines as they are found in the texts at hand, and occasionally depart from the lectionary (in those denominations where preachers have this liberty), perhaps at regular intervals through the year to preach a topical or doctrinal sermon or sermon series.

One Theme Statement (The Tiny Dog Now Is Mine.)

The second sign that preachers often do not observe is the one where they have to identify a focus or theme statement. Recent scholarship, especially of Hans Frei, has emphasized the danger of reducing biblical texts to propositions instead of allowing the biblical narratives to function on their own to communicate their meanings in their own ways. Some preachers have assumed that this means they should avoid a theme in a sermon; they advocate preaching images or stories that avoid rhetorical persuasion and leave a sermon open-ended for the hearer to draw a conclusion and apply it to daily life;[3] they envision preaching as conversation around a table where everyone is valued equally and truth claims are avoided.[4] There are merits in such an approach. They underline a shift that has taken place in homiletics and in society in general away from doctrinal absolutism, preaching as lecturing, and hierarchical models of ministry. Perhaps Eugene L. Lowry is right, that it all comes down to the inability of our language adequately to capture the truth; preaching, he says, "declares the truth, all the while knowing the truth cannot be uttered."[5]

Still, as Lucy Lind Hogan has argued in response to Lucy Rose, persuasion cannot be avoided; to attempt to do so in the pursuit of greater inclusivity is to misconstrue both the nature of speech and the nature of persuasion, which in itself is not authoritarian.[6] The case can be taken further. Even stories and movies have a focus that can be stated in a sentence. At minimum the congregation needs to know what the preacher means in telling a story or speaking about a doctrine, in order to know how it connects with what came before or what will follow. The sermon still must be about something that listeners can identify and engage. Clear communication will not have listeners asking, "What are you saying? What was that all about?" A theme statement is not an authoritarian rule about what listeners must accept. It helps make conversation possible. It is a community-assisting guide that allows listeners to know what the preacher is actually saying so that they may better discern their own understanding; and as such, it is an important goal of biblical exegesis in preparation for preaching. Moreover, the theme statement is an attempt to identify clearly one formulation of what the preacher discerns God wants to communicate through the sermon.

A theme sentence will not stand as an adequate summary of the text; it is rather a clear marker of one path, amongst other possibilities, through what the preacher interprets to be the heart of the text. It will not stand as an adequate statement of who God is or what God is doing: the whole sermon is our attempt at that—to the degree that our words are ever adequate in this regard. As with most theological statements, the theme sentence needs qualifications, illumination, exemplification, and explanation. It will be a key to the sermon from the preacher's perspective but it may not even stand as an adequate summary of the sermon, for individuals will vary in their interpretations of what they have heard. The theme is simply a statement of what the preacher chooses as a handle for the text and as an organizing principle for the sermon. Images and stories will help to develop it but they are no substitute for it in effective communication.

As a statement about the text, a theme sentence should be posed as a declarative sentence, not as a question. When a question is used, it functions: (a) to mask or blunt a more direct statement the preacher is reluctant to make, but nonetheless wants the congregation to hear, (e.g., the preacher says "Who are we?" instead of "We are the Pharisees"); or (b) to identify a general topic and avoid saying anything specific about it. Thus, on preaching about the Good Samaritan a preacher might ask, "Who is your neighbor?," which identifies a topic (i.e., neighbors) but says nothing about it and makes no theological claim. In contrast, a declarative theme sentence makes a specific statement about the topic and its relationship to the text; it makes a connection between the topic and a theological claim.

Even a theme statement is not enough, although in homiletics in the last few centuries often this was all that was required. A sermon is not about anything you feel like talking about; it should be about God—in the maxim some preachers were taught, "Preach about God and preach about twenty minutes." Translations, word studies, and commentaries may leave the text functioning merely at a literary or historical level. Preachers often miss one essential planning step that makes all the difference in the outcome of the sermon. For the text to be functioning at a theological level, and for it to lead into good news that casts listeners upon God's resources as well as their own, the actual starting place must be a theme statement that answers: What is God doing in or behind this text?

When we ask what God is doing in the text, we imply that God, in one of the Persons of the Trinity, is an active agent in the text. For example, when God is calling Jeremiah to speak, the verb "to call" clearly identifies God's action. The stronger the verb we choose for our theme statement the better, provided it gives an accurate reflection of the text. A stronger verb might communicate good news more readily: God equips Jeremiah.

We most often ask what God is doing behind the text when God is not mentioned explicitly in it. The biblical theology movement used the term "behind the text" in a different manner, to give priority to the historical events behind the text, or to the text's earlier form or meaning, bypassing or diminishing the text as it has been received in the canon. In fact, one problem with biblical theology was that it considered the Bible as a theological interpretation of God's action, not as a record of God's actual acts themselves.[7] A surprising number of texts do not explicitly mention God, and a surprising number of preachers, in preaching those texts, do the same, or only get to God in the last minutes of the sermon. When a text (for instance, the Good Samaritan) is silent about God, preachers need to seek God behind the text in the purpose or function of the text, or in the larger sweep of events to which the episode belongs. Such prayerful study might lead a preacher to say: God works through the outcast (thinking of the Samaritan); or God tends to the victim.

Alternative questions to "What is God doing behind the text?" can be "Whose action in this text is like God's?" or "What does this text tell me about God's love?" This multifaceted approach to the text ensures that preachers handle it theologically, and that the sermon points to God, for there is no other reason to preach.

There are three main objections to the practice of looking for what God is doing in or behind the text. First, some people might say that to focus on God when God is not mentioned in the biblical text is eisegesis, reading something into the text that is not there. It distorts the text's meaning. In response let us remember that the Bible is the church's book, and is to be read in light of its purpose as Scripture. We read the Bible appropriately when we read it to learn who God is and how we are to live in faith before God. Calvin said, "The Scriptures should be read with a view to finding Christ in them."[8] Many passages imply something about God without mentioning God, and we can discern what this is only if we stop long enough to consider the possibility. If the passage still seems mute concerning God, we might be better to put it away for a future day and greater insight, and instead choose to preach a text that has fruits ripe for picking.

The second objection arises from the traditional idea that a biblical text has only one meaning. This understanding was common prior to the advent of hermeneutics and literary criticism. When ideas of the single meaning of Scripture were originally voiced, for instance by reformers like Luther, it was to support the "plain" or grammatical sense of Scripture and was in opposition to the four senses of Scripture that were the standard hermeneutical tool of the church until that time: every text had several possible meanings (literal or historical; allegorical, having to do with church and faith; moral, concerning the soul; and anagogical or eschatological). Luther said, "But we are not . . . to say that the Scriptures or the word of God have more than one meaning,"[9] although he did not abandon the allegorical and other methods of interpretation he inherited. Calvin spoke of the secret witness *(testimonium internum)* of the Holy Spirit inspiring the reader to the meaning of Scripture. Even when the single-meaning theory was popular, scholars could not agree on what that meaning was.

Today we recognize that every text has a multitude of meanings, some legitimate from the church's perspective, and some not. Thomas W. Gillespie conceives of the relationship between the text and its sense or meaning to be like the relationship of an anchor to a harbor buoy that can move and shift, but only within the circumference allowed by its chain.[10] Every time we restate the meaning of a biblical text as a theme statement for the sermon, we may be offering a different meaning. In the worst cases, preachers grasp a meaning of the biblical text that has little to do with God and thereby effectively exclude God from any significant role in their sermons.

A third objection to finding God behind the text comes from another sector. Narrative has been recovered in the scholarship of diverse disciplines: literary studies, history, sociology, psychiatry, and preaching. In these postmodern times, some writers have embraced the postmodern as something to be imitated rather than as a paradigm for society that needs both appreciation and critique from a Christian perspective. Some have been ready to discard ideas as 'modern' and idea-centered preaching as a throwback to the Enlightenment. Rather, they say, preaching should be about plot.[11]

They are partially right. Plot is essential for contemporary preaching. Even more important than plot, however, sermons should be about character—the character and nature of God. As Charles L. Campbell says, "It is the central character [of Jesus Christ] rendered by the gospel narratives, not narrative plot in general, that is at the heart of preaching shaped by the biblical story."[12] Sermons can be an event or encounter with God, not just information or abstraction about God, and preachers ought not structure them as though they are lectures to postdoctoral specialists in logic. For preachers to communicate a lively sense of God in the midst of life as people experience it, they may strive for sermonic flow and organic unit—like that of a river bending and moving through a delta—not for the static unity of points and subpoints—like the system of pipes and plumbing joints in a house. The theme sentence, as I am conceiving it, is a concrete idea—words cannot help but generate ideas—but it is not to remain abstract, nor is it meant to be detached from the biblical narrative, inviting the preacher to offer an academic lecture in disregard to the needs of the hearers.

The theme statement may be called the sermon-in-a-sentence (e.g., Ronald J. Allen); or "what the text is saying" (Fred Craddock); or the focus statement (Thomas G. Long); or what the text says in response to the Fallen Condition Focus (Bryan Chapell—i.e., our "trouble"); or the homiletical idea (Haddon W. Robinson); or the controlling idea (Henry Mitchell); or the God-statement or the major concern of the text (Wilson)—whatever it is called, it is the one statement that will help the preacher to shape, mold, or choreograph everything that is written. Preachers need to test it in the process of exegesis and scholarly study to ensure that it is, in fact, an accurate or fair reading the text, according to the best wisdom of the church (i.e., what is known in history as the rule of faith). Once a preacher has tested the theme sentence, it provides a solid path to follow. It may seem too plain a path at this early stage just starting out, yet this can be its strength—it encourages the preacher to say more, to walk through the center of the text along a certain route, to develop the character of humanity and God through the action or plot, and to explain things that need clarification. A good theme sentence leads the preacher to restructure and retell the biblical passage, to add nuancing, qualifications, stories, explanations, and grounding in experience and doctrinal tradition. These necessary additions are the elements of the sermon beginning to write itself.

Without asking, Where is God in or behind this text?, the preacher is likely to speed away on the sermon journey leaving God behind. In many sermons it is as though Jesus never said, "For my yoke is easy, and my burden is light" (Matthew 11:30). Claims that identify human responsibility and the need to respond to God's grace with thanks are essential for the sermon—they develop an important theological emphasis of trouble in and around us. However, if God's action and nature are not the focus in sermon preparation, God will not likely end up as the focus of the final sermon, and the good news will be hard to find. The good news is what God graciously has accomplished in Jesus Christ on our behalf through no merit of our own except for the fact that God loves us. With good news, the burden of the action falls on God, not on the listener, and the cross and resurrection are a symbol of the difference this makes for us today.

The following statements from a miscellany of biblical texts put the burden on humans, not on God. Do not sweep these texts from the desk as though they are unpreachable. Rather, keep working with the texts to discover how God empowers:

God wants Israel to change (i.e., it is still up to Israel). **Try:** God brings Israel to a new place.

Jesus calls us to repent (i.e., we must repent). **Try:** Jesus brings us to repentance.

The Holy Spirit convicts Saul (i.e., we are convicted). **Try:** The Holy Spirit acts for Paul.

God invites Jeremiah to act (i.e., Jeremiah/we will have to find the resources to accept the invitation). **Try:** God equips Jeremiah.

If we . . . then God . . . (i.e., good news is conditional upon human ability). **Try:** In Christ, God has completed the conditions for God's love.

God can act in your life (i.e., God has not acted already? God is waiting for us to do something first? Good news is only in the future?). **Try:** God has already acted in your life.

Let God . . . (i.e., God never acts to overcome our determination to say no). **Try:** God will not be stopped.

Choose a strong active verb for the theme statement wherever possible—something that creates an image in the mind. God does judge, but it is not the judging actions we need to focus on for the theme statement, because these actions in the first instance mean trouble for humans. Even if a text genuinely is a judgment text, from a theological perspective I would still affirm that God's word is never only condemnation, thus I would still seek to identify the empowerment God graciously provides—if not in, then behind, the text. As preachers, we are to identify God's gracious actions that enable listeners to face their judgment and trouble. God not only asks you to take responsibility, God also empowers you with the means to do so.

Often preachers say things like: God listens to your cries; God hears your problems; God knows your needs; God understands your pain; God feels your anguish; God cares about your difficulties; God sees your trouble. These perceiving, nonaction verbs are fine if we use other, stronger verbs in the sermon. However, too often they provide all the good news that there is and they point to our own North American fixation on "how God can help us feel good." Such a message is a distortion of the gospel. Moreover, Sunday after Sunday such a message can become cloying and sentimental, more of a weak hope in the fading light of weary day than the dawning light and exuberant hope of a brand new era.

Those who are in crisis need to know that God is doing something on their behalf, something that brings joy to where there was death, healing to where there was illness, peace to where there was violence, justice to where there was injustice, reconciliation to where there was enmity, and awareness of the active presence of Christ through the Holy Spirit to where there was a sense of being all alone. Listeners need strong verbs to reinforce the theological truth that God is not passive and remote but active and involved, loving and compassionate.

Here, then, are quick rules to guide formulation of the theme sentence or God-statement:

Keep it short.
Make it a declarative sentence (not a question).
Make God the subject of the sentence.
Focus on God's action of grace.
Use strong, active verbs.

One Doctrine (The Tiny **D**og Now Is Mine.)

There is a third sign that preachers tend to ignore in their late rush to the homiletical highway. Most preachers fail to choose one doctrine arising from their theme statement. A doctrine is a teaching of the church, and theology is commonly the systematic reflection on that teaching. As one scholar succinctly notes, "When we state the meaning of a biblical idea we have created a doctrine. . . .For Christians, a doctrine is the teaching of Scripture on a particular theme."[12] Preachers often have difficulty knowing how systematic, dogmatic, or constructive theology relates to preaching.

Clearly, we go into the pulpit ready to share meaty portions from our favorite theology textbooks and biblical commentaries. But often the academic language of essential preaching resources is too abstract and sounds like theological jargon to most church members. Occasionally we may paraphrase a helpful passage, but generally these books were written for their own academic and rhetorical purposes. Preaching speaks to a different audience. Nonetheless, biblical studies and theology exist to help and inform preachers. For our journey they function as essential maps and travel guides. We simply need help knowing how best to use them. In particular we need to know how to get from one place to another and what to say along the way.

Doctrinal sermons are devoted to explicating a doctrine, rather than a biblical text. These may have their place in the church, though they are not the norm, nor are they the focus here. We are trying to select a relevant doctrine or set of church teachings for every sermon—which one best relates to the theme sentence for Sunday? Turn to a table of contents in any theology textbook and you will immediately see the kaleidoscope of standard church doctrines: atonement, attributes of God, authority of Scripture, community of the church, Christ, creation, eschatology, evil, humanity, and so on. Different authors or denominations name doctrines differently, but a biblical passage of some length typically may suggest half a dozen doctrines. Even one well-known verse, such as John 3:16 ("For God so loved the world that he gave his only Son, so that everyone who believes in him may not perish but have eternal life"), offers numerous possibilities: atonement, justification, the nature of God, salvation, sanctification, redemption, revelation, and perhaps others. With so many possibilities for just one verse, no wonder students and many pastors are confused about how to integrate theology with preaching.

Most doctrines can be summarized in a few sentences, and preachers can use a simple procedure with their theme sentences. They can ask themselves which doctrine most accurately "says the text in other words"—even though that is not our goal and we do not actually substitute propositions for the Bible in the sermon.

That doctrine as it is discussed in an introductory theology text-book can inform our thinking for that particular sermon. However, as preachers we are limited in what we can offer by the time available for the sermon, the ability of the congregation to comprehend doctrinal discussion, and the need for the sermon to offer some practical applications to daily life. Much instructional material that we might like to include in the sermon must be left to an evening service or to Christian education events. The sermon normally should not become an essay on the doctrine, and one sermon cannot normally explore much doctrinal territory. But because the doctrine offers the best reflections of the church on a particular area of thought and experience, it may have a direct, obvious impact on a portion of the sermon, or it may simply help clarify and deepen our thought.

At its best, doctrinal expression adds humanity, not abstraction, to preaching—for deep thought is often the product of suffering and healing, blood and balm. Preachers who follow a weekly program of reading in theology will experience the excitement of ongoing growth and facility in theological expression over the years. Moreover, they will be able to represent, engage and critique the church's teachings with greater confidence. As Gerhard Ebeling once said, "theology is necessary in order to make preaching as hard for the preacher as it has to be."[14] Among the preachers who are most likely to be rejected or experience meltdown in ministry are those who think they can get along without doctrine or excellent teaching in preaching, and depend instead on relational skills in day-to-day ministry. Relationships, however, are not separate from theological tasks at the heart of the office of preaching.

The most immediate benefit of choosing one doctrine that comes out of the theme statement is more focused depth and greater clarity in the sermon. Instead of going all over the theological map, as may be tempting with the array of doctrinal possibilities in John 3:16, we find guidance in one direction by selecting the most appropriate or obvious doctrine.

Doctrine is important but preachers should never try to impress listeners with what they know, for instance by presenting complex doctrinal arguments that leave hearers scratching their heads or staring out the window. Nearly everything that a preacher says should be understandable to a twelve-year-old. The purpose of choosing a doctrine is not to make sermonic thought more difficult but to make it more simple, clear and deep. Simplicity that is superficial is worth nothing, but simplicity that emerges on the other side of complexity we should treasure as knowledge grounded in experience.

Below are a number of Bible texts, God-action statements, and a doctrine that could help shape sermon development. The key is to keep the sentence short:

Bible Text	Theme Sentence	Doctrine
"God so loved the world" (John 3:16)	God pays the price.	Atonement
"In the beginning . . ." (Genesis 1)	God created all things.	Creation
Jeremiah's call (Jeremiah 1)	God chose Jeremiah.	Calling/ Vocation
"O Lord, you have searched me and known me . . ." (Psalm 139)	God already knows.	Omniscience of God
The Ten Bridesmaids (Matthew 25:1-13)	God comes at any moment.	Eschatology
Feeding of the 4000 (Mark 8:1-10)	Jesus provides for all their needs.	Providence of God
"I planted, Apollos watered, but God gave . . ." (1 Corinthians 3:5)	God nurtures the church.	The Church/ Mission
"Gentiles have become fellow heirs . . ." (Ephesians 3:1-7)	Christ reveals himself to Paul.	Revelation
The new Jerusalem (Revelation 22:9-27)	The angel shows John the heavenly city.	Eschatology

Once we have completed our study and confirmed that the doctrine has a legitimate connection to the biblical text, the doctrinal teachings of the church upon which to draw are open. Starting sermon composition without it is like setting off in a car without a map.

One Need in the Congregation
(The Tiny Dog **N**ow Is Mine.)

Along the preacher's route to sermon composition there is a fourth sign. We have already chosen (1) a text, (2) a theme statement that focuses on a gracious action of God, and (3) a doctrine that arises out of that theme statement. Now, at this fourth sign, we identify a need that this doctrine will meet in the congregation. Too many preachers write their sermons without ever pausing to ask: Who cares? What difference will this make to anyone? What need does this meet in anyone's life? As O. C. Jones, Jr., says, "The devil's favorite Sunday morning entertainment is the sermon which does not disturb. The pulpit must have something relevant, serious, and honest to say on perplexing problems and subjects."[15] Moreover, the devil probably loves a sermon that offers no hope. When we offer no hope, we may be like the comedian who said, "Folks, I'd really like to end my show by giving you a positive thought, a positive message, but I can't think of one. Will you take two negatives instead?" There is little point to our journey on the homiletical highway if we are simply going to be negative and offer no hope or help.

Every effective sermon must have relevance and address a need in the lives of the congregation. This is not necessarily the need that the preacher thinks a congregation has, for example, "My people need to know more about the Bible," or "They need to know more about this doctrine." The need also is not necessarily a need that the people in the congregation feel or perceive themselves to have—for instance at Christmas to have fine gifts. Rather, the preacher ideally addresses the real need of people. As Christians we affirm that human needs are determined on the basis of our wants but in our relationship to God—for instance, the need to know God born in our midst. Each time we preach we should try to identify some need in the congregation that our message seeks to meet.

Here are two ways to identify congregational need. First, ask of the theme statement, "What question does this answer in the life of a person or people in the church?" Be sure the question is from the perspective of the person or people, not couched in theological jargon. Include that question in the development of the sermon. Here are a few examples from the previous chart. Note that the theme sentence answers the question.

THEME SENTENCE	QUESTION
God pays the price.	How can I begin again?
God created all things.	What has God to do with anything?
God chose Jeremiah. (i.e., God in Christ chose you.)	Why should I/we go on?
God already knows.	Who can understand?
God comes at any moment.	Why should I/we persevere?
Jesus provided for all their needs.	What if I do not find work?
God nurtures the church.	What will happen to our church?

Christ is revealed to Paul.
    (i.e., Christ revealed himself
        to you.)
	How can I trust what I know of God?

The angel shows John
    the heavenly city (i.e., God has
    a larger purpose than we can see).
	Why not end it now?

A second approach uses the doctrine selected from the theme statement to determine a question. Shirley C. Guthrie, in the table of contents of his *Christian Doctrine,* identifies excellent questions that each doctrine answers.[16] Here is a sampling:

DOCTRINE	QUESTION
Revelation	How can we find God?
Predestination	What does God want with us?
Creation	What are we doing here?
Sin	Why don't you just be yourself?
Incarnation	Where is God?
Resurrection	Who's in charge here?
The Holy Spirit	What's new?
Eschatology	What's going to happen to us?

These and similar questions can help a preacher early in the sermon-making process to imagine scenes in everyday life to which the message can speak with particular relevance. Be sure to include the question somewhere in the sermon, at least twice.

Note that the need generally is not any need the preacher may determine the congregation to have. Rather, it is a need that the theme sentence and/or doctrine point to in the congregation. The need thus serves sermon unity.

One Image (The Tiny Dog Now *Is* Mine)

The fifth sign for preachers to observe before proceeding onto the homiletical highway is not mandatory but can be important nonetheless: Choose one image to become dominant in the sermon. From a practical point of view, most preachers on Monday will only begin to search for an image to function in this manner, and they may not find it until much later in the week, on Wednesday or Thursday perhaps, when the sermon is nearly written. In such a case, the preacher sees how an image from one story can be repeated effectively by inserting it on pages where it had not previously appeared.

Ways to use dominant images

Of course most sermons have many images—there are as many images in a sermon as there are pictures for the mind to see. Yet one of these might become dominant and unifying simply because we repeat it in different locations. Such an image is not essential for each sermon; a sermon can function quite well without one even as any sermon might be enhanced by including one. However, use of a dominant image is essential for those preachers who tend to emphasize images and cram their sermons so full of them they are distracting. One single image can add unity to a sermon and can make it more memorable. This dominant image, if there is to be one, should first appear on Page One.

For our purposes, an image is a word picture. The difference between an image and an abstract idea is that an image presents a specific picture created to the mind's eye. Some words are picturesque and refer to specific concrete objects that easily function as images: road, maple tree, cup, loaf of bread. By contrast, abstract words like love, anger, or justice, do not present a specific picture to the mind. They are usually conceived apart from any concrete instance, actual event, or specific object. An image of a hand extended to help someone from a car provides a picture of love.

The best test of abstract language is this: does this word present

a specific picture to my mind? If it does not present a specific picture then it is abstract. For example, "beautiful flowers" presents a
nonspecific picture: we may think of a floral arrangement or of a
field. "Beautiful roses" is a little less abstract, but the picture is still
unclear: are they cut roses in a vase or on a bush outdoors? By contrast, "twelve long-stemmed yellow roses in a vase" presents a very
distinct picture. If yellow roses kept reappearing in the sermon, that
image would start to become more central than other nonrepeating
images. Duane Litfin used the strong dominant image of a hot air
balloon as an imag e of life in a sermon entitled "Riding the Wind
of God":

> Have you ever ridden in a hot air balloon? They say it's a lot like sail-
> ing with the wind. You may be moving very quickly, but there is
> complete silence and no sense of any wind . . . as you travel with the
> wind, there is no sense of your own motion except as you see the
> earth glide by beneath you. The journey is startlingly quiet and
> peaceful.
>
> That's the kind of thing Solomon has in mind . . . one who lives
> with the wind of God at his back. . . .[17]

Such an image of doing the will of God can be more effective than
speech that is more straight-forward. At the end of the day, when
we reflect on the day's events, abstract principles do not normally
come to mind—we visualize people and places and replay conversations. Much of human thinking is in mental pictures, and most
people remember best what they can visualize.

A dominant image in a sermon is a repeated image and when listeners see it over and over, it begins to stand out in their minds.
Because preaching is oral, repetition is the preacher's equivalent of
the highlighting marker or colored text on a computer screen.
Listeners should see the same image in a sermon introduction, on
one or two other pages, and in the conclusion. A recurring image
can add conceptual unity to the sermon. However, it becomes of
greatest force and usefulness if by the end of the sermon it adds theological unity as well. In the course of the sermon the image should
become theological; it should become united with the theme statement and thereby become a visual and memory aid for God's action.

An example of what I mean can be found in a sermon involving
the doctrine of salvation (which I determined from my theme state-

ment). In the introduction I told of taking a youth group on a bus to a Detroit church service. In dealing with the gospel lesson I inserted a bus into my biblical text, and had Jesus boarding it. It was so obvious an insertion that no one would have thought that the text actually said it, and I was not anxious about whether I had distorted the text. By the end of the sermon I said: "You may have thought of going to your car in the parking lot after the service. But when you go out to the parking lot, I hope you will see something else. You see, a bus is there. It's destination, written above the windshield, is SALVATION. The door to that bus is open for you. Jesus Christ is the driver and he has already paid your fare. . . ." Ideally, every time the listeners see that image of the bus or recall it during the week, they will recall the heart of the sermon.

Some people may conceive highly visual people to be more imaginative and creative than others. They think primarily in pictures and images come easily to them; they are walking movie cameras. But they are not necessarily more creative and they will not necessarily be better preachers. Too many people mistakenly think of imagination and creativity as some kind of intuitive ability or inspirational energy that one simply has and can set free—like the girl who, when asked if she could play the piano, replied, "I don't know. I never tried." Some imagistic thinkers who have great potential as preachers end up as poor communicators because they regard discipline as the enemy of creativity. O. C. Jones, Jr., may have this in mind when he refers to "butterfly preaching—a perpetual fluttering from one flowery text to another."[18]

Yet, without discipline there is no creativity. This was the insight gained by the young poet Stephen Daedalus at the end of James Joyce's novel *Portrait of the Artist as a Young Man;* he could perceive the beauty of the young woman who looked like a bird on the beach, but he could not yet communicate this beauty to others. Unbridled imagination in preaching is nothing more than free association, with random images exploding with unharnessed energy at numerous places in a sermon that has no evident structure, point, focus, or direction. What use are horses set free from a corral if they run without harness in different directions and leave the wagon behind?

Perhaps the term imagination in preaching should be reserved the way we try to reserve the terms art and music. Imagination in preaching is best if its tasks are clearly defined, restricted, and directed to a theological purpose. It should be evaluated theologically. In other words, it is not mere decoration or simple entertainment. Anselm defined theology as faith seeking understanding; we can adapt this for preaching. Imagination is faith seeking expression.

Sources of dominant images

Briefly, there are three sources for finding dominant images. The image we choose to become dominant can come from the biblical text. It may be something obvious, for instance, Jesus opening the eyes of the person who is blind. One Bible passage may contain several possibilities. Preaching from Isaiah 51:1-10, our theme statement might be, God's salvation lasts forever (see v. 6). Several verses contain rich images: "Consider the quarry from which you were mined, the rock from which you were cut!" (v. 1 NLT); "The LORD will comfort Israel again and make her deserts blossom. Her barren wilderness will become as beautiful as Eden" (v. 3); "my justice will become a light to the nations" (v. 4); "for the moth will destroy them as it destroys clothing" (v. 8).

Some preachers may be tempted to repeat all of these wonderful images throughout the sermon just because they are in the Bible passage. They think that the congregation will appreciate them weaving so much of the Bible text into the sermon. Instead, unless people know this passage well, they will not know where the images came from. People listen for a unifying line of thought, story, and images and they will be bewildered as to why the preacher is talking about rocks in quarries, flowers blossoming, lights shining, and moths devouring cloth. The only thing that connects these diverse images is the Bible passage itself, which for many in the congregation is as good as no connection. The preacher alone has the clue to their unity, which even in Isaiah is tangential. Rather than assisting the proclamation, these random images embedded in the sermon will be like land mines waiting to explode, destroying whatever path the listener's thought was following.

A recurring image in the sermon should be like water fountains in a park: they are found in different settings but are basically the same. A dominant image forms a chain through the sermon and adds to its unity.[19] When listener's associate the image with the theme statement and the sermon as a whole, they will recall what God does.

Concerning Isaiah 51, the image of rock ("Consider the quarry from which you were mined, the rock from which you were cut") has good potential links with the theme statement "God's salvation lasts forever" (i.e., both rocks and salvation endure). We might speak early in the sermon about the flip side of the theme statement, about something not lasting forever, including reference to a rock to anticipate unity. I recall as a child going on a path through woods and being hit by a rock thrown by another boy. I was dazed and bleeding behind the ear. It seemed like the mark and the bump would last forever, but in fact they only lasted for a couple of weeks. But that rock may still lie in the area where it landed years ago where it has lain for untold centuries.

In developing the image in a sermon, I would picture the rock in Isaiah and would include passing discussion of the other verses and their images, provided they served the theological angle being developed. (For instance, I could say: Israel is in exile in Babylon and they want to go home. They are cut off and it is hard to remember the quarry from which they were cut. Even God seems remote. The deserts are rocky and barren. Israel is scorned among nations, not revered. Moths have eaten at Israel's clothes.) There may be other occasions to use the picture of a rock by the end of the sermon. Look for ways to link that image to the larger Christian story and the theme statement. Think of other rocks in Scripture (the cleft Rock of Ages, the stone rolled from the tomb, Peter's confession) that might be mentioned in passing. By the end, we should wed the image to the theme statement: Even the rocks will pass away, but God's salvation lasts forever.

In addition to taking the image from our biblical text, as described above, we may take the image from our world. Bible writers used numerous images from their world, but many of us find it hard to use images from our own culture in our sermons. But potential images surround us: a telephone booth, a broom, a potted plant, a flashlight, a fishing pole, a bicycle, a lace tablecloth, a snow tire, a crystal bowl, a boarded storefront, a bouquet of flowers, a magic marker, a sign outside a schoolyard saying 'Drug Free Zone,' and the like. If our biblical text would allow it, we could preach a sermon on the suburbs of our faith and the downtown of our faith.

We might begin a sermon with a story from our world and find an image in that story that we repeat throughout the rest of the sermon. Thus if the story is of a woman who sews for a living, the sewing machine might become the recurring image. Unity is not served, however, if the sermon keeps returning to the precise and entire story of that woman sewing, for that keeps taking people back exactly to the beginning of the sermon and is merely confusing and disruptive. Only the image of the sewing machine itself should be brought forward, and nothing else. An adventurous preacher might even find a way of putting a sewing machine into the text—because it obviously does not belong, listeners will not be confused concerning what the text actually says. (Preaching on Paul, one might portray his tent ministry in the market square and have him working on a Singer machine.) Again, by the end of the sermon the preacher would need to wed the image to the theme statement and the broader Christian story (e.g., God sews the patchwork of our lives into a quilt of perfection).

A word of caution: when we use contemporary images for God, we need to be sure that they communicate clearly what we intend. One student said that Jesus was a red Porsche; however, the image does not work. There is no clear or appropriate point of comparison—moreover, a Porsche is generally a symbol of material wealth, and Jesus stood alongside the poor.

The third source for a dominant image is for the preacher to use a refrain or a rhetorical phrase. In this case, the refrain need not contain an actual picture, though by its repetition it functions like one, presenting a recurring aural or acoustic image rather than a pictorial one to the mind. The theme statement is an excellent candidate for this repetition. (Even if we do not use it as a refrain that occurs in each episode of the sermon, we must still repeat it, over and over, in one version or another, to make it absolutely clear.) Or the refrain may simply be a familiar memorable phrase or advertising slogan adapted for theological purposes, and closely related to the theme statement. Thus if the theme statement is "God's salvation lasts forever," early in the sermon, we can use the refrain "Nothing lasts forever." By the second half of the sermon we might amend this refrain to say, "Nothing lasts forever, but God's salvation is forever."

There are, then, three possibile sources for the dominant image: an image from the biblical text, an image from our world, or a refrain (or rhetorical phrase). If we use a dominant image, it should not take over or compete with the theme statement but support and strengthen it. Frequently in sermon composition, an image that can

55

function this way will not present itself on Monday but will do so later in the week, perhaps when we are working on Page Three or Four. In that case, a preacher can go back and work it into Pages One and Two in appropriate revisions.

One Mission (The Tiny Dog Now Is **M**ine)

Monday also may be too early in the sermon preparation process for the preacher to determine exactly what mission or action of Christian service the sermon might invite, but it is not too soon to start thinking about it. God does not ask us to fret about the millions who are needy, but does ask us to be of practical help to one or more. The primary places for mission to be expressed in the sermon are Pages Two and Four, for they both deal with our world and will be the subject of our attention later in the week. How we speak of mission will vary according to its location: when we speak of mission in the first half of the sermon, we identify specific ministries that God commands or wills, things we are to do. In the second half of the sermon, we identify the manner in which God enables us and others to perform these ministries—not that we must, but that we are privileged to have the opportunity. We might also make a suggestion concerning how listeners might express their thankfulness to God in the coming week—again as an invitation and example, not as an obligation that turns the faith into a new law. Here, mission is closely aligned with Calvin's third use of the law, an excitement to obedience, treating the law as beloved instruction.

By mission I mean primarily one act, one action of ministry that listeners may contemplate doing as a result of the sermon. This act of mission is merely an example or symbol of other actions that the congregation could contemplate. Some acts of mission are general and may speak to all people in a congregation, such as some of these: we must pray more; we must work to end racism, sexism, and poverty; we must dream how we can help our youth. Other acts are more specific to individual circumstances and may function as symbols or concrete examples of the kind of action an individual or group might undertake, such as one of these: "This week pray for your enemies; arrange to take a lonely person out for a meal; make one visit in the hospital; write a letter to someone who is in prison;

volunteer for duty at a food bank." Such suggestions can also be modeled in the stories that we tell.

In identifying one mission, we affirm that a sermon should result in faith and action. Christ makes us disciples not to form a country club, but to serve our sisters and brothers near and far. By naming one action, listeners can begin thinking concretely what they might do. Still, as preachers we should strive for balance. Listeners are led to mission by the Holy Spirit and any part of the sermon may function to awaken an individual to service. The mission that we name most frequently is just a possibility. Individuals must determine for themselves within the context of the community of faith how best to be faithful. We may name one mission as a way of being helpful, but it is not up to us to turn the faith into a law when Jesus came to fulfill the law. Laity often remember best those sermons that communicate one simple task clearly, forthrightly, yet without a hint of judgment or moral superiority.

Conclusion

The sermon journey has barely begun. We have pulled out of the local neighborhood and stopped at six signs: we have chosen one text, one theme sentence, one doctrine from that theme, and one need from that doctrine. Although we may not yet have made a final selection, we are also looking for one image to wed to the theme, and one mission. In stopping where we should stop, in not being overeager to get out on the highway of sermon composition, we have performed six essential tasks that help ensure that we will arrive at our destination safely. So many preachers unknowingly run through these signs without stopping and their sermons show more than a few dents and crushed fenders. While, we do not need to spend much time stopped at each sign for us to save time throughout the week, we do need to come to a complete stop and look before moving on.

CHAPTER THREE

Introducing the Sermon

The introduction, like the opening scenes of a movie, signals what the sermon is about and where it is headed, with some promise held in store. Listeners use the introduction as a time to adjust to the preacher. During it, members determine whether the preacher is still upset from the board meeting or is suffering from a cold. Visitors ask, "Who is this person? Do I agree with the approach he or she is taking? Can I trust what is being said?" Throughout the sermon listeners continue to make decisions about the preacher's character, or ethos, in relation to the subjects discussed. Ethos is the character of the speaker in the moment, as it is communicated through the sermon in relation to various subjects as listeners experience them, not overall character, which is experienced over time, in meetings, hospital visits, and other pastoral or social activities. Overall character is relatively stable whereas ethos fluctuates within a sermon.

In the history of preaching, prior to this last century in North America at least, introductions were not a strong point of sermons, at least by contemporary standards. We do not find preachers asking, "How did Calvin start his sermon on Titus 1:10-12?" Sermons normally were much longer than they are today and introductions— where they were used—were functional: they set before the congregation the table of contents of the sermon. Preachers would define the topic (*logos*) and perhaps preview, in outline form, the argument that would be presented, indicating the logical appeal of the sermon. Pulpit ethos was more narrowly considered then and had to do with correct doctrine, good moral principles and intellectual acumen. Making a personal or experiential connection with the audience seems to have been a less than urgent concern—or at least was achieved differently—in that culture. During this past century, sermon introductions generally have shifted from primarily a didactic function to a more holistic one.

Introduction means "to lead in." An introduction is a gate that we open, a path that we reveal. Within the first paragraph or two, the preacher needs to make the theme statement or topic clear, with some hint to both its relevance and the destination of the sermon. The introduction generally is not the time for weighty or dense material. And variety from week to week is important. As one preacher put it, "Don't jump out from behind the same tree every week. Some weeks I'll use a visual for an introduction; I may use an illustration from life; or something right out of the morning paper. I may plant someone in the audience to ask a question. I may show the congregation a slide or picture."[1]

Already readers may anticipate that an introduction may have little to do with the biblical text and we have indicated that Page One of the sermon is devoted to trouble in the Bible. This may seem to be a contradiction. However, I encourage students to envision the sermon introduction as a "preface" to Page One if it is dealing with nonbiblical material. In other words, if the preacher uses contemporary material to introduce the sermon, it should not be more than a short paragraph or two, and need not alter the notion of four distinct pages of equal length.

Six Simple Strategies for Writing the Introduction

1. **Tell a story that suggests the flip side of the theme sentence or God-action statement.** If we were preaching on Elijah and the Widow of Zarephath (a passage in which the prophet meets a starving widow who is miraculously fed as a result of the encounter; 1 Kings 17:8-16), our theme statement might be, "God fed the widow." The introduction might tell a story of an opposite situation, an incident in which God did not seem to feed the hungry. The distinction between God 'not seeming to do something' and 'not doing something' is crucial: stop short of saying the opposite of what we affirm in faith, for God does provide for all, but sin and evil have disrupted God's plans. In other words, the introduction (and perhaps beyond) can reflect how listeners commonly view

life, that is, detached from God. In classical rhetoric, introducing a theme in this inverse manner is referred to as the *via negativa,* the negative route. This purpose is different from preaching against God, which we should never do unless we are simply repeating someone's expression of anger at God. Even when we identify an experience of God's apparent distance we speak from a faith perspective. By acknowledging life as people commonly experience it, yet never departing from the faith, we pique listener interest and introduce the main theme.

We might choose the theme sentence, "Jesus healed the person who is blind;" it is a strong, simple sentence with God as the subject doing the action. The sermon introduction thus might tell a story of someone who longed to be healed and for whom God seemed silent:

> A woman named Ruth lived several miles from here in a small two-bedroom house with no real yard and one lilac bush, where she raised seven children on her own after her husband's death. Each day she arose early, worked a full-day shift at the local bakery, and when she got home on the bus, she put on supper and helped the kids with their homework. She had no car. The children had nothing extra. They rarely bought anything new. But there was always fresh bakery bread on the table. One by one the children grew up and left town for work in other parts of the country. Coming home late one night, the elderly Ruth slipped on an icy step and broke her hip. What should have been one operation turned into four operations over a long period of time. Her children kept in touch by phone, and a couple of them came for short visits. Friends occasionally visited. Nonetheless, through much of that time Ruth felt alone. No one would have been able to convince her at that time that Jesus could heal; for God, like her children, seemed far away.

The advantages of such an introduction can be several. First, it signals the subject of healing: any introduction needs an obvious connection to the theme statement of the sermon. Second, it names a common experience: most people remember times where they sought healing but God seemed absent. And daring to name life as we all experience it, the preacher is likely to earn trust. Third, it will set up the audience to listen for how Ruth's story ends. At the end of the sermon, the preacher will give the conclusion of her story (or one very similar to it), and thus highlight a new awareness of God's healing presence. In that location, her story ideally (1) will help the congregation to recall the many times God has touched them with healing power in their daily lives and (2) will bring the sermon full circle, to the place it began, and hence to a fitting close.

2. **Start with a not-too-serious experience of the general theme.** An introduction is not useful if it shoves listeners into the deep end of a swimming pool when they are not prepared. The sermon should be experienced by the listener, not as swimming for one's life, but as an invitation to wade in shallow water. The sermon should also reflect the viewpoints and experiences of many people heard through the week. Normally we do not relate anything in the sermon's introduction that we would not say after being introduced to a stranger, such as our gastrointestinal ailment. Build trust instead. Thus, in a sermon on healing, we would not describe a horrible accident that left six people dead and twenty-seven injured (unless such a crisis had overtaken the community). Instead, we might tell of the first time a child got a cut, or the night when ice-skating on the pond ended in the minor emergency room.

Barbara Lundblad, a Lutheran pastor in New York City, opened a sermon on John 17:1-11 (especially Jesus' words in v. 11, "so that they may be one as you are one") in the following manner:

> Last fall, friends of mine took their daughter Kate to college. . . . Kate knew that her room-mate would be a young woman from Turkey—she knew nothing more. . . . They discovered that they had brought the same tapes of the same bands . . . and found out they also had the same favorite songs on each tape. . . . How small the big world seemed, how insignificant the distance of ocean and language and culture. They had the same song in their ears before they even met.
> Yet we know this smaller world is not singing in harmony.[2]

Haddon W. Robinson has a sermon on Genesis 3:1-6 entitled, "A Case in Temptation." Here is his compelling introduction:

> A few months ago I received a letter from a young man in a penitentiary in Texas. He is serving from ten to twenty years for attempted rape. He is a Christian, and he asked if I would send him a book that was not available to him in the prison. I gladly responded to his request. But his letter deeply disturbed me, because the young man had been a student of mine when he was in seminary. . . .
> When I read that letter and knew what had happened, I found myself wrestling with all kinds of questions and emotions. What hap-

pens in a person's life who does that? What went through his mind? What was it that caused him to turn his back on all that he had given his life to?

I realized as I was asking those questions that I was not simply asking about him, but about myself. . . .[3]

Note that Robinson retains empathy with this young man, even while he struggles to understand. It is very important in preaching to treat with empathy (which is not the same thing as sympathy) even the worst person mentioned, whether it is Jezebel, Judas, or a contemporary rapist or terrorist. All people deserve empathy as fellow human beings, yet not all should excite sympathy, particularly if we may appear to condone the deed. God never allows us to write off anyone and we do not preach hatred. All are God's loved ones, though we condemn their deeds. Note, too, how Robinson brings himself and all of his listeners under the same scrutiny he offers the convict.

Robert J. McCracken of Riverside Church in New York City began a 1950 sermon telling this story on himself. (It is a good kind of story to tell, because it does not put the preacher in the spotlight of glory, nor is it a private story that belongs only with a partner, counselor, or confessor.)

Some time ago, walking on Riverside Drive, I saw a truck pull up sharply and draw to the side of the road. The driver climbed out of his cabin and made for a small boy who was struggling with a tricycle at the curb. "You can't get it up, Sonny," he said, and with one movement of his arm and the pleasantest of smiles he put the machine on the sidewalk. On the way back to the truck, happening to glance in my direction, he good-humoredly shrugged his shoulders and yanked his thumb in the direction of the boy who was already on the tricycle and riding away. Though I was close to the lad I hadn't noticed him or his plight. I had been busy with my own thoughts and, until I heard brakes being applied, oblivious to what was going on. My heart warmed to the truck driver. What he did was a little thing, and a simple thing, but it showed that he hadn't lost the human touch.

With the rush of life so fast and feverish we are apt to lose the human touch, to forget that, next to bread, kindness is the food all mortals hunger for. . . .[4]

3. **Start with the biblical text.** If the preacher starts directly with the biblical text, the introduction for the sermon may be conceived

as part of Page One. Robert P. Waznak, S.S., Professor of Homiletics at Washington Theological Union, opened a homily on John 8:1-11:

From the beginning, folks have been more than curious about what Jesus traced on the sand. St. Jerome was one of the first serious speculators. He suggested that when Jesus bent down, he traced the sins of those men seeking to stone the woman to death. . . .[5]

Susanne Vanderlugt began thus on Matthew 5:21-37:

I imagine that many of those who gathered to hear Jesus were completely shocked when he quoted a law from Deuteronomy—"You have heard that is was said to those of ancient times"—and then revised that law—"But I say to you. . . ." After all these were God's words that had been passed down through the great leader Moses, and Deuteronomy's injunction against altering any laws was always honored. No one ever rewrote legislation.[6]

Karl Barth focused broadly, and doctrinally, on the meaning of Easter in introducing this sermon on Ephesians 2:1-2, 4-6:

What is Easter? The Bible answers: resurrection, resurrection of Jesus from the dead; and that means: the living God, forgiveness of sins, the empty tomb, conquered death—in a word, Jesus is victor. But really, are these answers? . . . Are these clear, plain, understandable words, from which light streams forth? Are they not rather hard to understand, hazy words, which follow one another, which only involve us in deeper enigmas? May we not say to ourselves, "Life is hard and dismal. We have little enough light."[7]

Note that even in Barth's heavily doctrinal introduction (and in spite of his own claim that sermons should leave congregational needs to the Holy Spirit) he is addressing a need in the lives of his congregation. He is asking of his text: What question does this answer in the lives of my people? What brokenness in their experience does it address?

4. **Start with a social justice issue.** Starting a sermon by moving directly into a social justice issue, without warning or preparation, can alienate listeners. However, in this sermon by Raymond L. Brown, preached in an African American setting, the issue is one on which congregational accord is clearly established. Brown uses a key image of opposing weather fronts to give drama and interest to his words:

We have come here this week facing the reality that the storms of life are raging across our nation and world with a fierceness that suggests the convergence of opposing fronts. The searing heat of urgency to redeem the social and political economic plight of our communities collides with bitter cold winds of racism and injustice that never seem to abate. These are not just isolated and separate occurrences. Upon the landscape of human activity and interaction these storms are developing along well-defined lines of frustration and futility every-where.[8]

In the following sermon introduction, Carlyle Fielding Stewart III confronts the drug problem head-on through his narrative focus on one individual:

Sweat swarmed and beaded the palms of his hands as his heart thumped and pulse escalated. Bulging eyes blinked rapidly as his face twitched. His brown, swollen hands rumbled nervously through the inside pocket of his urine-stained tweed overcoat. . . . "I got to find a match," he whispered, half screaming. "If I don't find that match, I'm gonna kill somebody!"

Finally the match. Now the pipe and that little white ball of crack. Now he would take leave of his five senses. Now he would take refuge in that white ghost; the white witch that promised to be the answer to his deepest yearnings. Now he would do the solemn death dance and prepare himself to go as high and as far as the junk would take him.

The hostage crisis is not where terrorists, brandishing semi-automatic weapons, heap scorn and scourge upon the innocent by making them captive. The hostage crisis is not where planes are skyjacked. . . .

The hostage crisis today is where the people of God are taken prisoner by evil and spiritual decadence. . . .[9]

5. **Start with a news item.** Starting with news or other contemporary cultural items can be an excellent way of capturing interest quickly and leading people into the biblical text. But not just any news story will work. At the beginning of a sermon, listeners are trying to adjust to listening, to the preacher, and to the subject matter. A story about people that involves humor can work well, but a tragic story rarely does. The exception, of course, is when the church community has been overtaken by such an event, such as the riots in Los Angeles or the Oklahoma bombing, then to speak about

something else would be absurd. In such cases, the sermon has close parallels to the funeral sermon.

One of my favorite classic sermon introductions is by Harry Emerson Fosdick of Riverside Church in New York City several decades ago:

> Recently the newspapers carried the story of a man who boarded a bus with the full intention and desire of going to Detroit, but when at the end of a long trip he alighted at the destination, he found himself not in Detroit, but in Kansas City. He had caught the wrong bus. Something like that goes on habitually in human life. People on the whole desire good things—happiness, fine family life, competence in their work, the respect of their friends, an honorable old age. Nothing is more common in our consciously held desires and intentions than such good goals, but after a long trip, how many, alighting at the destination, find themselves somewhere else altogether!
>
> That man who started in Detroit and landed in Kansas City would not at first believe it. Stepping from the bus, he asked for Woodward Avenue and [when] told there was no Woodward Avenue, he was indignant. He knew his Detroit; there was a Woodward Avenue; and protesting against inhospitable failure to direct him, it was some time before he could face the fact that despite the clarity of his desire and his intention, it was not Detroit. He had caught the wrong bus.
>
> The Prodigal Son did not start out for a swine pasture. His desire was centered on happiness. . . .[10]

We could find our own examples in the news. Stories in the introduction should not be so long that they leave the congregation wondering about our purpose in telling it. If it is too long, we can use it later, or interrupt it, as Fosdick did above, to make relevant connections. This next news story is similar to the kind Jesus told, and could easily be adapted to a variety of themes:

> Three orphans in Sierra Leone recently made world news. They had just been returned to their tiny home village for the first time in weeks since their parents had been killed by rebels. Now they were alone and had no one to care for them. They had had no food for two days when they went looking for wild yams. Although they walked for miles they were unsuccessful. On the way back they were successful beyond their wildest dreams. One of them said, "On the way back we found a yam under a palm tree and dug it up. Right under the yam we found the diamond. It was easy to see because it

was shining and sparkling." The diamond proved to be a flawless 100-carat diamond worth $650,000.[11]

Some preachers mistakenly might think that such a story could only be told when introducing a sermon on the parable of the pearl of great price, or on the danger of riches. But such thinking would be too narrow. Jesus' parables were connected to the realm of God, and that is a broad field that includes justice, mercy, righteousness, healing, reconciliation, homecoming, and the like. We can make similar application of our stories. In this case, perhaps the story could be an analogy of the surprising nature of God's love when we least expect it. Analogy assumes some point of correspondence or likeness. In the above story, we might want to stop short of offering the diamond finding as an example of God's action (which it might also be), lest the congregation fall into the danger of equating material wealth with God's love.

This next story goes as far as may be advisable in using a story that contains violence in the introduction—or anywhere. The general rule for the entire sermon is this: use no details of violence beyond the simple fact of it. Violent images are too powerful and may be difficult to counter. Moreover, we do not preach evil.

> Some of you may have read a story recently that would be funny if it had not involved a death. [This kind of disclaimer is helpful as a signal to the congregation that the preacher is sensitive to the death in this instance and is intending to focus on the lighter side of the present story.] In Fort Walton Beach in Florida two young men suspected of murder in a drug deal were fleeing the police. They deserted their Nissan Stanza, and in their haste one of the young men left his pager behind in the car. The police recovered the beeper, traced it to the young man, called him, and informed him that they had found his beeper, although they did not tell him they found it in the back seat of the car. They invited him to come down to pick it up. When he arrived, they arrested him.[12]

Again, a simple sentence attached to the end of the story can link the story to the theme statement. Something about foolishness (if the theme is wisdom), or greed in not wanting to lose the pager (if the theme is God's generosity), or being discovered (if the theme is identity before God) are obvious possibilities. By the end of the sermon it might be good to come back to this young man, or someone like him in another story, to extend God's mercy even to him.

6. **Start with a fictional account.** Occasionally a fictional event, if well-developed, can make a powerful introduction. Alvin O. Jackson began a sermon in the following compelling fashion. The time and place references are to his own congregation:

> Have you heard that on January 16, 1994, at 70 North Bellevue, The Mississippi Boulevard Christian Church, Memphis, Tennessee, around 11:30 a.m. a robbery was committed? An undetermined amount of money was stolen. This doesn't appear to be the first time the crime was committed. The evidence strongly suggests that this is only one of many unchecked offenses that have been going on over a long period of time. The evidence also suggests that it was an inside job. There were no signs of forced entry. Thirty-five hundred people were present at the scene of the crime and at least three thousand are suspected of actively participating in the robbery. None of the suspects has been apprehended. The authorities are still investigating.
>
> One of the authorities commented that in all of his years of investigating robberies, he has never seen anything like this one before. A large sum of money is missing, but no money seems to have changed hands. The money appears to have been stolen from God . . . address unknown. No indication of weapons used and no visible signs of a struggle. It appears to have been a robbery without a weapon.
>
> I have just come today on behalf of the authorities to issue the warrants for arrest. But I have also come to announce that the Judge in the case, who is also God, is willing to suspend the sentences and pardon all who will vow never to commit this crime again.
>
> This is the message that the prophet Malachi delivers to the people of Israel. . . .[13]

One of the reasons this works so well is that it leads so tightly into the biblical text. We must take care with fictional accounts not to manipulate the listeners into believing and feeling something that is just a trick. The most obvious example of this kind of manipulation is to tell a story that ends up being a dream the preacher had ("And then, I woke up").

Common Problems In Introductions

Five problems are common in introductions. One problem is starting with a question. For instance, a student recently began a sermon with, "Have you ever been to the beach? Well I have." The question was, of course, rhetorical, for in that group there were none who would say no. The student wanted to take listeners to the beach, but instead of painting the picture, creating the waves and sun and hot sand with words, he took the lazy route. He made the listeners do the work of conjuring up a vision of the beach on their own. It is far better to avoid questions in the introduction. The best way to involve listeners is to give them something involving. A question can say, You do the work. I'm nervous about being up here.

David Buttrick identifies three other problems in introductions: One is telling a joke at the beginning of the sermon; this, he says, is often disconnected and requires a second introduction to refocus the congregation.[14] Another is what he calls "oblique suspense," in which the preacher withholds relevant information as a false means of obtaining suspense: "The audience does not know what 'it' is, or who 'they' are, or where the action is happening."[15] Another problem is the step-down introduction,[16] in which the preacher keeps narrowing the subject, almost as though looking for a focus. He gives the example of an introduction that begins by naming the apostle Paul as a "brave champion of faith" and in successive sentences shifts first to his journeys, then to Corinth, then to the problems of the Lord's Supper, instead of just starting with the Lord's Supper.

A fifth, related problem is telling a story or event chronologically, rather than beginning in the place of action. (This can be a problem anywhere in the sermon, yet it is particularly apparent in the introduction.) A student told the story of going to South America with his wife and family to do mission work. He told of receiving the phone call, telling the family, going to the airport, landing, meeting the people, and eventually of a transforming experience that changed his judgmental attitude toward the people he had come to serve. Each time he started a new episode, his listeners expected something to happen that would disclose his purpose in telling the story. Instead, listeners kept being disappointed and became impatient. When he finally got to the heart of the story, interest had flagged.

The student was given another chance. He revised his story, this time beginning with the key event, which was the particular experience that transformed his attitude. He did not start at the chronological beginning of the story, but with the event and place of the main action he wanted to relate. Now, instead of pulling the hearers through the laborious earlier scenes, he simply made brief passing reference, in the middle of developing the action, to what his earlier reaction to the news had been and to his hopes and fears in the flight south. The homiletical principle: start at the place in the story where the key action takes place, with whatever has occurred already (i.e., the flight south) referred to as the action unfolds. The classical term for this is in *media res,* into the central things or the middle of the action.

Conclusion

In this section devoted to Monday's task, we considered how to start composing the sermon by attending to sermon unity—one text, one theme, one doctrine, one need, one image, and one mission (and we composed as a memory device the sentence, The Tiny Dog Now Is Mine). We identified six ways that a preacher might introduce a sermon by starting with: (1) a story that suggests the flip side of the theme statement; (2) a not-too-serious experience of the general theme; (3) the biblical text; (4) a social justice issue; (5) a news or cultural item; or (6) a fictional account. If we started with the biblical text itself we would consider the introduction to be a part of Page One; otherwise it should be treated as simply a paragraph or two prior to it. Now we move to Tuesday and the theological considerations that are appropriate to each of the sermon's four pages.

SECTION II
PAGE ONE: TUESDAY

CHAPTER FOUR

Trouble in the Bible

Earlier we briefly discussed the content of the four pages: Page One (trouble in the biblical text), Page Two (trouble in our world), Page Three (grace in the Bible: what God did), and Page Four (grace in our world: what God does). Now we will examine the content of these pages in greater detail.

In this four-page model of preaching, two pages—Pages One and Three—develop the biblical text with as much attention to biblical scholarship, theology, and creative expression as possible. Yet each has its own theological thrust, hence each has its own biblical material and resources upon which to draw. Page One, one-quarter of the entire sermon, considers the trouble in the biblical text; it examines human sinfulness and its consequences, together with human responsibility for corrective action in light of God's will. Page Three, another quarter of the sermon, examines God's active response to human trouble in the same text and in light of what God has accomplished in Jesus Christ.

An introduction might precede Page One since this page is devoted to the Bible. Why have I designated Page One as biblical? Why not simply devote the first page of the sermon to analyzing what is wrong in the world? This is an appropriate way to start a sermon; we can aim our homiletical movie cameras at much that needs correction from a Christian perspective without starting with the Bible—and in Chapter Thirteen we will consider various options for reordering the pages. However, the best reason for starting with the Bible (apart from the introduction) is theological: the sermon is God's Word, not merely a human word. As Christians, we seek to be instructed by God, thus from a theological perspective we do not presume already to know or to understand what is wrong. Even the knowledge of sin and evil is often a matter of revelation. We rely upon the Holy Spirit and Scripture to illuminate our individual and societal wrongdoing, and we approach the Bible with open minds and prayerful hearts, ready to discover and be discovered. A preacher can start a sermon with Page Two (trouble in our world) and then move to Page One (trouble in the Bible), but to do so the preacher has to have gone to the Bible so that Page Two can lead to Page One. Since the Bible normally provides the preacher's cue for trouble, I devote Page One in our sequence to the Bible.

A Theological Focus

In any biblical passage, something is wrong in human affairs because then, as now, sin is present. The text is included in the Bible for a reason. No matter how positive a text may seem at first, trouble is present and waiting to be discerned. Sometimes the trouble is explicit, as with David's sins of adultery and murder against Bathsheba and Uriah; sometimes it is implicit, for example, trouble in Corinth is never far from any of the passages in Paul's letters to the Corinthians. While knowledge of human wrongdoing is in part a matter of conscience ("what the law requires is written on their hearts, to which their own conscience also bears witness" Romans 2:15), the depth of human trouble is a matter of divine illumination, not mere individual observation or opinion; thus we depend on the Bible to illuminate trouble. Page One will lead to Page Two and a discussion of that same trouble in our own world.

On Page One preachers must do more than narrate what a biblical writer is saying. The agenda is theological. As Bryan Chappell says, we must determine the reason for the words or cause or occasion of them—"the mutual human condition that contemporary believers share with those to or for whom the text was written that requires the grace of the passage."[1] He calls this the Fallen Condition Focus (FCF) of a biblical text. It points to human sinfulness, our fallen condition, or the world's brokenness. Without an FCF, he says, we are unable properly to interpret a biblical text. It provides the "So What?" of the sermon: "A message that merely establishes 'God is good' is not a sermon. However, when the same discourse deals with the doubt we may have that God is good when

74

we face trial and demonstrates from the text how we handle our doubt with the truth of God's goodness, then the preacher has a sermon."[2] Chappell says that a biblical text may provide several possible FCFs. He offers three questions to ensure faithfulness to the text in determining an FCF: "(1) What does the text say? (2) What concern(s) did the text address in its context? (3) What do listeners share in common with those to (or about) whom it was written or the one by whom it was written?"[3] Chapell is imposing the kind of theological judgment on the text that preachers are constantly called to impose; there is no theological neutrality in preaching, for even to avoid making theological claims is to make a statement that can be evaluated theologically.

Page One is about one idea and one idea only—a theological idea about trouble in the Bible. This biblical trouble will lead to trouble in our world on Page Two and must prepare for God's action on Pages Three and Four. Page One thus must provide the occasion or reason for God's action. Every page serves the theme statement yet has its own discrete theological focus. The focus of Page One, in a short sentence, might be: Adam and Eve are expelled from the Garden (Genesis 3); or, The Corinthians are divided (1 Corinthians 1:10-17); or, The man was blind (John 9:1-12); or, The disciples were afraid (Luke 8:22-26). Whatever the sentence, it should be short and sharp. The preacher on Page One should focus only on it and develop it biblically and theologically, deepening the congregation's understanding and helping the listener to see the biblical text from this perspective. To stay focused on this one idea of biblical trouble, the preacher may be wise to write the short sentence across the top of Page One.

Page One and a Traditional Method of Preaching

An traditional, respected, and still common method of preaching is structured as exposition/application. In some ways Page One corresponds to this expository stance and Page Two corresponds to its application to our world. To exposit or exegete a text is to interpret it critically, or to develop a theme or understanding. The merits of a two-part structure are obvious: it is simple. It ensures that the sermon arises from the Bible, which is our primary authority. Preaching has one foot in Scripture and the other in contemporary situations (or as Karl Barth once said, preachers should have the Bible in one hand and the newspaper in the other). Because the preacher must seek an application, the message not only will be relevant, it will appear to the listener to be relevant.

The basic form is as ancient as Scripture: rabbis in Jesus' time provided "an exposition of the text that compared and contrasted earlier interpretations and then applied the text to the hearers."[4] The two movements are essentially one, as tossing the ball and hitting it with a racquet constitutes a serve. As T.H.L. Parker says of Calvin's sermons:

> Expository preaching consists in the explanation and application of a passage of Scripture. Without explanation it is not expository; without application it is not preaching. . . . Calvin believed in the universal relevance of Holy Scripture. There was not a man, woman, or child in the congregation to whom each book and each passage did not apply. It was just a question of trying his best to bring it home to them.[5]

In the history of preaching, a sermon in this format could be *exegetical,* moving verse by verse (e.g., many of Calvin's and Barth's sermons), yet more often was organized around a number of points with the development of one unifying idea. Sermons following this format were often long. The introduction itself could be a few pages and frequently included a preview of the sermon's key points (the technical name is the division of the argument). The exposition is not of the historical-critical sort that is common in the past century; instead it is commonly doctrinal discussion of theology found in the text and elsewhere in the Bible.[6]

Following exposition, the preacher then made a bridge to an application of the text today (our Page Two). George Herbert, in England in 1652, described the exposition/application method: "A parson's method in handling the text consists in two parts: First, a plain and evident declaration of the Meaning of the text;—and secondly, some choice observations, drawn out of the whole text, as it lies entire and unbroken in the scripture itself."[7] The sermon in those days often might last well over an hour; in fact, Herbert cautioned preachers not to exceed an hour for "who profits not in that time, will less afterwards."[8] This exposition/application model and its shorter variations are still used today throughout the world. In recent years, it has become identified, perhaps unnecessarily, with the negative practice of reducing a biblical narrative to propositions that are then applied to our time; the significance of the narrative often is either lost or distorted in the process. The fault lies not with the form itself but with the hermeneutical practices that have been implemented alongside it.

However, there is another disadvantage of equal importance that few people have noted. Preachers were tutored that sermon structure or form was one thing and content or theology was another. They were not made aware that using this form often predisposes one toward a theology that has dominated sermon content for centuries.

The Impact of Sermon Structure on Pulpit Theology

Sermon structure has never been considered in detail in the theological outcome of sermons. If a preacher goes exegetically into a biblical text only once, trouble in human affairs is going to be the normal theological focus. A preacher will emerge most of the time with a message that concentrates on human sin, or brokenness, and human responsibility to change. In this regard, it matters little whether the preacher follows a conservative or liberal path; nor does it matter much whether the biblical text seems to emphasize trouble or grace. The message is commonly one that states what people must do. The reason is simple: generally we cannot speak of God's grace without first identifying human brokenness and sin. We cannot speak accurately of the significance of Easter, without first speaking of the passion of Christ and his crucifixion. To attempt to do so is to void the cross and empty tomb of their significance. God is sovereign and communities have responsibility before God to behave in certain ways. Preachers have responsibility to identify with their congregations—not to stand over them as "holier than thou"—and to name where all people fall short before the Word of God. Such words of address, reproof, and correction are essential; they initially come from the biblical text and then must be applied to the contemporary world.

In other words, Pages One and Two play an important theological function without which a sermon would be much diminished. But when preachers have stopped there, sermon form normally predetermines a theology of trouble. *Trouble at the simplest level puts the burden on humans to change.* This burden is appropriate, yet in itself it is only part of the Christian story: God acted in the cross and resurrection and did everything that was required. At the heart of our faith is this very important paradox: the burden God places upon humans is the burden that God has already accepted in Jesus Christ. Obviously, trouble and grace are related and cannot entirely be separated from one another. Even identification of trouble and revelation of human sin is a saving word. However, grace is God's action and *grace at its simplest level puts the burden on God, not on humans.* This is our true source of good news, hope, joy, and celebration.

The old model of exposition/application predetermines theology in another way. It prevents the caring preacher from naming trouble in a strong voice: if there is no balm in Gilead and no physician who can bring healing, why operate? Or to use another metaphor, when most preachers bring out their blues trumpets to play the tunes of trouble, they use a mechanical device known as a mute to muffle the sound *(con sordino),* instead of playing full volume. However, when preachers know that they have a way to proclaim good news, the fullness of both the trouble and the gospel can be heard by discarding the mute *(senza sordino).* In preaching, we discard the mute by adopting a second exposition/application movement (Pages Three and Four) that focuses on God's action. As we compose Pages One and Two, we should remember that Pages Three and Four will follow.

Preachers have used numerous other approaches to preaching without questioning how structure affects theology: exegetical sermons, which develop the biblical text chronologically or verse by verse; expository sermons, which develop larger portions of Scripture, aiming at the overall structure of a passage; doctrinal sermons, which develop a Christian doctrine; thematic or topical sermons, which develop a theme or topic from life; and narrative sermons, which often retell the biblical story or employ narrative principles such as plot to structure material. Any one of these could employ a theological principle that is sensitive to the need for preaching to be good news. A number of teachers of preaching across the theological spectrum have spoken of this need, including Frederick Buechner,[9] Eugene Lowry,[10] Richard Lischer,[11] and Bryan Chappell.[12] For the most part, however, preachers have given priority to literary matters over theological ones: that is, they preach good news only if their biblical text sounds to them like good news, and frequently they fail even then. At best, God's action is mentioned only in the closing moments of the sermon, with no opportunity afforded to experience God in the Bible text or the world. But here we are getting ahead of ourselves.

When Trouble Seems Absent

In the sermon journey, good news is on the other side of the land of trouble, or as Frederick Buechner baldly says, "The Gospel is bad news before it is good news."[13] We cannot get to a strong theology of grace except via a strong theology of human trouble. While essential for the first half of the sermon, we simply do not want our tour of it to be the entire journey. Trouble, after all, does not have the final word in faith.

Some Bible texts may seem to have no trouble in them, or may seem to emphasize trouble to the exclusion of grace. For now, let us simply affirm that when one or the other seems not to be present, we need to read the text more closely. The portion of the text we have chosen to preach may be too small, or we may not have explored the larger background of the text. Even a text like "Rejoice in the Lord always, for again I say Rejoice" (Philippians 4:4), has trouble behind it: the Philippians need this instruction because they do not always rejoice. Who is able on their own to rejoice always? God's Word is always double-edged—binding and freeing, trouble and grace. The word that condemns also liberates. Our sin and brokenness is always in tension with the grace God freely gives to us. The two do not negate each other, nor are they meant to by the end of the sermon. Both are not only true, but can be shown to be true, and in that tension faith is fostered and life is lived.

Most preachers have not been taught or encouraged to look for both trouble and grace, thus for some it is easy to forget that the Christian message is hope. We have been conditioned by our culture, perhaps even our churches' culture, not to see both. Both are readily present in biblical texts if we train ourselves to see them and are open to the guidance of the Holy Spirit. As John Wesley once said, every law contains a hidden promise. Every door of judgment is an opening of grace; every sinful act of humans is met by God in

79

Christ. When we exclude trouble or grace from a sermon, we make a choice. We opt for a theology in preaching that is an incomplete expression of the faith, a less than full encounter with God's Word.

Guidelines for Page One

There are similarities between the old exposition/application approach and our four-page model. There are also important differences, as should become apparent in the following guidelines for developing Page One.

Preachers should choose a complete pericope (i.e., a complete unit of Scripture; often this is a single narrative or portion of an epistle) as the Bible text for the sermon, not simply a verse, even though a single verse may seem most important. The congregation should have the opportunity to hear enough of the Scripture read and interpreted to get a sense of the context. Equally important, we have to find enough in our text to speak at length upon it, enough to fill two pages (Pages One and Three). We preach primarily on only one text, even if we read more than one. For to present one text with scholarly integrity and imaginative power, and to apply it to our world is often barely possible in the time available. We might mention other texts in passing once the main one is clearly established, but we do this only if we will not confuse the congregation about which text is which. Again, reference to other texts is not for purposes of detailed exegesis but for obvious connections of story, image, or idea. The congregation is in church not to worship Bible texts but to worship God, and to this goal we dedicate our efforts.

Listeners need a substantial focus of several minutes in one area to "get the picture." Recreate the biblical text (as much as is needed for Page One) as though it has not been heard in the first reading—even if the biblical text was read immediately prior to the sermon. Often by Sunday we preachers have become obsessed with the biblical text and see everything in terms of it with three-dimensional clarity; unfortunately we assume that church members will also have it seared into their minds in similar fashion, though they will have only heard it in one oral reading. Normally we cannot discuss a piece of music with house guests if we have not first played it for them. In retelling a portion of the text, in recovering the lived situation of the biblical text, we are already interpreting and affecting it.

Although we will not fully focus upon and develop the theme sentence until midway in the sermon, on Page Three, for the sake of sermon unity we are best advised not to begin Page One without it. Once the theme of the sermon is in place, we can determine the focus of Page One.

If we are unsure how to connect Page One with the theme sentence, we could try a focus for Page One that is the inverse or flip side of the theme statement. For example, the theme sentence, "Jesus heals the person who is blind" (John 9), can yield for Page One, "Many people needed healing" (a reference to the Pharisees as religious authorities). We must make sure that the focus for Page One is a legitimate interpretation of the text, however. For example to say "Many people were not healed" is probably not a fair reading for purposes of proclamation since the text makes no mention of it. While we need Ricoeur's hermeneutical suspicion in reading texts, obscure interpretations— though they may be legitimate from a literary perspective—are rarely helpful. Generally a fair interpretation is established when three or more separate pieces of information in a text all point in the same direction. For example, we can say the Prodigal Son matured while he was away: he realized the stupidity of his own actions as he ate with the swine; he confessed that he had sinned against his father; and he returned with the desire to be his father's slave.

We should be able to identify the focus of every page in a short sentence. In fact, at the beginning of sermon composition, students are wise to take all four blank pages and write at the top of each one a short sentence that is the focus for each page. In order for each page to be devoted to its topic sentence, preachers are wise to discuss that sentence early on the page, rather than getting to it at the end of the page, where it will be hard for listeners to hear it as an organizing principle.

For example, with the woman at the well (John 4), we choose as the theme sentence or God-action statement for the sermon, "Jesus gave the woman living water." For Page One we want some focus on trouble in the text that will lead to that statement and serve it as directly as possible. Thus Page One might focus on "The woman needed water" or, stronger from a theological perspective, "The woman needed more than water." This would allow the preacher on Page One to speak of the woman's various needs and troubles. Thus a sketch of the sentences one might put at the top of their respective pages might look like this:

Page One: The woman needed more than water.

Page Two: Many people today do not know what they need.

Page Three: **Jesus gave the woman living water.** (This is the sermon's theme sentence)

Page Four: Jesus has given us living water.

More examples and explanation in later chapters will help clarify this process (see pages 123, 171, 200-201; see also my *Practice of Preaching* [Abingdon, 1995], pp. 146-50, 164-71). For now we may remember that everything we say about the text on Page One is ultimately to lead toward and eventually serve the theme sentence, the God-action statement. We may need to ration textual material, thereby saving some fresh material and insights for Page Three.

Student preachers may have difficulty finding enough to say about a biblical text to keep the focus on it for an entire page. However, preachers should regularly consult Bible atlases, Bible dictionaries, word studies, commentaries, and other related sources. Moreover, experienced preachers train themselves to keep speaking for a paragraph or so without moving the discussion very far, keeping the focus in one place. We need to recognize just how small is a unit of thought and move one small step at a time, without becoming laborious or tedious. In the next chapter we will review many examples of Page One in published sermons.

Though we speak about trouble in the text, acknowledging such things as the apparent distance of God or the ongoing suffering in Israel, we always speak from the perspective of faith. While we admit the reality and importance of doubt, the difficulty of faithful living, and lament the failures of the world and the church, we never merely attack the faith or stand outside it in our proclamation. We are not striving to present the text in a neutral manner, thus theological reflection upon events and people in the text is entirely appropriate. Such reflection can help to build the sustained focus that we need.

Movie Making—Exposition with a Difference

Perhaps the single most important guideline for Page One is this: as much as it is wise and possible, approach the task of composing the text as a movie director might shoot a film, through the eyes of the viewer; likewise the preacher must craft the sermon with the listener in mind, recognizing that the listener is accustomed to getting information visually through computers, televisions, and movies. As preachers, we strive to present essential exposition of the biblical text in a manner that will communicate effectively to our listeners. The manner of doing this needs to be different from former times, for the needs of our age and culture are different. We can no longer assume that congregations will return if, week after week, we launch into reading an essay, no matter how good that essay may be. We are compelled to find ways to communicate to the generations born since World War II, who have grown up in "electronic culture." This means we should also avoid writing an exegetical assignment for a biblical class and avoid treating the text primarily as a history text concerning ancient times. We need a way to treat biblical texts and events as though they are about real events involving real people who in many ways are like us. We need a means of recovering the lively concrete nature of most biblical language itself.

To accomplish this difficult task, preachers might begin thinking of themselves as movie directors. I recall speaking to a woman who wanted to be a writer. I had seen some of her writing and I knew she wrote well. "Do your think of yourself as a writer?" I asked. "No," she responded. Perhaps that is what she needed to do—until she claimed that she was a writer, she might not be one. Similarly, we may need to view our own tasks of sermon composition as movie directing tasks if we are to see a change in the manner of our composition. As movie directors we place ourselves on the "set" of the text, somewhere in the Middle East that the text identifies or suggests. Real geography surrounds us. Listeners should meet the main character (e.g., Paul, or the community members from or to whom he writes), observe his behavior, and overhear a few spoken words as a means of establishing realism.

Dangers of Making Movies

I make this movie-making suggestion with a certain amount of trepidation because ideally we should simply present the text as it is, unsullied by any of our interference with it. Unfortunately, that is not possible, and every great preacher who advocated this principle—like Luther, Calvin, Barth, and others—violated it. We cannot preach the pure text. In fact, we alter a text by translating it, or by lifting it out of its context, or by treating it exegetically, verse by verse, or by expositing it, or indeed by making a movie of it. This is no excuse for abandoning caution: we must minimize distortion of a text as much as possible. Since we cannot interpret a text without sullying it, we must simply acknowledge that this is part of the process of preaching and seek to minimize it as much as possible.

We affirm that the word we proclaim both witnesses to Christ and is used by Christ to reveal God's nature to God's children. In fact, we can only render the divine and human nature of God's Word through the human dimension of our words used for divine purposes. We take a risk even by treating a biblical text as an essay— we render the Word of God in an abstract manner that may communicate poorly in our age. We take the risk of movie making for a good reason—to communicate effectively to the youth as well as the adults of the church. A safe way of preaching the gospel is not available, and the best way, whatever it is, will be ventured in faith, informed by scholarship, and will render the word in a lively engaging manner that is as faithful to the text as we can make it.

I am also hesitant to suggest movie making because some of the worst sermons I have heard have been those that have long descriptive passages, and boring, lengthy, or unrealistic monologues or dialogues. The only solution to protect against these poor sermons might be for preachers either to abandon reaching people in a manner that will interest them and us, or to become great novelists—an impossible feat for most of us. However, making a video is more achievable and less daunting. We can readily begin to visualize what is needed: geography, people, action. We immediately have a mental model of what we are after from television: listeners should see action happening the way that we see the action happening in or behind the Bible text.

I am also aware, however, that sermons in most traditions are not the most vital form of communication and that, as preachers, we owe it to God to strive to do better for the sake of the gospel. Churchgoers today are accustomed to watching television, and their thought processes are shaped by it. To reach people effectively today, preachers must use a style that is largely visual, yet that addresses the other senses as well. The movie that we make will speak in the present tense (as much as possible) as a way of making events vividly present to the listeners. Marshall McLuhan, in his book *The Medium Is the Message,* refers to cool and hot media. An essay-style lecture is a cool medium. Long descriptive passages and corny dialogue are also cool media. A good movie is a hot medium. We can make vibrant pictures with words for listeners to see, not by larding our prose with descriptive passages, but by using occasional picture and sensory words in economic, almost minimalist fashion.

Our goal can be to direct movie experiences that do more than merely convey information and that effectively reach even the youth in our churches. Creative writing has an old maxim, "Show instead of tell." Instead of giving listeners mere exegetical facts, data, abstract ideas and propositions, we can process this information visually to help inform the filming of the text. Our purpose is not to eliminate abstract conceptual language from the sermon, for some of our self-understanding is provided by essential doctrinal language that we use; we simply want to reserve it for important doctrinal matters so that listeners, when they encounter it, are not already exhausted or inattentive.

Aiming the Camera: Scenes

David Buttrick suggests that the sermon be composed of a series of moves, or shots, with each move like camera lens taking a photograph that fixes an image or thought into consciousness.[14] If we think of a moving picture instead of a photograph, we are closer to what is needed for a television generation. Yet this poses a problem. Particularly youth, but now most people in society, are heavily influenced by the programs and movies they see. Viewers expect frequent shifts of camera angle and rapid scene changes, as often as several per minute, and they are accustomed to holding a remote control device for additional variation and choice in channel selection. How can preachers begin to compete with such high-powered, technology-assisted communication?

The simple answer is that preachers do not and cannot compete directly with such media; we should not try to make the sermon into a sound and light show. Self-conscious concerns about whether we are "hot" or "cold" are not entirely appropriate, given that we are simply called to be faithful proclaimers of the gospel. Moreover, apart from situations where we speak to seekers, we preach to a group of people who normally are present not so much to listen to the preacher as to listen for God speaking through the preacher's words. Still, there is no reason for us to be complacent, or for us to bring to our task of communication less dedication and skill than speakers elsewhere bring to their topics; Jesus reprimanded his followers concerning "the children of this age [who] are more shrewd in dealing with their own generation than are the children of light" (Luke 16:8 RSV). We can improve our preaching. Television teaches us to be visual and engage the other senses. Yet if we try changing scenes in the sermon as often as on television, or if we keep changing the angle of our camera lens, we will lose our hearers for the simple reason that we depend upon them to make the camera and scenery changes in their minds. In fact, we must keep the focus in one place for several minutes in order for the congregation to get on board, and this is one reason for our pages.

Rapid scene changes are not an option for us, but we do have a highly effective alternative at our disposal. Instead of shifting the scene, every few sentences we can use a word that is sensory. We can film in color and provide through our words something for the congregation to see, hear, touch, taste, or smell. Preachers can practice using concrete language, even as seminaries perhaps should train students in all courses for this kind of effective communication.

Every time we make a scene change, for instance, at the beginning of each page, we will need to set the stage for the listener. People cannot picture a boat accurately if they do not know whether it is bobbing in a bay or whipping down the highway on a trailer. A few quick details will establish the location. Do not compose a paragraph of description (that is too much!) and then a paragraph that deals with action. Action should be an early focus. Description should filter through the action. If we introduce a place, we should depict something distinctive about it (for instance an evocative detail, that it is by the sea or in a desert). Paul's letters often seem to be about abstract ideas, yet much of his language is concrete, and we do have some knowledge of the lifestyle, architecture, economy, vegetation, and location of his people and their communities.

Place essential scholarly or exegetical material within the story the way a movie maker would do this, allowing it to be seen or heard. One of the characters can say it; or something in the setting or action can communicate it. The concrete details we seek are not drawn out of thin air. Research resources can help us to make a biblical scene real for listeners. A Bible dictionary or a travel book for the Holy Land often can provide otherwise hard-to-find information about Middle East flora, fauna, geography, architecture, economy, and climate of biblical locations; perhaps the best travel resource is one edited by Catherine Fouré, *The Holy Land*.[15] Again, our purpose is not to load the biblical text with extraneous detail, for that is simply bad writing, but is to provide occasional one-word pictures that assist in our filming of an authentic biblical setting.

Aiming the Camera: People and Action

The setting is important background material, and should remain in the background:. We ought to focus on people and action; description and conversation are essential but we should keep both brief, weaving them into the action. Beware of adjectives and adverbs: many of us mistake them for description and creative writing. We speak of "the beautiful road" instead of being specific, "the road ran alongside the beach." Or we say, "she ran quickly," instead of saying, "she scrambled," or, "her feet pounded down the trail." We also should try to avoid using clichés like, "she ran like the wind."

Instead of relying upon adjectives and adverbs to paint our scenes, people, and actions, we can be observant and concentrate on small details like gestures and objects, particularly those that give clues to characters and relationships. Paul writes as one person to other people about events that are taking place in communities that can be named. We should provide a few details about a biblical person concerning clothing (clothing gives clues to personal interests, profession, or economic situation), or manner of walking, or age. If we actually were making a movie, we would have no choice but to make these decisions. We make these decisions here because we are trying to reach the widest age-group possible. Listeners can visualize someone if we give them visual clues, such as gray hair or the elegance of movement. In general, we should be as visual and sensory with the Bible as we are about current events, when we speak of someone today wearing jeans (name the color and the specific label) and a tee shirt from the Hard Rock Cafe, or of a hospital room with a single birthday card on the window ledge, for these small details paint bigger pictures of individual lives.

Our focus should stay on the biblical characters' words and

actions yet we should stay out of the minds of characters as much as possible. Too often preachers, using narrative instead of movie making as their model, will tell the story from inside someone's head, and will relate all of the character's thoughts and emotions. Again, as a general principle, stay out of the minds of the characters. Monologues or extensive dialogues are rarely as effective as a brief quotation here and there to give a sense of real people speaking. Concerning what information to communicate: let the camera be your model. We overstate the case here, but in movie making, if you cannot see or hear something, you cannot say it. You speak primarily through words that provide the actions and speech of the characters. Movie directors rarely can use the voice of a narrator to explain things, if at all. As much as possible preachers ought to let the events happen instead of reporting and commenting on everything. The hearer must be able to attribute motive to a character according to details uncovered in the plot, not by the narrator explaining it. When you are not certain how to communicate something, ask how a film director would communicate it without a narrator. In portraying a character we should not psychologize, psychoanalyze, or reduce the person to one dimension, for instance, by implying that someone is all good or all bad, with no inner conflict or ambiguity. Allow the listeners to experience the characters by providing brief events or episodes where we have a chance to experience them. Still, the entire sermon does not have to be a movie. But when we are making movies with our sermons, we should be striving to make them well. We are not making "B-grade" movies.

Conclusion

We spoke earlier about one doctrine and one congregational need from the theme sentence or doctrine (in fact, all of the components represented by "The Tiny Dog Now Is Mine" ought to be in our minds as we compose, to assure sermon unity). Now we might begin to use these to influence, shape, or instruct Page One and other pages. Again, if the theme statement is, God reaches out to those in trouble, the doctrine is the nature of God, and the congregational question might be, "Where is God when I am in need?" This question or need can be used in the course of Page One with the biblical text, or elsewhere in the sermon. It can be a legitimate question to put in the mouths of the biblical characters in the movie we make.

We also discussed how to aim the camera to set the scene and to focus on the people and their actions by attending to small details to make the biblical characters come alive through use of sensory words. The reason we rely upon movie making through words is not to be part of a fad or to be trendy. We do it to be good communicators, by imitating the concrete and often sensory language of the biblical texts themselves. Many of these texts resemble movie scripts, complete with brief dialogue. Most important, we are ensuring that new generations have the opportunity of hearing the gospel message. We now turn to practical examples of Page One in published sermons.

CHAPTER FIVE

Filming Trouble in the Bible

Page One is a metaphor for theological function and imaginative endeavor appropriate to the first foray into the biblical text, thus any biblical sermon is likely to have material on trouble appropriate to this page. This chapter is devoted to reviewing published sermons to discern how various preachers have filmed the biblical trouble in their sermon composition. Of course we should try to make movies only as much as this is possible and wise, for important propositional or abstract material still has an important place in preaching. Not all of the categories below directly relate to filming the text, but they all contribute to the final product. Readers might use these review samples to stimulate their own creative ventures with biblical texts.

Develop Trouble

Each sermon has one theme sentence, and each page of a sermon is about one focus that serves that theme sentence. (In other words each page has its own subtheme that can be stated in a short sentence at the top of each page—one theological task that relates directly to the overarching theme.) On Page One the single focus is an idea or story of biblical trouble. Too often in sermon delivery preachers will spend no time on their text. They will cite it briefly and hastily move on, without considering the time listeners need to appropriate what is said. In order to have enough to say, preachers need to learn to expand discussion of a Bible text.

Samuel D. Proctor expands his discussion of the trouble in the text of the Good Samaritan (Luke 10:25-37). All of what follows is on just one verse: the first paragraph concentrates on the mugged man's anonymity; the second establishes the lack of physical clues to his identity; and the third focuses on his suffering. Yet all are about one idea or event of trouble: "a certain man" (KJV) was robbed and beaten and left by the side of the road. Proctor incorporates material from scholarly research in his narration:

[Jesus] started out, "A certain man. . . ." He wouldn't give away the identity of the man's tribe, his race, his clan, his social class, his dialect, or even the language he spoke. We don't need to know any of that! Why do we need footnotes on him? Jesus left all that information out! Just *Homo sapiens*, that's all. A certain man, it could have been anybody, was simply on his way from Jerusalem to Jericho. If we ask about the man's background and all of that, we start ruining the whole story. Jesus wants to leave the subject right there.

The journey was seventeen dangerous miles through lonely, rocky, rough desert, and it is still seventeen lonely miles even today. Robbers and muggers were known to attack travelers, and this man was beaten by thieves and left half dead. In the story Jesus had the man's clothes torn off and had him unconscious so that we can not identify him by his clothes; we can't tell anything by the cut of his garment, the depth of the border, the hem of the cloth, or the color of the cloth. We can't tell whether he was a poor man with a cheaply woven piece of cloth or a rich man with a cloth of smooth purple and a deep hem. We don't have the advantage of getting our prejudices working. He was a 'certain man.' Jesus left him naked so we wouldn't have any clue whatsoever as to his status; and he was unconscious so we can't hear his accent. We don't know whether he said "sibboleth" or "shibboleth."

So, since he was lying without clothes and was unconscious, we can't tell who was lying there. Jesus was trying to fix it so that all we have to deal with is the man's suffering. Jesus removed every other detail. He was hurt! Without clothes and unconscious, there the man lay. He could have been a person of our own race and class, and we might have helped out of ethnic pride and loyalty, not out of pure compassion. He could have been one of another race and class. Jesus made the story tell of nothing but a human being in need, half dead, beaten, and robbed. We don't know how well educated he was or how poor he was. We don't know what family he came from or what side of town he lived on. Barely breathing, bloody, and near death the "certain man" was left to die.[1]

Beginning students or inexperienced preachers might think that this pace is too slow. Not so; this is excellent communication of the sort that is most helpful for preaching. It can take years to unlearn good habits for writing that are bad habits for speaking, and to shift into oral/aural ways of communication. By the same token, it can take years to unlearn bad habits of speaking and to write well for the pulpit.

Choose One Doctrine

The purpose of Page One is not just to introduce the biblical text in a lively and animated manner, but to introduce it theologically—from the perspective of trouble in the text. An experienced preacher should be able to listen to the trouble on Page One and deduce from it the flip side, the grace of Page Three, the theme of the sermon. Ralph J. Wallace develops the doctrine of salvation in a sermon on Galatians 3:16-22; his Page One focuses on the flip side, excessive reliance upon the law. Pauline passages are difficult to present creatively as a movie yet here strong visual images contribute to the theological strength. Wallace's thought progresses in small steps from paragraph to paragraph, instead of remaining on exactly the same point or leaping from one place to another, yet he always serves his one focus:

> They were Judaizers, those who believed that to become a Christian was first to become a Jew. It was not enough to accept God's promise, "believe on the Lord Jesus Christ and you shall be saved." One had also to observe the laws and customs of Moses. . . .
>
> Salvation by the gracious promises of God sounds uncomplicated enough but promises are intangible, nebulous, ethereal, hard to catch and hold. And the Judaizers demanded something into which they could sink their hooks, something in which they could see their conversion, and hear their compliments, and feel their climb toward heaven. Promises demand an eternity of standing on tiptoe, an eternity of neck stretching, in order to glimpse their fulfillment. The Judaizers had to do something then, something on which they could rest, something in which they could find concrete comfort. The Judaizers of Galatia wanted more than promises so they turned to the Law.
>
> However, in our scripture, Paul insisted that promises are primary and that they precede the Law. The short and bow-stemmed Apostle had his feathers ruffled by the Galatians. We can almost see his dark

eyes flashing and the nostrils of his . . . nose expanding and contracting as he writes searing words something like this: "You stupid Galatians! You have been spellbound by the wrong people. . . . You look to the Law to make you perfect."[2]

Here the theme sentence of the sermon might be, God's promises are our fulfillment. On Page One a preacher could start to use that theme sentence, or a challenge to it, as a means to develop the sermon's unity of purpose. Even if the listeners are able to predict where the sermon is going, this is not a bad thing. Too many preachers believe that the drama arises from the question Where is this going? The point of the sermon is not, How is the preacher going to pull this off? The appropriate point is, What is God doing and how am I empowered to live better? This is a theological question the effective preacher seeks to raise in listeners' minds. They need to know where they are being taken, and that the destination is worthwhile, in order to follow willingly. Usually a detective novel involves a murder and a romance, and readers know this before they start reading. To know this is not to know the plot. How we get to the destination is the plot and how the preacher gets from trouble to believable empowering grace is the theological and imaginative drama of the sermon.

Use One Dominant Image

Barbara Brown Taylor uses the image of Luke as a doctor to unify a sermon and give it its title, "Gospel Medicine." She uses background information concerning her text to make it come to life:

> I like to think that Luke never resigned his job as a healer. He just changed medicines. Instead of prescribing herbs and spices, hot compresses and bed rest, he told stories with power to mend broken lives and revive faint hearts. Instead of pills and potions, he carried words in his black bag, words like, "Weep no more," "Do not be afraid," "Your sins are forgiven," "Stand up and walk." His medicine was gospel medicine, which was Jesus' medicine—medicine that works, strangely enough, through words.[3]

James O. Rose devises a clever image of "giant troubles" from 1 Samuel 17:1-51, and uses it to bring the trouble in the lives of his people into sharp and amusing biblical focus. Because trouble is the focus, some preachers may think they should steer away from humor; but when dealing with trouble, appropriate humor can assist it to be heard.

> Saul is looking at life from ground level. Giants are overwhelming to those who look at life from that level. Giants are terribly hard to handle on your own. Israel ought to know: they've had giant troubles before. The report of Goliath's imposing ancestors stopped a whole generation of Israel at the door to the Promised Land. When the new crew finally did enter the Promised Land, only Caleb invaded giant country. He handled most of them, but at eighty years of age, we wouldn't expect him to get them all. Goliath is a leftover, a big leftover. And it only takes one giant leftover to unglue folks looking at life from ground level. From ground level giants fill up our screen. The closer we get, the bigger they look. We shouldn't consider giants unusual or unexpected. They roam in every generation—theirs at 1000 B.C. in Elah Valley and ours at A.D. 2000 in our valleys. I'll bet you've got one in your valley, a valley you must cross, if you're going on with God. I do, too. My giant has been waving at me lately.
>
> The issue is: What are we going to do about our giants? Those locked into ground level living refuse to face them. . . .[4]

The danger of having more than one image is demonstrated in this closing paragraph of a sermon that is constructed around three images—locks, rocks, and key. Because the image is triple, no clear picture of anything is presented to the mind (how are a rock and a key to connect?). Do not imitate this.

> Locks and rocks, that is why Christ came. He is the sure Rock to guide your life. He is the Key that came confessing the love of the Father. He is the one Rock and Key that helps us to cope with life and not collapse. When Peter was in prison and looked at his cell, he could sing, and that night Christ, the Key of David, sent an angel. The doors were opened, and chains and locks were opened, and Peter was free to proclaim his marvelous Master. We have been freed for the same.[5]

Employ the Senses

Even a short passage can have movie-like features. Raymond Bailey uses a tracking camera and includes a couple of relevant, historically accurate visual and sensory details to make more real his brief account of Jesus going to the pool of Bethsaida in a sermon on John 5:1-6. One or two sensory details in any paragraph can add vividness and interest. Obviously preachers must observe suitable decorum and avoid using material simply to shock or manipulate listeners. In this example, Bailey is wise in saying no more than he does and in keeping his words brief: he briefly establishes the necessary effect and moves on.

> Here is Jesus on a religious holiday coming to the holy city of Jerusalem, but does he go into the Temple to worship? Does he seek out the wise men of the town for discourse? No. He goes with haste to this place where the clientele are the blind, lame, or paralyzed. It was a place that would not be beautiful by our standards. The odors of illness and unkept bodies are not pleasant to our noses. The sight of uncared for, broken bodies in their own waste turns weak stomachs.[6]

In a sermon on Hosea and Gomer, Barbara Brown Taylor captures this vivid motion-picture of Israel's relationship with God. Notice the numerous sensory words Taylor uses to make the scene come alive. Notice also the remarkable compassion in the child image of the last sentence.

> The moment the rains failed or the cows ran low on milk, [Gomer] was gone, leaving nothing but a note on the kitchen table: "Gone to see if I can't do better than this."
>
> Where did she go? To other lovers, who promised everything her heart desired. . . . With Ba'al, there was no dreary talk of commitment or honor, no Where-were-you-last-night? and Have-you-thought-what-this-is-doing-to-the-children? Everything was spontaneous. You did what you felt like doing when you felt like doing it, and the only rule was to do what felt best at the time. No one knew your name and you did not know anyone else's, but it did not matter. All that mattered was giving in to the sweet, hot pulse of life.
>
> Israel always came home again, once she had taken the edge off her appetite, once she had been reminded for the umpteenth time that the grass of the other side was never as green as it looked. One morning Yahweh would hear the screen door slam and he would smell her before he saw her: cigarette butts, musty sheets, stale beer. Then she would come into the room and lean against the door jamb looking at him, a cut on her upper lip and the fading bruise of some-

one's strong grip on her arm, home to the husband who took her by the hand and drew her bath and tugged her torn clothes over her head while she held her skinny arms up for him like a child.[7]

Create the Geographical Setting

Geographical resource material from a Bible atlas or dictionary (or actual experience of the Holy Land) also can add sensory and other forms of interest to a biblical account. Normally, geographical setting can be established in one or two sentences. Laurie Haller develops a form of a brief travelogue and appeals primarily to senses of sight and space in a sermon on Mark 8:27-38.

Jesus and his disciples were in Caesarea Philippi, which is in the northern part of Palestine at the source of the Jordan River. In ancient history, Caesarea Philippi was a center for the worship of Baal, but it was also the place where the Greeks found one of their most prized gods. According to Greek mythology, the birth of Pan, the god of nature, took place in a cave from which sprang the Jordan River. So you see, Caesarea Philippi was a place associated with many pagan rites and traditions, and it competed for the attention of pilgrims from these two religions. The town used to be called Panias, after Pan's grotto, but because Baal's altar was also there, the name of the town was changed to Banias, which seems to have been a linguistic compromise.

By the time of Jesus, Banius was the site of a magnificent marble temple built in honor of Caesar Augustus. Caesarea Philippi, the Roman name for Banias, at the headwaters of the Jordan River, was the religious fortress of the pagan world. So why did Jesus and his disciples end up in Caesarea Philippi? Actually, Jesus was on his way to Jerusalem, and Caesarea Philippi was definitely out of the way. It was eighty miles north of Jerusalem and about twenty miles north of the Sea of Galilee.[8]

Film the Text from a Fresh Perspective

Haddon Robinson treats the encounter between Eve and Satan in Genesis like a movie. He uses the device of a debate and takes creative license with the text in order to communicate it in a lively manner, but he does so without distorting the central message he has gleaned from it. And although he is developing trouble in the text, he still is open to using good humor. He weaves exegetical insights into the retelling of the story. He includes brief conversation with the central character, Satan, and thereby makes the story more immediate or life-like.

> Not only is he [Satan] disguised in his person, but he disguises his purposes. He does not whisper to Eve, "I am here to tempt you." He merely wants to conduct a religious discussion. He would like to discuss theology; he doesn't intend to talk about sin. The serpent opens the conversation by asking, "Did God really say, 'You must not eat from any tree in the garden'?" You can't argue with that. Satan asks only for clarification. "Look, I want to be sure of your exegesis. I want to understand the idea God was trying to get across. Did he really say you can't eat of any of the trees of the garden?" You see, he is a religious devil. He doesn't come and knock on the door of your soul and say, "Pardon me, buddy, allow me a half hour of your life. I'd like to damn and destroy you." No, all he wants to do is talk about a point of theology. He only wants to interpret the Word of God. It is possible, isn't it, to discuss theology to our peril. We can talk about God in an abstract way, as though he were a mathematical formula. You can concoct a theology that leads you to disobey God.[9]

Nancy Hastings Sehested makes a movie of Exodus 1:8-22 from the fresh perspective of midwives. Some allusions to our time add richness to the biblical details and expressions; other details are not necessarily from the Bible text or scholarly resources but are the product of a well-tutored imagination. The phrase "let pharaoh go" will become a refrain by the end of the sermon that carries her theme sentence, "We follow the life-bearing God, not Pharaoh":

> Pharaoh had no idea what he was asking. . . .
> But Shiprah and Puah knew who they were. They knew their vocation meant assisting in life, not death. They knew they had no power before Pharaoh. So they let Pharaoh go—to think his own thoughts—to go his own way—while they followed their way assisting in life.
> It didn't take long for Pharaoh to get news of their defiance. Hebrew mommas were strolling boy babies up and down the streets showing them off, proud to have a son. The midwives were called in for the scolding. "Can't practice civil disobedience in this country," said Pharaoh.

The midwives looked Pharaoh straight in the eye and told him a cocka-
mamy story about the Hebrew women delivering their babies so much
more vigorously than Egyptian women that the babies were already
being burped for their first feeding by the time the midwives arrived.
Shiprah and Puah must have surely thought that such a noble lie could
easily pass by Pharaoh. After all, what did he know about birthing babies?
Who are our pharaohs?[10]

Create the Event, Don't Report It

We can revise the maxim "show, don't tell," into "create, don't
report"—provide an experience, don't just summarize the relevant
facts. There are places, such as in newspapers and some meetings,
where the bare facts are needed; occasionally this is true in preaching, for instance, when providing brief social statistics to support a
claim, but generally this is not the case. This sermon by Martin B.
Copenhaver (Excerpted from The Library of Distinctive Sermons, ©
1996, by Questar Direct, and reprinted by permission of Multnomah
Publishers, Inc.), follows the "create, don't report" maxim in quickly creating a dinner party with guests (instead of simply reporting
that a dinner party took place) in dealing with Luke 14:12-24 (RSV):

> Jesus offered his guidance on how to throw a party while he him-
> self was attending a party at the home of an important person, one of
> the right people, a ruler. Around the table were influential priests, suc-
> cessful lawyers, and other people of note. In short, it was the kind of
> party that would have done a first century Emily Post proud. . . .
> It was in the midst of this gathering, as they were beginning to pass
> around the kosher quail pâté, that Jesus said, "When you give a dinner or
> a banquet, do not invite your friends or your brothers or your kinsmen or
> rich neighbors, lest they also invite you in return and you be repaid. . . ."[11]

In another sermon Copenhaver uses his imagination to create a person the listeners can meet, again instead of simply reporting the facts.
He develops a fresh perspective on the text by introducing the widow
of the fool who stored up riches in Luke 12:16-21 and, through this
device, listeners experience more of the rich fool himself.

> I try to imagine what it would be like to make a pastoral call on the
> widow of the farmer in Jesus' parable of the rich fool. That in itself

would not be too difficult because I have made many such calls. The farmer has just died. His wife is in shock. She asks, "What is a person to do now? No one has told me what happens next." Her talk wanders, and I follow, mostly just listening. Then we turn to the memorial service, and I ask a few questions about the man who has recently died. You see, I didn't know him too well, although on one of those rare occasions when I did see him for a moment or two I genuinely liked him. But now, as we anticipate a memorial service, I know that it is up to me to speak of him as a whole person, not just of those few, fleeting moments that I have shared with him.

And so I ask, "What was important to him?" And his widow answers, "His family is—was—very important to him. He was really proud of his children, although I'm not sure they really know that. But he spoke of them often. His wallet was thick with their pictures. . . ."

I ask, "How did he spend his time?" She replies, "Oh working up on the farm. And he was very successful. As for other parts of his life, well they were put on hold for a while. I didn't always make things easier for him either. I would frequently ask him when it would all end and we could get on with our lives. And he would always try to reassure me, mostly by using words like *tomorrow* or *soon* and phrases like *this won't last forever* and *some day* and *I promise*. And he meant it. I know he did. . . ."[12]

Film the Story in Contemporary Idiom

Here is a portion of my own attempt to film the story of Joseph (Genesis 45:1-18) in contemporary idiom. To attempt this kind of retelling too often could offend some members of a congregation, but occasional use can offer interesting variety and can help to reach especially young people. I generally recommend avoiding preaching as a character in the biblical story, a form of first-person preaching in which the preacher takes on a role. While it can be effective if done well, it is often alienating. Nearly always, however, excessive textual distortion occurs, for the character in role becomes the center of the text. A general rule for homiletics is not, "does it work?," but "can something work better?"

When making a movie, continue to think of the exercise as theology, and include theology as part of the story where possible, such as in the last paragraph here. In other words, include God as much as possible. I place words concerning the nature of God in Joseph's mouth and repeat them to emphasize the difficult doctrine being developed:

> If Hollywood were writing the Bible script, events would not take place in Israel, but in Cape Cod, and Joseph's family would be a good Roman Catholic family of eleven sons. The opening shots would be aerial shots of the Atlantic surf crashing against the beaches of Cape Cod houses, dunes and boathouses. We would then see people playing on the beaches. Finally the camera would come to rest in front of an in-line-skate shop where seventeen year old Joseph and his friends are doing skating tricks. He is a ruddy, handsome boy with an easy smile and longish hair blowing in the wind. He does not notice his father Jacob driving up in the Mercedes. The window glides down. "Joseph. Joseph, come here. I want you to take these supplies to your brothers. They are out building the hotel on the island. Take the cutter, but be careful across the Sound. You know how much I love you."
>
> His brothers see Joseph coming across the water and the look on their faces is not one of pleasure. They show none of their contempt as they greet him. But that evening, when he is asleep in the boathouse, they pull his sleeping bag up over his head and tie it. They take him, not to a dry well in the desert as in the Bible story, but to a cave in a cove that will be covered by water at high tide. Their work done they decide that they have made a mistake. They cannot kill their own brother. They phone a man on the island who does frequent runs to South America on his boat who has connections with the drug trade. They arrange for him to take Joseph and sell him as a slave in South America. . . .
>
> . . . We do not know the exact words that Joseph said when his brother put him in the bottom of a well to die, but they were probably something like this: "O God, I know that you are not the source of evil, and that you can take even evil acts and bring good from them." We do not know what he said when he was thrown into slavery, but they were probably something like, "O God, I know that you are not the source of evil, and that you can take even evil acts and bring good from them." And he said the same words when he was thrown into prison. And when his brothers came to him asking for food, he said in our text, "Oh God I thank you that out of all the evil that has been done to me you have brought the possibility of my saving many lives."

Helmut Thielicke retells his biblical text, the parable of the rich man and Lazarus, in a daring manner that begins to blend Page One and Two, exegesis and application.[13] In portraying the rich man, he follows a very important principle for preaching: never portray someone as all bad. Find something in the character with which listeners can empathize.

> Very likely there were times . . . when the rich man felt clearly that there was something wrong about his life. And then the anxious images would loom up in his mind. The miserable wretches would troop past him, staring at him, and suddenly his fine villa became a dirty hovel. What he repressed during the day came out in his dreams and accused his hard, unfeeling heart. So he did what most people do in such cases: he looked for a moral alibi. He tried to prove to himself and to others that he actually did have a heart for the poor, that he really was an openhanded fellow. So he begins to contribute to charity balls, which produce not only a lot of high jinks but also considerable sums for charitable purposes. He also forks out considerable contributions from his bank account to the social missions and the organized charities of his city. . . .
>
> . . . the rich man dies. And when he thus quite literally "comes to an end" he sees that he is absolutely separated from God. Now it becomes apparent how dreadfully different are the standards by which God measures our life. How foolish was our own assessment of ourselves and how foolishly we allowed ourselves to be assessed by others!
>
> There the rich man is in hell, and from there he looks at his own funeral. . . . It's all so oppressively different from the way it appeared to his coquettish fantasy. True, it is a magnificent funeral. But it no longer pleases him. It only gives him a pain because it is in such screaming contradiction to his real state.
>
> He hears a shovelful of earth come thumping down on his coffin and one of his best cronies saying, "He lived life for its own sake." And he wants to interject (though nobody hears him): "I failed to live; I am in anguish in this flame."
>
> Then the second shovelful falls and again the clods of earth come thudding down on his mahogany casket. "He loved the poor in the city," says another voice. And the rich man wants to shriek, "Oh, if you only suspected what the truth is; I am in anguish in this flame."
>
> Then the minister, the popular and beloved abbé of society, casts the third shovelful: "He was so religious. He donated bells, windows, and a seven-branched candlestick. Peace be to his ashes." And again the clods of earth come rumbling down on his coffin. Or is it the rumbling of the crater of hell? "I am in anguish in this flame."
>
> How different, how dreadfully different are the judgments of God! Then we come to the poor man. His name is Lazarus. . . .[14]

Know the Characters

Aloneness is an important aspect of trouble that many people experience today. When a preacher mentions a biblical person, or any person for that matter, the preacher should have a lively sense of that person as a real person, with all of the complexity and contradiction that operate in everyone. Suzan D. Johnson in 1985 was pastor of Mariner's Temple Baptist Church in New York City when she introduced her congregation to Esther. She asked of her the kind of question preachers should ask, What is it like to be this person? In describing Esther, she is also describing many people in the pews, in fact, she is naming all those who feel alienation and aloneness today. Notice that she does not go inside Esther's mind to discuss her feelings, but mostly stays with the things a movie camera can film. There is no question that Johnson knows Esther.

> Esther was a Jewish woman living in Persia. She was in that land through the same circumstances that Black people came here: by enslavement. She was the second generation of those who had been enslaved, and so no one but an old cousin named Mordecai knew that she was a Jew. It was a secret however. If the truth had been known. . . .
>
> Have you ever felt that you had to hide your identity? Have you not been able to let yourself be known? . . . It's sad when even in the church of God, you feel all by yourself. Oh, it's a terrible feeling.
>
> If you have felt this way, you can identify with Esther's predicament. Being a Jew and living in a Persian empire didn't really mix well, like oil and water. But Esther had to deal with life as it was presented to her, just as we must. . . .
>
> Esther had no real support system with which to identify. She had no mother to "reach out and touch" and no sisters or brothers that she knew of; she had no one but her old cousin Mordecai. This cousin helped to support her and take care of her. He worked in the king's court. He didn't have a big job; he was just a little civil servant who had to work each and every day to help make ends meet, just as you and I must do. But Mordecai loved his people and wanted the future generations to live in freedom and have a better life than he had had, just as many of us hope and pray that life will be easier for our children. . . .[15]

On July 13, 1969, after a brief introduction to a sermon entitled "The Case for Reparations," Ernest T. Campbell of Riverside Church in New York City gave the following treatment of his Zacchaeus in Luke 19:8.

Note the care with which he reconstructs Zacchaeus' character and the biblical text to ensure that the congregation is with him. He tells the story with imagination and humor and includes interesting exegetical material within the story, along with details such as the walk to Zacchaeus' house that the text does not mention. Campbell does not try to deal with the whole text; portions are left out of his account, such as the reaction of disapproval from the onlookers. Campbell does not go into the mind of his character or present an abstract discussion of feelings:

> One thing I need not do today is win you to an affection for Zacchaeus. You already like this friend of Jesus. Most everyone does. Handicapped by a lack of height, he draws us out. With a name like Zacchaeus he probably sat in the back row in school and missed a lot of what went on up front. But chiefly we warm to Zacchaeus because in his zeal to see the Man from Nazareth he was willing to abandon his dignity by running down the street and climbing a tree.
>
> Jesus rewarded Zacchaeus' zeal by stopping before that tree and bidding the publican come down. "Zacchaeus," said Jesus, "make haste and come down; for I must stay at your house today."
>
> It must have been a walk to end all walks, that walk of Jesus and Zacchaeus to the publican's house. If only we could have bugged that conversation. Zacchaeus was a tax collector. His job was to raise money from his own people on behalf of the occupying country, hated Rome. As I understand it, it was a cost-plus operation. He paid so much for the franchise and all that he made beyond that price was his. It was a case of "all the traffic can bear." Apparently Zacchaeus saw to it that the traffic bore plenty.
>
> But now it's different: Zacchaeus sees his job in a new light. He sees other people as he had not seen them before. He sees money in what for him is a startlingly fresh perspective. Listen to him now! "Behold, Lord, the half of my goods I give to the poor; and if I have defrauded any one of anything, I restore it fourfold." Walking with Jesus will do that to a person.
>
> More important than this remarkable resolution of Zacchaeus is the response of Jesus. He pronounces words of unqualified approval. He gives it his blessing. He speaks the reassuring "Amen." For Jesus said to him, "Today salvation has come to this house, since he also is a son of Abraham."
>
> There were two elements in the reclamation of Zacchaeus: Generosity ("Half of my goods I give to the poor"), and Justice ("If I have defrauded any one of anything, I restore it fourfold"). To put it differently, Zacchaeus made reparation. . . .[16]

Campbell is using a two-page, not a four-page, format. From the perspective of four pages, he has told the entire biblical story on Page One. If we do that we will have nothing left to say on Page Three. If the sermon were mine I might use Page One to develop the idea of reparation. On Page Three I would speak of Jesus blessing Zacchaeus.

Preaching on trouble does not mean that we preach without faith on Pages One and Two and preach with faith on Pages Three and Four. Even when we develop trouble we preach from a faith perspective. One temptation when preachers use Page One is to let trouble take over in the sermon and to keep the focus on human action. The purpose of developing trouble on Page One is to prepare for what God is doing about that trouble on Page Three. By the end of the sermon listeners should rely not upon their own inadequate resources and strength to make the needed reparations in their lives, but on the strength of God in Christ who empowers all people both to discern and carry out what is required.

A Checklist for Page One

Is the introduction (which may precede Page One) interesting?

Does it state or signal the sermon's theme?

Does Page One focus on one biblical text?

Have I reconstructed the text, saving some material for Page Three?

Do I develop trouble in the text?

Is the trouble theological (as opposed to psychological or sociological)?

Is this page clearly about one idea?

Is it exegetically sound?

Did I film the text from a fresh angle?

Does the trouble here connect to the grace on Page Three?

Is this page mainly a movie?

Do I focus on people in action?

Do I avoid going into the characters' minds?

Have I created the event rather than reported it?

Have I found ways to speak about God on this page?

Have I allowed my one doctrine to inform my filming of the text?

Is there an image from this page that might become a dominant image for the sermon?

Does this page appeal to logos, pathos and ethos?

SECTION III
PAGE TWO: WEDNESDAY

CHAPTER SIX

Trouble in the World

Ideally the preacher will compose Page Two of the sermon on Wednesday. Page One was devoted to God's sovereign commands that disrupt the expectations or behavior of God's people, as well as to their failure, sin, brokenness, and responsibility to act. Page Two interprets similar trouble in the world today. In turning to this page, we span a chasm of thousands of years and leap other gaps between the Bible's geographical setting, culture, language, and worldview—and ours. Obviously, if we are to learn something from an ancient culture, we must assume that in spite of all of the changes between then and now, some things remain the same. The primary elements of consistency are the unchanging nature of God and the continuing nature of human behavior. These are the preacher's two primary bridges to today. God continues to speak through the Bible in the church; and people continue to come to church with complacency or trouble in their hearts, and concerns about a range of human suffering and injustices near and far.

The Bible is a fixed canon, and in that sense it is unchanging. Its meanings for us do change to a degree, however, because our world is always changing; we read the text from different circumstances and needs that affect our understanding of it. No two sermons on a given text will be identical, or will take exactly the same approach. In fact, how we interpret a text will be different each time we preach it, given that each text has range of legitimate possible emphases.

And all texts—not just Scripture—will vary in the meanings they disclose each time they are read. The uniqueness of God's Word is that God is uniquely active in the process of our study of Scripture.

The proclamation of Jesus Christ is not possible without the assistance of the Holy Spirit (1 John 4:2); moreover, God's Word is a living Word. Origen said that Christ reads the Scriptures to us, an insight rooted in Jesus' resurrection appearance in Luke 24:45, "Then he opened their minds to understand the scriptures." Calvin, addressing the same text, said that the word of God "cannot penetrate into our minds, unless the internal teacher, the Spirit, make way for it by his illumination."[1]

The Need for Trouble to be Preached

One area of experience that we rely upon the Holy Spirit to illumine in the sermon is the area of trouble. When we speak of trouble in the sermon, we speak of human failure to live as God ordained and of the ongoing consequences of allowing that which is not sovereign to supplant God's place in our lives. God wills to be in loving relationship with us and wills that we also be in loving relationship with one another and those portions of the created order of which we are stewards. This radical kind of interrelationship with God, others, and creation is part of what being human means.

As Christians, we need our world to be discussed in the sermon because our ways are not God's ways. The status quo is inadequate: there is trouble in us and we are in trouble. In God's sight, we stand guilty of wrongs, which include violation of the greatest commandment to love God and our neighbors as ourselves. However, we easily lose sight of this. We need to be convicted of our sin, convinced that our ways are often the way of death, shown that we misuse our freedom to trust other than the gospel, persuaded of our broken social systems, unmasked of our pretensions, shown the world as it really is, known in the depth of our saying no to God.

Likewise, many in society and the church are victims of suffering, oppression, and evil. They endure ongoing hardship because of natural disasters, accidents, illness, or violence; or they are denied opportunities because of race, gender, poverty, or nationality. Jesus said, "Truly I tell you, just as you did it to one of the least of these who are members of my family, you did it to me" (Matthew 25:40). God is on the side of those who are in need. Suffering continues, often on broad societal levels, and is a judgment against all in that society, even though the action may be unintentional and there may be no immediate or obvious solution to the problem. Liberation theologians speak of Jesus' "preferential option for the poor." As Christians we can try to deny the concept of societal guilt, preferring to speak only of individual sin, but a more responsible approach is to be open to such chastening, welcoming the opportunity to make our lives correspond more closely to what God wills for creation, and to turn with even greater dependency, determination, and faith to Jesus Christ for our salvation.

Faithful Proclamation of Trouble

Robert G. Duffett wants to call a moratorium on sermons that are

. . . guilt-provoking, negative, "beat up the folks" messages. No matter what church I attend, no matter what its denomination or theology, most messages that I hear are trying to "spank" listeners overtly or subtly. On the theological left I am scolded for voting Republican, for lacking a social conscience, and for noninvolvement in social issues. On the right I am chided for not loving God more, not winning my neighbor to Christ, not attending Sunday evening services, and being too "cosy" with secular humanists and New Agers. Both right and left have consensus in one area: they "beat up people". . . .[2]

What alternatives are there? Some say that preachers should preach judgment because that is what all people face before God. Others say that we should toss out the old-fashioned idea of a judging God as irrelevant to the needs of the contemporary era. Others say we should make the sermon into a "message" modeled on talk shows that are popular, so it will be more appealing.

None of these is a real solution. Innovative homiletical techniques, of which there have been no shortage in our time, are also no substitute for addressing the heart of the problem. We can change our forms, adapt our means of communication to a high-technology, visual society, and still have no fundamental improvement in the overall quality of preaching. The problem here is theological and as such needs theological solutions. I propose three solutions here to help preachers present trouble effectively in the contemporary context: develop a three-part theological understanding of trouble, preach with global awareness and, most important, preach grace in tension with trouble.

Develop a Three-Part Understanding of Trouble

We devote the first half of the sermon to trouble and may conceive of it in three categories: transcendent or vertical trouble, immanent or horizontal trouble, and human trouble in which all of the responsibility for change falls on humanity.

1. Transcendent Trouble

Many preachers feel most comfortable with a transcendent understanding of trouble: God in sovereignty on high sits in the throne of judgment, while humanity is down below, guilty as charged, in need of corrective action, to be sure, but also in need of forgiveness. Herman G. Steumpfle calls this type of judgment a "hammer," for it hits listeners like one and brings them to their knees in prayer.[3] Transcendent or vertical understandings are an important kind of trouble. With them we have to be careful not to end up with Duffett's description of "guilt-provoking, negative, 'beat up the folks' messages." Here are some typical judgments of this sort:

> You must repent.
> You have failed God.
> You have not loved your neighbor as yourself.
> Give up your addiction.
> Go to church.
> You should do more.
> Honor your parents.
> You are wrong.

Note common elements of transcendent trouble, at least as it is commonly preached: the mood is imperative; the sin tends to be personal or individual sin before God; a sentence of judgment is passed from on high; the recipient experiences guilt (or anger); repentance and forgiveness are the only way out; responsibility for change rests

110

mainly on the individual; the only recourse is to turn to God for grace and mercy.

Preaching transcendent trouble does not need to be limited to the individual, though it generally is in practice. Biblical scholar James A. Sanders reminds us that in the Bible transcendent trouble tends to be social, is dominantly theocentric, and primarily presents God as sovereign Creator.[4]

As preachers, we can preach transcendent trouble with different degrees of confrontation and challenge, from imperative to indicative. In its imperative expression, "you should," "you must" or "you have to" is stated or implied. We may think of this kind of trouble as index-finger-wagging, or scolding preaching. We can also preach transcendent trouble using the indicative mood, which is more factual and descriptive and less confrontative and accusatory; it merely indicates, suggests, or points. This stance is empathetic or understanding yet is not condoning.

Excellent preachers generally prefer the indicative over the imperative, recognizing that authority, including that of the preacher, is challenged in most quarters of society today. Many well-meaning people do not respond positively to being told what to do, as though they have no choice in the matter and must abandon their own God-given ability to think for themselves. The Bible has many imperatives. The danger of an imperative stance arises if the preacher is perceived to be on a high horse—righteous above the fray or always imposing a solution. Generally preachers are best to reserve use of imperatives for those texts and rare occasions on which they are necessary. Children learn to tune out parents who constantly criticize and the same is true of parishioners before critical pastors. Congregations are made up of God's children, and children need affirmation in the process of correction.

What does trouble sound like in a sermon? We will see many examples in the next chapter. Eugene H. Peterson uses transcendent individual, indicative trouble in this sermon. Backsliders, he was taught, are people

> . . . who lost their footing on the ascent to Christ and backslid.
> My Uncle Harry was a backslider. He was a warm, ardent Christian. In his middle years, on the basis of a mere wisp of rumor, he acquired hundreds of acres of useless land. Not long afterward the

Department of Interior decided to build a hydroelectric dam on that land. Suddenly my uncle was a rich man. The excitement of making money got into his blood; attendance at worship became infrequent. He became impatient with his children and with me, his nephew. His work habits became compulsive. That is when I first heard backslider applied to someone I knew. He died of high blood pressure and a heart attack. Everyone in his family visibly relaxed. . . .

Backsliding was everywhere and always an ominous possibility. . . . The mood was anxious and worried. . . . I got the feeling that back-sliding was not something you did, it happened to you. It was an accident that intruded on the unwary or an attack that involved the undefended.[5]

The trouble here is mostly vertical: his uncle made choices that violated his relationship with God. It is indicative, dealing with the problem descriptively and empathetically—an imperative approach would condemn the uncle rather than describe him and condemn us for our own backsliding. It is individual—a social approach would condemn all society of backsliding. Transcendent troubles become problematic for preaching only if they are our exclusive practice. We need other understandings as well.

2. Immanent Trouble

Immanent trouble is a very important understanding of trouble that preachers do well to cultivate alongside the transcendent. As preachers, we are identifying immanent trouble when we examine the world horizontally for evidence of the fall and when we reflect in our words the brokenness of the world and the suffering of the innocent. Humanity fails to live as God intended and continues to seek salvation in the wrong places. Herman G. Stuempfle calls this kind of trouble a "mirror of existence."[6] Simply by holding a mirror up to the world, the preacher can show that there is a discrepancy between the world as it is and the world as God desires it to be. This function of trouble is immanent because it surrounds an individual and permeates society; the consequences of social behavior are evident. Humanity proceeds on its route to destruction as though it has no need for God, and as though God is distant and passive, incapable of entering and overturning history. Here are some typical statements employing immanent trouble:

Our times are anxious.
Life seems meaningless to many.
Many have been left unemployed.
Wars continue in the world.
Racism continues.
Global warming threatens life as we know it.
Cycles of child abuse go unbroken.
Many are homeless in the streets.
Welfare dependency is passed from generation to generation.
A woman suffers from cancer.
Entire nations are suffering.

In the case of immanent trouble, individuals share guilt with society and the primary thrust of guilt tends to be social, though individual guilt and responsibility before God comes into play. The result can be a feeling of collective guilt, of shame, of mourning, and of a renewed awareness of surrounding needs. People become conscious of those who have not been served well by society's collective decisions. This kind of trouble creates a sense of urgency, because people are suffering. Some social analysis is needed for the power of evil is present in human systems. Even if everyone in an institution (such as the church or a multinational corporation) were saintly, some people would still be hurt by well-intended programs; individual people cannot avoid systemic evil and corporate sin. Moreover, a change of individual hearts is not enough to accomplish God's will on earth. People need to commit themselves to social change, even as God is committed to overturn the powers of the world that may seem to be having the final say. The resurrection pronounces the ultimate defeat of even these powers.

On Page Two of the sermon we portray the powers of this world that seem to have the final say or appear to be stronger than God—although we never allow that they are stronger and we always preach from the perspective of faith. These powers seemed to have the final say on Good Friday, and at times, this is how all people experience life. Immanent trouble focuses on God as a Suffering Servant and Savior (or to use the title of Henri Nouwen's book, *The Wounded Healer*), and is thus primarily Christocentric, employing the incarnation, suffering, and crucifixion of Christ as key ways of understanding.

Immanent trouble tends to be indicative, pointing to situations of suffering, the descriptions of which more or less speak for themselves, though they often need analysis. But this kind of trouble can become imperative, such as when it becomes a command to social action or protest. This happens across the theological spectrum, on issues ranging from abortion to the environment. When the imperative takes over, the preacher's task becomes more difficult: shoulds, musts and have-tos are more demanding of listeners and therefore potentially more alienating and divisive. A rule of communication and persuasion is that when one is pushed, one is likely to push back. Preachers always ought to ask themselves what is the best way of achieving the desired result and what is the best way of speaking given varying viewpoints amongst committed Christians.

The vertical plane of transcendent trouble and the horizontal plane of immanent trouble cannot be entirely separated; they are held together by the great commandment of Jesus. If the preacher speaks of someone addicted to drugs, that individual person has responsibility before God to change (vertical); yet at some level all people are guilty in being a society that apparently tolerates drugs (horizontal); and to a certain extent our nations come under prophetic condemnation (vertical). Alternatively, when the preacher speaks of a homeless woman who is evicted from her cardboard box shelter under a bridge, it can be to condemn society before God (vertical); to awaken the conscience of the congregation to society's collective responsibility for the poor (horizontal); and to arouse individual guilt before God in relation to personal wealth (vertical)—independent of whatever obligations the woman herself might have before God to change aspects of her own life.

Transcendent and immanent trouble, while related, are two distinct categories in theology and preaching. Many preachers fail to preach on social ills, simply because individual repentance by itself cannot correct the situation. But by doing so they short-change the fullness of the gospel message and make God irrelevant to the large issues of the day. We need to name individual and social evils so that they can be addressed in the second half of the sermon. One individual may not be able to make a lot of difference to racism; although one cannot do everything, one can still do something. An individual can make a difference; several individuals can make a bigger difference; a congregation can make even more of a difference. And many congregations can begin to make a large impact, of the kind God both desires and empowers. If we are attentive to both transcendent or vertical trouble and immanent or horizontal trouble—and their respective primary emphases—our preaching of trouble can be more fulsome.

3. Human Trouble

In addition to transcendent and immanent trouble, a third kind of trouble, human trouble, flows from the first two and is often preached yet is overlooked as trouble. It is concerned only with human responsibility to act. We might protest that human action is simply what is required in light of God's Word. What humans are required to do is not trouble but a way out of trouble; that is, it is action that will be pleasing in God's sight, as in Micah 6:8, "What does the Lord require of you but to do justice, and to love kindness, and to walk humbly with your God?"

But human responsibility in the sermon does function as trouble. If a right relationship with God is dependent upon human fulfill-ment of God's laws, all is lost. As Jesus said, "apart from me you can do nothing" (John 15:5). Paul says, "For I do not do the good I want, but the evil I do not want is what I do" (Romans 7:19). For this rea-son Luther and the Reformers emphasized Paul's justification by faith. Human actions cannot fulfill God's demand. But through the accomplishment of Christ on the cross, God enables people to meet the requirements placed upon them. If as preachers we are aware of what we are doing theologically when we call people to act, we will be less likely to highlight human actions as the singular thrust and final outcome of the sermon.

Even though God's judgment may be proclaimed in such ser-mons, they remain dominantly anthropocentric. God is essentially remote from the human predicament, judging it, and waiting for humans to change. Since humans cannot do what is required, how-ever, and since these sermons point only in the human direction, as though the law is all there is, these sermons preach false hope. They preach the impossible as though it is possible; they thus preach our utter destruction. The primary doctrine they imply, when examined from a distance, is the doctrine of human limita-tion and condemnation. Humanity needs "to get its act together" and do better. Change of the sort that is required will not take place, without God.

Dominant Preaching Emphases

TRANSCENDENT TROUBLE Vertical judgment	IMMANENT Horizontal judgment	HUMAN TROUBLE Vertical and horizontal judgment
Addresses the guilty conscience	Awakens consciousness of others	Awakens a sense of duty
Individual sin	Social sin	Individual and social sin
Law as hammer	Law as mirror	Law is all
Broken commandments	Broken society	Broken commandments and society
Theocentric	Christocentric	Anthropocentric
God as Creator/ Sovereign	God as Suffering Servant/Savior	God as remote/forsaken/ irrelevant
Doctrine of creation/fall	Doctrine of incarnation/ crucifixion	Doctrine of human ability
Preacher seems above the Word	Preacher stands under the Word	Preacher is an agent of the law
Individuals must repent	Society must change	Human ability to change is the only hope
Individuals need God's forgiveness	Society needs God's intervention	Humanity needs to do better

Is there a norm for preaching trouble? Preachers who keep hammering congregations with individual responsibility to act, when individuals can do little apart from God's empowerment (even if they do not know this), risk becoming agents of God's anger at the expense of God's love. Listeners more readily respond to an empathetic posture and an invitation to action, rather than the musts, shoulds, and have-tos of imperative trouble.

Collections of sermons demonstrate that the best preachers use vertical and horizontal trouble in their indicative forms. Both are important. If we focus exclusively on individual relationships with God in Christ, we communicate an absence of God's concern for issues of injustice and suffering, and we fail to treat our neighbors as ourselves; if we focus exclusively on corporate sin and social responsibility, we ignore individual responsibilities before God. Together, vertical and horizontal trouble help to ensure that the God we preach is not a narrow, parochial, or small god. Rather we preach the one transcendent and immanent God whom Jesus Christ taught us to call Father, who is concerned for all people equally, everywhere, and who abhors every kind of sin.

Preach with Global Awareness

The problem with many justice sermons is that they are judgmental and hard for listeners to receive. In addition to developing a three-part understanding of trouble, there is a second alternative to preaching that "beats up on people": preach with global awareness. Speak about the big and small issues of justice on the world stage. But does this not contribute to listeners being overwhelmed by the demands of the sermon? Who wants to come to church to hear the news? Some people feel church should be a "time-out" from worldly concerns, a time to be with God. Ironically, God is concerned for the world and loves the world (John 3:16). When the focus of preaching is sufficiently large, it becomes clear that the world's problems are beyond individual remedy, and thus reliance upon God becomes utterly necessary.[7] Such reliance leads to grace.

One of the biggest single problems facing preaching in North America is what I call the claustrophobia generated in too many pulpits: preaching that is inward-gazing, us-centered, or church-focused, as though worries about the church and what it thinks are the most urgent issues in people's lives, or as though exclusive focus on the local community is a faithful response to God's creation. By contrast, sermons should be open to God's love for all people, wherever there is crisis today, and should uphold God's redeeming justice anywhere in the world.

Concern for justice and the poor was essential in the Old Testament, where it was never separate from righteousness (*hesed*) toward God. One of the root meanings for the Hebrew word salvation is "wide open space"—the opposite of what is suggested by claustrophobia. Social concern and justice were also central to Jesus' own ministry and preaching. In fact, justice has been so much a part of the life and mission of the church at its best that it is hard to

117

account for the virtual absence of much preaching on the subject in surviving sermons from the history of preaching.

Some historic preachers come to mind for their obvious concern for justice: Chrysostom preached against the corruption of high officials; Thomas Muntzer preached against the slaughter of the peasants; Calvin's Geneva was organized for the welfare of all; in South America, Bartholomé de Las Casas preached against the decimation of Amerindians,[8] and Archbishop Toribio of Lima, Peru, anticipated liberation theology;[9] John Wesley preached against slavery, and his Methodist movement laid the foundations for the Social Gospel movement;[10] Phoebe Palmer was a founder of feminist theology and preaching; and Martin Luther King, Jr., of course, was part of a long tradition of preaching that led to the civil rights movement.

Still, there appears to have been little impetus for preaching on social justice through most of the history of the church. The reasons for this are hard to identify. One reason is that justice, which we tend to understand as the outcome of responsible decisions in human social systems, is a relatively recent concept, a product of the Enlightenment and the upheavals stemming from the Industrial Revolution. The primary focus of justice shifted from preconceived rights and powers ordained by God, and exemplified for instance in the divine right of monarchy, to the administration of fair rules of conduct that could be agreed upon by members of a social contract. David Buttrick, perhaps overstating his case, holds Karl Barth responsible for denying the social relevance of preaching in our own times.[11] Other factors were certainly involved. Karl Marx and the growth of social science gave legitimacy to class struggle and the voice of the poor and oppressed in this century; and many liberal pulpits, notably Riverside Church in New York, became identified with social justice. Other pulpits fell silent on some social issues because justice sounded Marxist, or because the Vatican or culture opposed mixing religion with politics, or because people counted on the government to deal with such big budget issues.

Important shifts are taking place that will have an impact on preaching. Many churches are in a period of decline. Between 1967 and 1984, the Presbyterian Church, U.S.A., declined in membership by 27 percent; and prior to 1995, 30 percent of Southern Baptist churches were experiencing growth while 18 percent were facing decline.[12] A surprising recent survey by sociologist Reginald Bibby in Canada indicates that, since 1975, evangelical Christians have become more convinced that religion should be concerned with politics—

while all other Christians have become less convinced.[13] Although Christian camps differ on their ideas and methods of achieving justice, calls for justice under law do not necessarily belong to one group or another. As one ethicist sees the difference, ". . . some [theologians] find individualistic, consensual systems of justice too permissive and inattentive to other moral questions. Others believe that the standards of justice that can be achieved by mutual consent fall far short of the human care that the love of God requires."[14]

Most preachers cannot allow partisan politics to set the justice agenda for preaching. From a Christian perspective, basic needs in society, such as caring for the poor, the hungry, the helpless, the sick, and the homeless, transcend denominational and political differences. Sermons are an essential place to discuss how people are facing these societal problems, and to portray the difference that individuals and congregations can make by helping.

As we move into the third millennium, we witness increasing gaps between the rich and the poor around the world. Preachers who narrowly choose between partisan approaches to justice, who use stories and illustrations coming from only one predominant ethnic background, social class, gender, or age group, or who remain silent on anything but relatively trivial daily issues in life—all of these can encourage claustrophobia because of the narrow confines of the sermon. By contrast, preachers who treat justice issues as though they are responsibilities that are entirely up to human endeavor and who leave God out of the picture, can also foster claustrophobia.

The perceived relevance of God to contemporary life stands in direct relation to a preacher's willingness to represent in story, image, and idea, matters encompassing the breadth and depth of God's concern in the local community and the world at large. The preacher who identifies God's nature and manner of action in and behind the biblical text can more readily show how the same God is working for the thousands of Rwandan refugees in central Africa who are depicted in the news reports, as well as for local needs in a community.

Develop Grace in Tension with Trouble

We have discussed how preachers might develop a three-part understanding of trouble and preach with global awareness as alternatives to preaching that "beats up on people." The third important alternative is to preach what God does in relation to the troubles of the world. The goal of the four-page sermon is not to preach trouble on Pages One and Two and then erase it with grace on Pages Three and Four, as though it can now be tossed into the wastebin. Rather, the purpose is to establish the tension between trouble and grace, the same tension that appropriately exists in faith—even though the resurrection signals the final outcome and resolution of that tension. Salvation is not merely something we humans experience at the end of time; we also taste it in the present, in worship, in the sacraments, and wherever the realm of God breaks into our world. Salvation exists not in trouble, or in grace on its own, but in the juxtaposition of the two. It is true that there are things we must do and we are condemned or doomed by our own actions; yet it is also true that God in Christ has accomplished our salvation on the cross. Between these two stances we work out our salvation, Paul says, in fear and trembling (Philippians 2:12).

Here is both the possibility and necessity of faith. As Christians, we cannot simply cling to our sinfulness and ignore the cross; nor can we cling to the cross and ignore the necessity of change. Both are real and thus both are essential for preaching. Christ has fulfilled the law and accomplished what is necessary on our behalf—Easter marks the end of the old ways—yet how can we speak of this without depicting the initial trouble, the need for God to act in Christ? As preachers, we seek to develop this tension in the sermon. We should separate trouble and grace, rather than blend them as in a food processor, because they are normally so mixed in daily life that most people are unable to see them or see God. We develop trouble on Pages One and Two from a faith perspective with the awareness that we are preparing for the grace of Pages Three and Four. We put grace after trouble, rather than interweave them, because (1) each needs to be heard in its own right; (2) trouble identifies the need for God to act; (3) the joyous message of Easter follows Good Friday; and (4) Christ offers hope, not despair—for the sermon to offer hope it must place its final emphasis not on human action but on God's. By the end of the sermon, the listeners ought not experience grace cut off from trouble, but experience instead the tension between them, and be cast on the full sufficiency of God's promise for lives of service in the coming week.

Something important happens by the end of Page Two that helps create the juxtaposition that we seek. The preacher takes seriously the questions people have uttered during the prior week and that they may have brought to worship. While people may have left God out of their consideration, the preacher does not; rather, the preacher reshapes their questions, which may well be religious questions, into theological questions. "Why is this happening to me?" may now become, "Why does God seem absent?" "Who am I?" becomes, "Who does God want me to be?" "What will happen to my children?" becomes, "In what way is God in control?" "Where is meaning in life?" becomes, "How may I find God?" or "Has God found me?"

Pages Three and Four will provide responses to those questions that will be more than just answers: they will be an affirmation, a proclamation, a benediction, an encounter with the God who is already encountering listeners through the sermon. We need not be hesitant the way some preachers seem to be, timidly tiptoeing the perimeters of trouble for fear of having no countering word of encouragement. Since we have good news to proclaim, we can go to greater depths in naming trouble, in exposing the sin and brokenness of the world and our people, and in calling them to responsible action, confident that God's will shall transform even these burdens into joy and hope.

Theological Use of Stories

Preachers can use three simple paradigms or basic theological motifs to help them apply stories theologically on Page Two. First, stories can be used as metaphors to speak about *God's judgment on humans*. These are hard stories to use well and some preachers have used them to manipulate and frighten vulnerable listeners, for instance, by depicting AIDS or other tragic events as God's punishment. However, God has rules in place to guide responsible use of human freedom, and people violate these at their peril. Moreover, God often thwarts the purposes of groups and individuals seeking to do wrong, and to those individuals, such divine action presents trouble. Anyone can tell a story of someone whose life is going to ruin, but preachers have the particular responsibility of grounding these stories theologically. Suppose two people are fighting; a preacher can use this story as a simile or metaphor to demonstrate what God's judgment stands against; or show the consequences of ignoring God; or perhaps even to claim that, while evil may claim victory in the moment, God does act to limit the power of evil on earth, and the death sentence on all evil has been pronounced. Occasionally, perhaps even rarely in sermons, a story like the collapse of apartheid in South Africa can be effectively claimed as God's judgment in action.

An easier paradigm for preachers to use is stories as metaphors of *the human condition after the Fall*. Humans have fallen from God's high purposes for them. Many situations indicate human sin and brokenness: wars, economic exploitation of others, and family abuse are among the worst and most common.

Third, stories can be told as demonstrations, similes, or metaphors *of the Incarnation, of God as the Suffering Servant, or of Christ being crucified today*. When the preacher lays this paradigm over many of the horrible stories of this world, listeners see the world in a fresh way that conforms to Jesus' word to his disciples, "just as you did it to the least of these . . . you did it to me" (Matthew 25:40). Most stories appropriate to Page Two fit one of these theological categories: God's judgment, the fallen world, or the Suffering Servant.

Guidelines for Page Two

Organization and Focus

Page Two reinforces Page One and should be roughly the same length, in other words, a quarter of the sermon. One sentence, written across the top of our blank Page Two, may help us in sermon composition to stay on topic, especially if we try to incorporate that sentence into our composition early on the page and find ways to repeat it, so that it can begin to serve as an organizing principle for listeners to that page. The focus for trouble on Page Two (our world) is determined by the focus of trouble on Page One (the Bible).

The sentence for Page One might appear in various places. For smooth transition from Page One to Two, it can also be nearly the last sentence on Page One. Its partner sentence can then be the first sentence on Page Two. Sentences for Pages One and Two might be paired as follows:

Page One	**Page Two**
Israel must change.	Our world must change.
Judah is threatened with war.	War confronts people today.
Useless salt is good for nothing.	Without God we are good for nothing.
Jesus challenged the religious authorities.	We challenge God.
Judas betrayed Jesus.	The world is filled with betrayals.
The woman needed healing.	Many suffer today.
Paul condemned disunity.	Disunity is our condemnation.

Obviously the above sentences will need much amplification and qualification. When we compose Page Two, we use such focus sentences to provide the subject of the page. If in composition we find that we have moved off the topic, we can take that as a sign that we must revise what we are doing or start again. Keeping on topic is important. If we drift here we will not only lose focus for Page Two and the links with the other pages, we will also lose our hearers.

As preachers we should repeat the focus on trouble in as many ways as possible so that listeners make no mistake as to its importance. Yet we always continue to speak from the perspective of faith: to discern sin we need faith and revelation; to name the problems in human relationships we need to be able to speak of God's love; to speak to trouble in the world we require a vision of God's will for the world. Of course one dimension of theological trouble is human inability to think as God thinks, or to see as God sees; our best attempts at naming what is wrong are flawed by sin, thus faith is required even at the level of daring to speak about it.

Trouble should have tooth and bite. As preachers, if we have strong grace to proclaim, we can proclaim strong trouble. This gives us the ability to address the depths of people's aloneness and despair. Alternatively, we can convict them and ourselves—for we stand with them under the Word, not over them—of individual and social sin. We can hold up the consequences of our individual and corporate actions. And we can show the suffering of others and demonstrate the need for us to act. These duties will be juxtaposed with grace on Pages Three and Four, as is appropriate in theology and faith.

Sermon Unity

We might also continue to keep in mind those elements that contribute to the sermon's unity that are designated by the memory device, The Tiny Dog Now Is Mine: one text, one theme, one doctrine, one need, one image, and one mission. Both Pages One and Two are preparing for the one central theme of the sermon, represented by the theme sentence that will be developed on Page Three. The theme sentence points to a doctrine and preachers are advised to develop Page Two (and each page for that matter) theologically, allowing the central doctrine to guide and inform what is said. The doctrine can point to a human need that belongs on Page Two, perhaps identified in relation to a particular story or situation. We may not yet have one image to unify the sermon, or we may have decided not to employ one. However, an image from the sermon's introduction or Page One might be carried over to Page Two. And Page Two is an excellent place to begin identification of a possible mission or action the sermon might encourage.

Mission

Mission is a specific action or act of ministry that the preacher encourages the congregation to take as a result of the sermon. Although at an early stage in sermon preparation we began to think of one mission that the sermon might promote; by now, Wednesday, we should be finalizing our decision. Mission, in part, arises out of the stories that we bring before God's word and, to a certain extent, every story the preacher tells has mission implications (a story about a homeless person often implies a need to care for the poor; a story about family troubles often implies a need to be more attentive to our own families). However, here we focus on explicit mission possibilities, specific acts that are offered for the congregation to consider doing. These are usually offered not to tell the congregation exactly what they must do, but to provide specific, concrete examples of what is possible by way of Christian life, and to stimulate them to identify further or alternative possibilities.

The preacher most frequently presents mission on Page Two as a duty; later, on Page Four, the demands of this mission will be transformed into an opportunity and privilege, and an invitation to meet Christ in the place of need. As a general rule, if the burden of the mission falls on the hearers, the material discussing it belongs on Page Two. If the burden to act falls on God, that material belongs on Page Four.

Preachers should also weigh the emotional or spiritual impact of the mission suggestion to determine where it best belongs. For example, if mission involves something controversial, about which members of the congregation are likely to say no, it should be raised first on Page Two, where resistance to it can be identified and discussed. Consequently, nearly all fund-raising requests belong on Page Two. The preacher can then devote the remaining half of the sermon to presenting the issue in the light of God's grace. If the preacher delays in introducing the issue until Page Four, its impact there may be so great as to sabotage the grace that one has worked hard to develop on Pages Three and Four.

Use Vertical and Horizontal Trouble

Vertical trouble is almost always harder for the congregation to hear than horizontal trouble. Vertical trouble tries to awaken a sense of guilt but, unless it is done well, it can seem like the preacher is manipulating the listeners to feel guilty. For example, the preacher might speak (a) of talking to a homeless person in the street, (b) of then going into the bank, only to overhear two people planning retirement investments, and (c) of the need for society to be more generous toward the poor. By implication, the people planning their retirement were judged to be greedy, the listeners were judged to be greedy, and the preacher desired to persuade them to take action by making them feel guilty.

There are times when vertical judgment is both necessary and effective, for instance when a community plainly acts in ways that defy God's Word. Generally, however, a horizontal treatment of the trouble can be more effective. To change vertical trouble into horizontal, the preacher can stand with the listeners, under the Word, and can strive to help listeners to understand the sin that causes them to behave in this way or that. The key is empathy. Thus the preacher in the example above could help listeners to understand what fears stand in the way of being as generous as we might like to be in relation to our neighbor (e.g., fear of not having enough;

125

fear of strangers; fear of being deceived). Later, the preacher can speak of these fears in light of what God has accomplished.

Use Stories

Preachers are wise over every couple of weeks to pick a range of stories from the following categories: personal (having to do with any person's individual struggle), local, church (at large), and world. Sermons that consistently focus on stories about the church, the local community, or even one's own region or country, foster notions of a smaller God who is seemingly less relevant to the larger troubles of the world, causing listeners to wonder what, if anything, God is doing about the larger world. Stories about big issues that omit the local scene foster the impression of a God who is too busy for the individual. At most, as preachers, we should tell no more than one story about ourselves in a sermon; otherwise, we risk being perceived as seeking attention, like individual spectators at sporting events who run onto the playing field. The story we tell about ourselves ought to be about a weakness that all people share, not a private confession; likewise, it should not be a recital of our wonderful deeds of visitation or inspired words at a bedside. We should avoid drawing needless attention to ourselves, and eliminate self-references in stories where we are not essential. For example, if we tell a story about someone, we can usually eliminate the fact of our being present with the person. Jesus teaches his followers to be humble.

We are also wise to introduce into our sermon some stories from the national and international news on television and in the news-papers. Increasingly, the stories that unite us as communities are stories we find on television. Normally we want to bring in stories about substantial, weighty matters, not about soap operas or cute commercials that show how nice the world is. We also want to maintain an important distinction between cultural values and Christian understanding. Our role in the pulpit is never simply to mouth discussions that can be held elsewhere, no matter how valuable these may be, but is always to bring a distinctly biblical and theological perspective to issues. If a sermon can as easily be delivered at a Lions Club, we might ask if it truly belongs in the church. Be mindful of major human needs that some people have on their minds and bring to church—health and family issues, starvation and wars in various parts of the world—and bring these before God.

After a story of substantial length, a sentence or two should connect that story, first, with the main thought or focus of the page and, second, with the listeners' own lives and experiences. For example, "You may have experienced this when you . . . ," or "This is not unusual . . . ," or "We have all had similar experiences. . . ." This linking helps listeners apply what is said to their own lives and helps them move to the next item.

As on Page One, preachers again need to create or show events rather than simply report or summarize them. Storytelling principles from Page One should be used: be visual and sensory; briefly locate the story geographically before showing an action; describe a person before describing the action; avoid adjectives for description but give details concerning objects, people, and action.

Attend to the Emotional and Spiritual Impact

As Christians we are always a people of hope, regardless of how our emotions work from time to time, and we affirm a story larger than the one immediately evident, and larger than the one the world likes to tell. In preaching we name the suffering of the world as it is without giving in to despair, cynicism, bitterness, or anger—for we know the one God whose story has the final word over all of our stories.

Evaluate the emotional and spiritual impact of stories before using them. Two or three instances of human suffering in most cases is enough; listeners may not be able to bear hearing more. Each story should take listeners a little deeper into the issue at hand, rather than merely illustrate the same point over and over. A good test for any part of a sermon can be to ask: Is this essential? What purpose does it serve? If I cut it, what would be lost?

Cut out details of violence. While we are still called to condemn acts of violence, we should avoid portraying them in graphic detail. Violent images usually are overpowering and readily come to people's minds even without presenting them from the pulpit. We do not preach evil and the impact of such images is hard to overcome in the remainder of the sermon.

Humor is helpful when talking about trouble. Page Two easily can become too earnest, intense, or depressing because we are trying to interpret serious matters.

Be Empathetic and Inclusive

Preachers do well to follow an excellent rule: be empathetic rather than condemning toward the worst person or type named in the sermon, because someone in the congregation may identify with that person and needs to be reached, not rejected.

Stories and experiences should be inclusive. In particular, both genders should be equally represented in sermons. For example, in delivering a sermon, a student spoke of his father, the Lone Ranger, Hercules, and a major football star; however, he had no stories of women, or even stories told from a woman's perspective. Similarly, a woman student told several stories, each of which put men in a negative light. We should ask of any of our sermons, What overall portrait of either gender have I presented in this sermon? Stories should never be told simply or coincidentally to put down members of the other gender. Similar sensitivity is needed with age, race, culture, relative wealth, ability, and the like. Just as the congregation may contain people of diverse ages, races, cultures, and so on, so should they be included in stories when appropriate, while at the same time not overrepresenting any one group.

Getting Beyond the Church

Here is a very important piece of advice that too many preachers disregard: Even if a biblical text deals with a situation in Paul's church, we should avoid making the church the sole subject of the sermon, except on rare occasions. We can discuss the church, but the church for most individual members is probably not the burning issue that it is for us preachers, nor is it the one people have been thinking about all week. Rather, preachers should take the disputes in Corinth into today's workplace or home, or onto the national or international stage, to listen for what God is saying. (Readers might review the sample focus sentences for Page Two, above, to see how each might apply to the church or to the larger world.)

Going Deep

Page One normally cannot be expected to touch listeners' deepest concerns because it deals with ancient times and people; Page Two brings those troubles home. By the end of Page Two, the congregation should be at a place of depth, struggling with the reality of human trouble, no longer pretending that everything is okay, but ready and yearning for the help that God offers. In other words, although Page Two is about one idea, there must be movement of that idea. One of the best ways for preachers to ensure that there is movement and depth in their thought is for them to spend some time each week reading systematic or constructive theology. This can have not only long-term benefits in providing the preacher with increased theological facility, but also short-term benefits for the sermon at hand. By identifying one doctrine from the theme sentence, a preacher can turn in a theology textbook to material that will suggest various dimensions of the topic that may need to be developed. In other words, no page of the sermon should end exactly where it began; Pages Two and Four in particular cry out for theological development, although we must remember also the need to be concrete and visual. A deepening awareness and broadening understanding must grow in listeners, creating increased theological depth and a quickened sense of responsibility or urgency of action. Each sentence and paragraph should takes listeners further along the road to a new perspective.

Our movie-sermon may have taken listeners to various places, near and far in the world; but immediately prior to Page Three the focus should be back on the listeners' own lives and experiences, if only for a sentence or two, for we are addressing them. We can check Page Two to see if it clearly answers, What is wrong today? What needs to be done? What does God want or demand? While mission will be an important thrust later in the sermon, this is the place for some specific instruction on the need for human changes, leaving the means of accomplishing them through God and with the Holy Spirit until later in the sermon, on Page Four.

CHAPTER SEVEN

Filming Trouble in the World

This chapter presents examples of Page Two in published sermons for the purpose of critical review. Page Two is a metaphor for theological function in a sermon, namely trouble in our time, thus no matter what sermon form is followed, almost any sermon will have some Page Two material. Numerous examples, below, demonstrate points from the previous chapter and may stimulate the creativity of preachers who are working on their sermons. Not all of the categories relate directly to making a movie but they all in some way contribute to the finished film. Each example models multi-sensory, especially visual, language appropriate for preaching.

Identify What Need the Theme Statement Answers

All of the various items identified by the memory device, The Tiny Dog Now Is Mine, are appropriate for Page Two, yet the one that we can least afford to ignore here is "one need." From the theme sentence or its doctrine we ought to be able to identify a need in the life of someone in the congregation. We do not have to devote the entire Page Two to identifying this need and we can address it either implicitly or explicitly. Sometimes this can be accomplished very quickly. With just a few quick strokes, Chevis F. Horne identifies that the need to which his sermon speaks is the fear or nearness of death. His theme is: Christ has gone ahead of us into our death. Most listeners would be keenly attentive to his frank and honest self-disclosure on a matter of universal human concern:

I, like all my brothers and sisters, am mortal. I am always walking into the night of my death. I am going to die, and I know two things about my death. It will come sooner than I expect it; I will not be ready for it. And it will find me with some unfinished task. I will lay aside my tools at the close of a day and expect to pick them up in the morning. But the morning will not come. I will not only leave some unfinished task but also an unfinished life.[1]

Usually the preacher must struggle to come up with the question the theme statement answers in the life of the congregation. However, sometimes the biblical text itself provides the question. Ronald D. Sisk was preaching on Psalm 121 to his congregation near San Francisco on the Sunday following the October 1989 earthquake. He imagined the people in the biblical text looking to the hills ("I will lift up mine eyes unto the hills from whence cometh my help" KJV) and added,

They raised their eyes like we stood in our homes last Tuesday and looked at our ceilings as they shook above us, like the victims on Route 880 must have done in that last terrifying moment of their lives. They looked around them like a lot of us have been doing in the shock and sorrow of this week. They wondered when danger might swoop down on them next. And they cried out.

From whence does my help come? How am I going to survive? How am I going to keep safe when danger comes? Isn't there anybody who's going to look out after me? It's been really encouraging this week to hear the response of so many in the Bay Area to the needs of those hardest hit by the quake. Neighbors helping neighbors. Strangers helping strangers. People going out of their way. People putting themselves into danger to help wherever help has been needed. We can help one another. That is one part of the answer to the psalmist's question. But the singer [of the Psalm] wasn't really asking about human help. He was really asking the question some of us in the Bay Area have been asking and others of us have been avoiding since Tuesday afternoon at 5:04. He was asking, Where does my help come from when human help comes to an end?

"My help comes from the Lord. . . ."[2]

Turn Everyday Issues into Theological Ones

In this development of trouble in our time, Jeffrey L. Ruff takes a common workplace dilemma, the issue of compromise of individ-

131

ual principles, and establishes it as a theological issue. He keeps working on it to bring it close to home. The question he asks in the last sentence is the deepest and best.

Does Zacchaeus's story ring any bells for you? I don't think you have to be a tax chief or an arms dealer or a government bureaucrat to feel the crunch of working in the world while trying to enter the Kingdom of Heaven, that is, of having a dirty job while trying to be clean for the Lord. As one commentator notes, "Zacchaeus' profession points up the problem of accommodating the structures necessary in the secular world to the call that comes from God." No job on earth is ideal or pristine, not in government, the business community, the service industry, or even the church. (Everyone knows the ministry's clean, right?) All work is dirty, fraught with compromise and ambiguity. And thus the dilemma with which we all must wrestle as people of faith, no matter what our vocation may be, is how best to minimize harm and maximize justice in our daily work. The issue often comes to us in the form of a question, Which is better, a job that allows me to keep all my ideals intact but that gives me little income or influence in the world or a job that yields high rewards and enables me considerable influence but that requires that I sacrifice many of my most cherished values and ideals?

This past week on the television series "ThirtySomething," the young couple, Michael and Hope, found themselves on different sides of this issue. Hope is offered a job at a magazine that will force her to compromise her ideals. She turns the job down but admits privately to a friend that she really doesn't see her high ideals making much of a difference anywhere. Michael, on the other hand, holds a party at their home to impress the boss, whom he despises. Hope is disgusted with him for selling himself in this way. Michael responds that he's only doing it to insure a solid financial future for their family. Hope counters that she also sees holding on to one's ideals as insuring a future—though not only for her family but for the whole imperiled earth. What good will a solid financial situation do their daughter, she asks, if there is no safe place for her to live? Michael responds with a question equally troublesome: What good will it do the earth or anyone if, in the name of high ideals, he fails at his vocation and allows himself and his family to lose everything?

Therein lies the dilemma of so many of us. How can I be responsible to God and also responsible to my family and my society? How can I be productive in the worldly sense and also productive of the fruits of the Spirit of Christ? And perhaps there is an even more basic question than these: How can I, as a follower of Christ, work in human society and still live with myself?[3]

Sometimes we can attain the most effective trouble horizontally simply by holding a mirror up to life and reflecting it as it is. Edmund Steimle, who taught preaching at Union Seminary in New York City, did this quickly and effectively:

> A run-down New York hotel, long overdue for demolition, is still inhabited by a handful of elderly people living there alone since there's no place else available which they can afford. One seventy-five-year-old resident, a woman hospitalized with Parkinson's disease who had no other neighbors or friends, pleaded to be sent "home" from the hospital to her shabby little room in that dilapidated hotel. "On her bedside table was a tiny figure of Santa Claus, and beside her on the bed was a child's stuffed animal, worn with hugging." When the bottom falls out of life, what then?[4]

Too many sermons avoid theological trouble (even as others have trouble only!). They talk about a theme or topic in a manner akin to mere social analysis rather than naming human sin, brokenness, or suffering before God. This is not the case in a sermon preached by Barbara Brown Taylor on the national radio show "The Protestant Hour." She begins by telling an innocent story about waiters. Instead of defining a good waiter, she takes time to seat listeners at the table and allows them to experience being served. The trouble creeps up on the congregation, and when it arrives, it comes as a surprise and with a bite.

> I still remember the best waiter I ever had. . . . He knew everything about the menu and the wine list, but only if I asked. He wore his name on a brass badge on his jacket, but he never announced it. He didn't want me to remember him. He wanted me to remember the meal, which arrived under a gleaming silver dome. He set it down in front of me, he lifted the dome, and I was left face-to-face with the prettiest salmon fillet I had ever seen. A fish knife appeared at my right hand. I dropped my fork and had not even bent to look for it when another was slid beside my plate. The water glass stayed three-quarters full and the bread basket was always heaped with warm brown rolls, but I was never aware of anyone doing it. The service was impeccable because it was invisible, and I left the restaurant that night with the highest regard for that waiter's skill.

He made me feel like royalty, but according to Jesus I was not the star of the show that night. My waiter was. "For who is greater, the one who is at the table or the one who serves? Is it not the one at table? But I am among you as one who serves."[5]

Allow the Trouble to Build

Many preachers are afraid to let the trouble build in impact and strength. Instead, they mention some aspect of trouble and rush in with good news to make things better. Thus the import of neither one is communicated or experienced, and each dilutes the other. To use a medical analogy, the wound is treated in a poor manner a little at a time, instead of cleansing the entire wound once and then applying the balm Elizabeth Achtemeier shows one way to build sustained trouble in this sermon. She identifies human failure to make peace, and failure to live up to God's expectations. She continues to build the indictment for several additional minutes, not as a way merely of making people feel guilty, but as a way of making an essential theological point: the problem (as with so many social problems today) has its roots in human defiance of God's will. She uses primarily vertical trouble. She is able to build trouble in this sustained and powerful manner in part because she has powerful grace to proclaim in the second half of her sermon.

But we have forgotten that, haven't we? We have forgotten that we can never be understood or ever understand ourselves except in relation to our God. And so now we have struck out on our own and decided to follow our own purposes and to run the world according to our own competing wills. And the result has been the chaos of which we read every morning in the newspapers.

But we are not responsible for that chaos, we think. No, it's the system—the system that is wrong. And if we can just fix the system— by reshaping our politics or economics or communications—we can create the peace we long for. And yet, we have the uneasy feeling that we are helpless to do just that—that we are, indeed, a race of impotent human beings trying to manage virile weapons, as one historian (Raymond Aron) put it, a race that always manages to come up with new and more imaginative ways of annihilating itself. When Captain Robert Lewis, copilot of the Enola Gay, looked down on Hiroshima, he asked in horror, "My God, what have we done?" But, of course, we did what we always do if we can get away with it: We kill one another—and we don't worry about what God thinks of it either.

Our Scripture lessons tell us that we shall never have peace as long as we reject our God, because, you see, our God will never settle for less than his abundant life for us, and he knows we cannot have that life except we obey and trust him. . . .[6]

In this sermon on Luke 14:25-33, Eric C. Kutzli allows the tension to mount, while at the same time he is sensitive not to push listeners so hard that they react defensively and stop listening. Trouble comes from people's inability to meet the demands placed upon them. Each paragraph moves—perhaps nudges is a better word in preaching, since it indicates the appropriate pace for listeners—a little beyond the previous paragraph:

Every time I read this text I stumble over that hard word in verse 26: "Whoever does not HATE . . . cannot be a disciple." It is so tempting to try to explain it away, to make it all right, but the text says, Hate, Deny, Despise, Disdain.

Disdain your father, your mother. Despise spouse, and children, brothers, sisters. Deny yourself.

I love my wife and kids, my friends and family. I just can't do this. But there is more!

Carry the cross. Take it up. Not a little gold cross on a chain but a real heavy wooden cross of death. If you want to become a disciple, go out and get yourself killed.

This is even worse! I am not going to be able to do this either.

Give up all your possessions. Get rid of everything. No money, no land, no house, no clothes on your back. Get rid of it all, tennis racquets to toothpicks. It has to go.

I tell you what. I will . . . if you will! Neither one of us will. Will we? Brothers and sisters, we have a problem. Have you ever arrived at the check out counter and discovered that you cannot pay?

I have to tell you that when I estimate the cost, there is no way that I can become a disciple of Jesus Christ, no matter how I try. That good old time value of pay as you go is stabbed in the heart. It dies hard and it hurts to admit it.

I can't become a disciple of the Lord Jesus Christ. Neither can you. How do we dare to call ourselves Christians? We have done nothing to deserve the privilege. What are we going to do?

[The sermon now moves on to Page Three and grace: "Someone else has paid for us."][7]

135

Tell Only One Story About Oneself

Trouble can come from personal experience, but preachers should take care to limit stories about themselves, lest they be perceived to seek the spotlight that belongs to God. One story about oneself, perhaps even every few weeks, is enough. Some stories that we observe personally we can use without including ourselves in the telling. Still, stories about our own brokenness can be important. Joanna Adams told this powerful story of brokenness in her own home. In telling this, she is vulnerable before the congregation and before the Word. The story she tells is of the right sort—neither too private (belonging to a counselor) nor one that makes her appear in a glowing light.

A year or so ago, I was sitting in our den at home watching the evening news. I was by myself. Everyone was away except for Sam, our teenage son, and me. Sam and I had earlier had one of those arguments only a teenager and a teenager's mother can have. It was a bellringer over one of the burning issues of our age: when the dirty clothes basket was going to be taken upstairs. We had, shall we say, not resolved our differences, and Sam had disappeared and the cat and I had the den all to ourselves. "CBS News" was doing a series that week on World War II, and that particular night the focus was on the Soviet Union. The statistics of the deaths, the losses that the Soviet Union experienced during World War II were mindboggling— 20 million people killed.

The cameras first panned the stark, mammoth war monument that the Soviets seemed to love so. Then they focused in on a young, bright-faced bride and groom who were laying a bouquet of red tulips at the foot of a soldier's tomb. It has become the custom there for couples as they begin their lives together. The bride and groom didn't look much different from American couples on their wedding day—same hopes, same dreams. Just as I was getting misty-eyed about it and thinking about the next Peacemaking Task Force meeting I could attend, I remembered our world's love affair with war. As I remembered, I got deeply frightened, and just as I remembered, Sam walked into the den and sat down. All of a sudden it seemed the most important thing in the world for us to talk and make our peace. . . .[8]

Develop a Fresh Angle on Trouble

In order to keep listeners' attention, preachers need occasionally to surprise them with something original or creative in thought, story, or image. Richard Groves tackles the tough and surprising subject, "Is Sex Ever Safe?" Of course the subject in itself will generate interest, but notice the twist that he uses to maintain interest at the beginning of the second paragraph below. He anticipates listeners' response and surprises them by taking a different, innovative, and insightful ethical turn.

> In the final analysis, love and trust are the only precautions we can take that will make sex in its deepest meaning safe. For love and trust create an environment in which we are free to be ourselves, to relax, to let down our defenses, to be vulnerable.
>
> "Oh, I can see it coming," I hear you say. "We finally got to the 'only in marriage' part." No, I'm not saying that. I'm saying *more* than that. I'm saying that even in marriage, sex has the potential for being dangerous. Talk to an abused spouse, if you don't think so. Sin separates the physical from the spiritual inside marriage just as it does outside marriage. And sex becomes superficial or coercive, shallow or threatening, inside marriage as well as outside marriage. Love and trust, which make "naked without shame" possible, can never be taken for granted, not even in marriage, especially not in marriage. They must be tended like the most delicate flowers. When they are so tended, they create a garden that is not Eden but that is, in its own way, even more beautiful.[9]

James Ayers brings a fresh and imaginative perspective to preaching on the consequences of human actions in Galatians 6:1-10. He ponders how some people became the way they are. His imagination could have been sparked by reading a sermon (for instance, Billy Sunday [1862–1935] once preached a sermon in which he noted, "No man ever started out with the intention of becoming a drunkard"[10])—we all need to read sermons for imaginative insights we might glean. Note his excellent pacing of ideas as each paragraph moves ahead just a little.

> But it isn't just the teens. It's all of us. Right now, we are each of us making choices about who we are. Right now, I'm caught in the act of being who I am. Right now, I'm caught in the act of sowing—

wild oats?—sowing, or planting, the kind of person that I am and that I'm going to be. Don't be deceived. God cannot be mocked. What we plant and cultivate right now is the kind of person that we will be.

Think about this for a moment. How often do you run into someone who says, "When I grow up, I want to be a mean and spiteful person. Miserly. Jealous. Greedy. I want to be the kind of person who always makes sure I get what I want, even if you've got it now, even if I have to step on you pretty hard when I take it away from you. When I grow up I want to be able to do whatever I want whenever I want to. If I feel like being ugly to people, I just will, just because I don't want to bother trying to be nice." Or someone who says, "I want to be an angry person. Vicious. Malicious. I want to be someone who holds a grudge. I want to have a memory that is supremely ready to remember what you did wrong and ready to put you on the rack for it all over again, ready to put in the knife and give it a good hard twist. That's what I'd like to be."

No one talks as if that's what they want. But a lot of us get caught in the act of becoming that kind of person. Why are there angry people? or jealous people? or bitter people? Did they say, "That's what I want to be when I grow up"? No. When they try to remember the fires of September of passion and hope from days gone by, it wasn't filled with longings for vindictiveness and spite. They dreamed of a life filled with love, joy, peace, patience, kindness, goodness, faithfulness, gentleness, and self-control. That's what they dreamed of. But those weren't the choices they made. And they got caught in the act of making those other choices over and over again. And what they kept on planting in their lives came to the harvest: They became the kind of people they had cultivated themselves to be.[11]

Exemplify Good Ethical Behavior

Stories modeling correct moral choices might belong either on Page Two (trouble) or Page Four (grace). They are appropriate for Page Two if they imply or state what listeners are to do and represent tough or costly choices in which the burden falls heavily on the individual or community. Often the story can be slightly revised to identify God's action and can be used most appropriately on Page Four. In the sermon on "God depicted in Scars and Beauty," John N. Jonsson tells several stories about his own mother and what she provided him by way of solid faith and good moral conduct. The story below involves a judgment call: what is its emotional or spiritual impact? The dominant initial impact it had on me in its current form was weighty, not celebrative, and related to the price of being good and the Suffering Christ.

When I was a young boy in southern Africa, my sister Elsa was involved in an accident and broke her back . . . [and] died. That was a scar my mother never seemed to be able to live with, and she would sometimes sob by the graveside. A tragic, ugly scar. But then there was the pharmacist in the town who asked my mother, "Mrs. Johnson, how can you believe in the love of God when tragic things like this happen?" My mother was able to reply through her tears, "We never as a family knew what the love of God was until this happened to us." What beauty! . . .

I came home from school one afternoon when I was a young teenager in South Africa. My mother was nowhere to be found. She was always there to meet me when I arrived home from school. I found her on her knees in an Episcopal church behind our home. She was crying. I went down on my knees beside her. "Why are you crying, Mom?" I asked. "John, we are very discouraged at the way we are being treated by our white neighbors. We are trying to educate the blacks towards self-subsistence, but this is felt to be a violation of our place in society, for the blacks need to be kept in their place." With my youthful exuberance I retorted, "Don't worry, Mom, you will one day get your reward!" After all, I thought to myself, isn't that why we do everything anyway? My mother replied, "But that is not why we are doing all this." I was a bit astonished and somewhat taken aback. "Well, why are you doing all this and being hurt by those who ought to know better?" My mother replied quietly but deliberately, "We did it all because we know it is the right thing to do." What scars, what beauty. . . .

I was in a minister's fraternal meeting. We were discussing the merits of the different translations of the Bible. We all had a turn at sharing what was our favorite translation of the Bible. "Well, what is your favorite translation of the Bible, John?" someone asked me. I replied, "I like my mother's translation."[12]

Use Appropriate Stories and Anecdotes

Stories and anecdotes obviously must be appropriate to the church and worship setting. They must be contemporary or crafted to sound contemporary, for listeners are seeking connections with their own lives and times; and the Bible presents enough temporal and cultural barriers without adding to them stories of the Duke and Duchess of Wellington during the Napoleonic wars. Furthermore, if most stories are from distant decades or centuries, the congregation will perceive the preacher as distant. Often a preacher can add a modern component to dated stories that will help them to connect more readily with the listeners (e.g., even the fact that the ABC television network this week was showing a documentary on the designated topic or person can help).

However, some rare anecdotal material seems so apt that it can be used without updating, as in this tale preached by Sanford Ragins in Los Angeles. It belongs on Page Two, not Four, because the burden falls on humans to act.

> We are told that about two thousand years ago, in Roman times, two rabbis, Rabbi Ishmael and Rabbi Akiba, were walking by the way when they met a sick man. Nearby they saw a farmer plowing his field, and Rabbi Ishmael called out to the farmer and asked him to go quickly to the nearest town and summons a physician.
>
> And the farmer said, "Oh, rabbi of little faith, it is God's will that this man has become ill. If God wants him to die, he will die. If God wants him to live, he will live."
>
> The rabbi was angered, and he said to the farmer, "What do you have in your hand?"
>
> "A plow of course," answered the farmer.
>
> And the Rabbi said, "Why do you interfere with the earth that God has created, O farmer of little faith? If God wants your crops to grow, they will grow. If God does not want your crops to grow, they will not grow. But what do you do? You plow, and you sow, and you water, and you weed, and you work. You enter into partnership with God in the work of creation. And so it is," the rabbi concluded, "with the physician who is partner with God in the work of healing. Now go and summon a doctor."[13]

Identify Important Issues

Some preachers may question the value of raising social issues in a sermon by saying, "There is little that this congregation will be able to do." The question relates to mission. The best response is the response of faith. In Christ all things are possible. Christ wills

140

that we lay down our lives for others, that all people may know justice, peace, security, and well-being. If dreaming God's dreams does not take place in the pulpit, where will it take place? We may never know what results will come from planting a seed. Moreover, what little that individuals can do on their own does not compare with what God can work through them. Here are several examples of how preachers have raised a variety of tough issues:

A sermon on *the environment and animal rights* may draw opposition from several quarters. Jonathan Massey, in a sermon entitled "God Is Concerned for the Oxen, Paul!," picks a small quarrel with Paul over 1 Corinthians 9:9. Massey cites John Wesley's sermon, "The General Deliverance," in his claim that animals have some measure of God's image stamped upon them, and Massey uses several stories designed to cut through the protest he anticipates from opponents. The use of several similar types of stories in a series to establish a case with increasing evidence (though technically not proof) is a rhetorical device called accumulation.

In October 1978, when [Koko the gorilla] was seven years old, *National Geographic* reported she looked at herself in a mirror and signed the word "woman." She had, at that time, a working vocabulary of 375 signs. Koko can respond to and ask questions, tells people when she's happy or sad, refers to past and future events, comes up with original definitions for objects, occasionally insults her human companions and sometimes lies to avoid blame! She lives independently in her own trailer, adopted a pet kitten, and was interviewed by *Life* magazine a few years ago. Does God care nothing for Koko, and can we do whatever we want with her and her kind, according to Aquinas? (I'll never forget watching a gorilla family in the Cincinnati zoo. The male was obviously hungry, but passed the first carton of milk given them to his nursing mate.)

The December 5, 1988, issue of *The Arizona Republic* told how, "for two days, a herd of elephants nursed a wounded elephant calf after nudging him along the road to the nearest human protection in the forests of eastern India.

"It took the elephants six hours to cover the two miles to a forest ranger's office. The staff administered first aid . . . but he later succumbed to the head wounds inflicted by a tiger.

"Tears rolled down the mother elephant's eyes as the rest of the herd formed a circle, raised their trunks and trumpeted over the body. . . .

"The elephants apparently thought the proximity of people would keep the tiger from returning for the kill, according to the news agency."

Does God care for the elephants? Does the Christian faith have anything to say about the slaughter of these creatures to increase the supply of ivory baubles?

These are the higher animals, but *The Arizona Republic* has also reported that even birds have thinking ability. According to University of Iowa scientist Edward A. Wasserman, "Pigeons commit new images to memory at lightning speed, but the remarkable thing is that they organize images of things into the same logical categories that human beings use when we conceptualize." Does God care for the pigeons? You will have to answer that for yourself, as I have to. We live in a world that is only partially redeemed. . . .[14]

Trouble should be developed in the sermon so as to lead to corrective action. Eugene Peterson sees *the lack of joy in contemporary society and the seeming futility of people's pursuits* as a sign of the trouble in our world. The problem is both social and individual. Even as he uses trouble to move his listeners to action, he offers a promise of joy (which would be Page Three and Four). Every sermon should offer something that will make a difference in the lives of listeners. Try to spot the promise here:

Inadequate sinners as we are, none of us can manage [joy] for very long.

We try to get it through entertainment. We pay someone to make jokes, tell stories, perform dramatic actions, sing songs. We buy the vitality of another's imagination to enliven our own poor lives. The enormous entertainment industry in our land is a sign of the depletion of joy in our culture. Society is a bored, gluttonous king employing a court jester to divert it after an overindulgent meal. But that kind of joy never penetrates our lives, never changes our basic constitution. The effects are extremely temporary—a few minutes, a few hours, a few days at most. When we run out of money, the joy trickles away. We cannot make ourselves joyful. Joy cannot be commanded, purchased, or arranged.

But there is something we can do. We can decide to live in response to the abundance of God, and not under the dictatorship of our own poor needs. . . . One of the certain consequences of such a life is joy, the kind expressed in Psalm 126.[15]

Large social issues can be difficult to tackle effectively in a way that sounds fresh and theological, that does not merely mouth what

142

may have been said in the press. Even social issues need a new angle each time they are preached. Samuel D. Proctor preached a powerful sermon that named *gambling as a social sin,* instead of just an individual one, and spent long enough on the issue to convince listeners of its seriousness. Part of the reason Proctor is convincing is because he includes a personal experience. In an academic essay, personal experience is not highly valued; but, in preaching, experience (which does not have to be the preacher's own) can sometimes be more important than statistics. Observe the excellent, slow pace of ideas and also the definite progression of thought from one paragraph to the next:

> In my home state of New Jersey, we face budget shortages. . . . And without any great controversy whatsoever, we installed gambling casinos in Atlantic City. When you go down there—if you thought this was not a social problem at first—see who's down there gambling: old folk with their Social Security payments, poor folk, women without husbands and who live alone, and people with the familiar signs of insecurity. There they are, taking this last chance at trying to augment their livelihood. We would rather take care of the poor like that than raise the money in other ways to take care of the needs of our state. I have seen Brink's trucks all of my life hauling money, but I had never seen a fourteen-wheel rig with "Brink's" printed on its side until I saw one coming out of Atlantic City one night. A truckload of poor folks' money! Our state has a budget that counts on several million dollars a year coming out of Atlantic City. That says nothing of what will filter out of Miami Beach and out of Las Vegas. We do this with casual ease: we walk by the other side.
>
> Here we are, rid of smallpox and yellow fever. We're finished with poliomyelitis and tuberculosis. We're able to reconnect severed limbs and to reproduce skin tissues. . . . But we cannot change the moral climate of our culture. We cannot change the hearts of persons. We cannot create a caring spirit among us.[16]

Brian L. Harbour told the following story about Clarence Jordan on the subject of *race relations* and the poor:

> In the 1940s he founded a farm in Americus, Georgia, and called it Koinonia Farm. It was a community for poor whites and poor blacks where they could farm the land and live together. There was, as you might imagine, strong resistance from citizens of the area. They tried

everything they could to stop Clarence Jordan. They boycotted him. They slashed his workers' tires when they came to town. For fourteen years, they relentlessly opposed and harassed him.

Finally in 1954, the Ku Klux Klan decided to make one more push and get rid of Clarence Jordan and his Koinonia Farm. They came in the middle of the night with guns and torches. They set fire to every building on Koinonia Farm except for Clarence's home, which they practically destroyed with bullets. They chased off all the families except one black family that refused to leave.

Clarence recognized the voice of one of the Klansmen to be that of the local newspaper reporter. The next day, the reporter came out to see what remained of the farm. The rubble still smoldered, and the land was scorched. The reporter found Clarence in the field, hoeing and planting.

The newspaper reporter said, "I heard the awful news of your tragedy last night, and I came out to do a story on the closing of your farm."

Clarence just kept on hoeing and planting. The reporter kept prodding, kept poking, trying to get a rise from this quietly determined man who seemed to be planning instead of packing.

Finally, with a haughty voice, the reporter said, "Well, Dr. Jordon, you got two of them Ph.D.'s, and you've put fourteeen years into this farm, and there's nothing left of it at all. Just how successful do you think you've been?"

Clarence stopped hoeing, turned toward the reporter with his penetrating eyes, and said quietly but firmly: "Sir, I don't think you understand us Christians. What we are about is not success. What we are about is faithfulness."[17]

Sharon E. Williams names *the issue of violence* in her own community. Her thought progresses steadily from the beginning of this passage to its end in an effective statement of her congregation's questions.

We know in our time that peace is broken by violence—even in the Christian journey. We are not exempt from rape, mugging, or murder. Our peace with God, family, and one another is taken from us by violence. I learned a while ago that a woman died on a subway platform in New York City during the Fourth of July weekend. Someone threw a cherry bomb at her to distract her and then snatched her purse. She was so frightened that she had a heart attack and died. . . .

Earlier this year our church funeralized a mother and two small children who had been brutally murdered in their own home. An older child in the family was arrested for the crime: a family's peace and joy were snatched away by violence. Unity and love were replaced by separation and grief.

From out of nowhere violence comes to assault the kingdom. From out of nowhere—attack! From behind masked faces—violence and destruction! From the skies and from under the earth—suffering and death. The kingdom suffers. The kingdom is taken.

It does not seem fair of God to create us for peace and love and then allow all this violence. It is not fair for the violent to be allowed to take the kingdom from us. Is God's kingdom that fragile and vulnerable? Is it okay for us—the meek and lowly—to take up armaments against this violence, at least for our own safety, in a violent world?[18]

Now we turn to a compelling portion of a sermon delivered by Gary A. Wilburn on *the subject of AIDS.* He speaks of his own doctor ordering him to have a blood test for HIV, and tells his congregation that he himself had no reason to be anxious. He uses the blood test scenario, however, to help us understand the experience of others who do have the virus. In dealing with a highly emotive or controversial subject like this, preachers should allow the congregation, through the words of the sermon, an opportunity to meet someone who is affected or infected, so as to make the issue human and personal, not abstract and intellectual.

I remembered horror stories of people being shunned years ago in this country because of the "Big C"; they were afraid even to whisper the word *cancer.* Now it is not only fear but shame, and shame is a worse killer even than AIDS.

Thankfully, my test came back negative. The liver test [that was the occasion of the test for HIV] was a fluke. My health is fine. I do not have the AIDS virus. But there are many who are not so fortunate.

One of those people is Elizabeth Glaser, the wife of actor Paul Michael Glaser of [the television show] "Starsky and Hutch" fame. Elizabeth was a happy wife and mother until two years ago when she sat sobbing on the steps of the hospital where a doctor had just told her that her daughter, Ariel, had forty-eight hours to live. In 1981 Elizabeth had received a contaminated blood transfusion after the birth of Ariel. During breastfeeding, she unknowingly passed the virus to her daughter and three years later to her son. Ariel died in March of 1988. Today both Elizabeth and her son have the HIV virus. "One of the things that my life has taught me," she said recently, "is that I have nothing to lose by being honest. I don't have the time to play games."

As your pastor, I feel the same way. It is unacceptable for a civilized society to act as though the problem will just go away if we keep pretending it isn't there or that it isn't our responsibility. . . .

The church has been silent for too long. We can be many things to many people. But if we cannot be the Church, the healing body of our Lord Jesus Christ, to those whose lives are destroyed by the tragedy of AIDS, then we have no right to call ourselves Christians.[19]

Foster Global Awareness

Few collections of sermons contain references to global events, and the results of such closed-in or claustrophobic preaching are evident. God is made small. If God is irrelevant to the needs of the sufferers people see on the television, how can they believe that their own more mundane troubles are of concern to God? Global references do not have to be lengthy. John Killinger speaks globally in this sermon and by doing so makes a powerful testimony to God's love. This catalogue or collage of various scenes speaks of God's "involvement" and this could be construed as grace, more appropriate for later in the sermon. The emotional impact of the paragraph, however, tends to be suffering and "the pain business." Frank theological discussion of human trouble on Page Two helps to put the world in perspective, for listeners start seeing things as they are. The need for divine action becomes obvious by the end of Page Two. (Excerpted from The Library of Distinctive Sermons, © 1996, by Questar Direct, and reprinted by permission of Multnomah Publishers, Inc.)

Moreover, God is involved in the pain and suffering of all people. God is involved in the hunger of a seven-year-old child in Africa who eats grass to put something in his distended belly. God is involved in the fear and loneliness of a teenage girl who's just discovered this morning that she is pregnant. God is involved in the agony of a young couple who buried their infant child last week. God is involved in the suicidal thoughts of an old man who desperately misses his wife of half a century. God is involved in the hurt and pain and bewilderment of a three-year-old child tortured to death by her parents. The words of the disciples are iconic: "Master, we are sinking! Do you not care?" Of course God cares. God is involved in all our problems. God is in the pain business.[20]

Similarly we can foster global awareness by relating stories from the international news on television. When we tell a story from another part of the globe, our purpose is to introduce listeners to a person there who is just as precious in God's sight as they are, and to awaken the congregation again to brothers and sisters around the globe. The preacher of the following sermon visited the Third World and preaches against landmines. But there is a potential problem here. Has the preacher portrayed the violence with too much detail, so that (a) the children or adults in the congregation will be upset, (b) the image of suffering and violence will take over the sermon, or (c) the proclamation of good news will be hampered? We must judge for ourselves.

One day I visited a hospital which many years ago had been established by the church at Chicuque in Mozambique in southern Africa. In the children's ward I saw a little girl about seven years old who was a victim of the civil conflict going on in her country. She had been in her village one day when bandit forces came. All the people ran into the bush to hide, but this little girl in her confusion ran into her parent's hut. The bandits stole what they wanted from the village without finding the girl. When she no longer heard any noise, she came out of her hiding place to look for her parents. Outside the hut she stepped on one of the land mines that the bandits had placed around the village when they withdrew. The explosion mangled both of the little girl's legs so that she could not walk.

As she lay in the dust in fear and pain, and alone, the thought passed through her mind that if she could just get to the United Methodist Hospital, those people could take care of her. And so she began to pull herself on the ground using her elbows to pull along in the direction of the hospital. She had traveled a distance of two or three miles when someone found her and took her to the hospital, where she was treated. When I saw her she was a patient in the children's ward.

She had truly walked through the shadow of death and had known great fear. But she found a source of comfort and healing. . . .[21]

Employ Doctrine

Explicit doctrinal reflection is appropriate on any page. By reading material relevant to the selected doctrine, for instance in a systematic theology textbook, preachers can find important insights and ways of adding depth to what they say. Penelope Duckworth keeps returning to the doctrine of resurrection in her sermon, "Disbelief for Joy." Note that the trouble here addresses the guilty conscience of listeners and thus functions primarily on a vertical axis. Here is a portion appropriate to Page Two:

> It is also clear that the resurrection body of Jesus had new properties as well as some very familiar ones. The resurrection body is a new creation of the divine will, but it bears the imprints of the suffering and sacrifice that we have done for love while we have lived on earth. Someone once said that the things we take with us when we die are the things we have given to the poor. It may also be that we will be recognized when we die by the scars of our moments of self-giving. . . .[22]

In the following sermon excerpt I use the doctrine of atonement to prepare for Page Three (that starts with the last paragraph here). I use the extended metaphor of Resentment Road to make the doctrinal discussion easier to follow and visualize. Trouble, here, functions primarily (although not exclusively) on a horizontal axis, for this passage speaks of the brokenness of the world.

> It is not just Hollywood that chooses violence. You and I choose it whenever we hang on to resentment, hatred and wish ill upon those who have done evil to us. We do not have to go far down Resentment Road before we start to see the work of others who have taken this route, the massive brick walls separating hated neighbors in Northern Ireland; the destroyed neighborhoods of ethnic violence in Bosnia, or Burundi, or Chechnya; or the bombed hulk of the Alfred P. Murrah Federal Building in Oklahoma City. At one twisted level, hatred of those who have done this seems right. Everyone walking on Resentment Road knows that the people who put them there should have to pay for their evil acts. Each of us has experienced wrongdoing at the hands of others, perhaps betrayal by a spouse or loss of a job. Some of us have experienced what felt like betrayal even by God in the loss of our health or the death of a partner. When things are not fair, someone should pay. God should not have let it happen. It is right to get even. Resentment Road is where we should be.

We should know, however, that Resentment Road is a dead end. It is well-posted. Dead End. No Way Out. Travel at You Own Risk. While others have determined the path, excavated the land, paved the route, erected signs, pointed the way for us, encouraged us on-- we are the ones who chose to go down it. We should pause before going further. Each one of us has done wrong to others. We have betrayed others. We are not innocent. We ourselves have helped nudge others down Resentment Road. If truth be told, at the end of Resentment Road is a killing field, and in the center is a hill, and on top of the hill stands the cross where Christ died. We have all with-held mercy. If there is no mercy for our enemies, there is no mercy for us either.

Of course there is mercy. It comes from a God who decided that someone should pay for the injustice of the world, from a God who has spread arms wide that all people may come to receive God's love.

Develop Mission by Naming What Listeners Can Do

Mission concerns the entire sermon, not just Page Two. But we begin to address it here. As listeners come to recognize the trouble they are in, the preacher can begin to address the question, What can we do? Gary W. Downing, in a sermon on the subject of racism, identifies three actions that congregational members could under-take as their mission for the coming week—acknowledge, believe, and commit. These actions are appropriate to Page Two for they emphasize human action, not God's (he does briefly refer to God's action). Downing's analysis is hardhitting and convicting, of the ver-tical sort of trouble (although horizontal is also present). He uses straight-forward, analytical, and propositional language that is fully appropriate. (Excerpted from The Library of Distinctive Sermons, © 1996, by Questar Direct, and reprinted by permission of Multnomah Publishers, Inc.)

We must choose whether we will view each other through natural, human, racist eyes or will love each other as brothers and sisters in Christ. We can reach out to others with a fist or a gun. Or we can embrace each other as children of our Heavenly Father.

There are three concrete action steps we can take in response to Scripture to overcome sinful racism in our lives.

First, we must *acknowledge* its presence. Have we ever told a racist joke, used a slur or behaved in a racist way? Have we ever made assumptions about another person just because of their skin color or economic status or gender? Acting in any of these ways is not only inappropriate, it is wrong! Racism is a sin.

Some of our racism comes from inherited family patterns. Some of it comes from larger societal and institutional racism. The human race has been racist from the beginning of history, and we continue to carry on that legacy in our lives. But some of our racism is a result of our own personal choices and behaviors. Can we admit it's there? That is the first step to dealing healthily and biblically with the evil of racism.

Can we also acknowledge that it is insufficient to try to overcome racism through our own efforts, relying on our own power?

The second action we must take is to *believe* that Jesus will give us the capacity to overcome racism through his power working in us. . . .

The third step to overcoming racisms is to *commit* yourself whole-heartedly to following Jesus for the rest of your life.[23]

If preachers try to take on the large sociological, psychological, and economic issues as though they are the sociologists, psychologists, or economists, they open themselves to criticism and the church loses its peculiar gift, which is always its theological perspective. The theological perspective is what makes Gardner C. Taylor's preaching powerful. In the following sermon, Taylor leaves no doubt as to what must be done: the people must return to God. His thought moves and develops, so that by the end of these two paragraphs he has increased the pointedness of the trouble.

There is a lot of sham religion in this country, people going through the motions, [people] for whom Christ is not a living, determining presence. Again and again people ask "What is wrong with us as a nation?" One word is the answer: godlessness. Never mind the churches and synagogues and mosques; godlessness is what is wrong with us. Never mind the public prayers and taking of oaths on the Bible. Godlessness is what is wrong with America. How does it come out? In the swagger of a gun lobby and money that stops congressmen from passing a gun law. In greed and bigotry and the attitude "anything goes." In lies and deceit in a nation that has no room for worship or things of the spirit.

You ask what is wrong with us as a people. Listen to any national telecast. See how all of our national interest is built around what some self-serving people in Washington do: crime, scams, confusion. See how little of the heart and mind, how little room for things of the spirit there is in our national telecasts. Godlessness! And until we turn to the Lord, it will not get better; it will get worse. And yes, one thing after another will go wrong.[24]

As these examples illustrate, by the end of Page Two in the sermon, listeners should experience not just the relevance of the issues or topics raised, but also the urgent need for help from beyond themselves. This is, after all, much of the purpose of having a Page One and Two: as preachers we are not just proclaiming human responsibility; we are preparing a means for understanding God's action. On Page Three, to which we now turn, we proclaim what God is doing in relationship to the trouble of Pages One and Two.

A Checklist for Page Two

Does this page develop trouble in our world?
Is this page about one idea?
Does this page clearly link with Page One?
Is this page mainly a movie?
Is one doctrine evident?
Is there a sense of deepening theological thought as the page
　　progresses?
Are everyday issues appropriately turned into theological
　　issues?
Is one need in the congregation identified?
Does this page lead listeners to their own possible struggle(s)?
Does it reflect their worlds?
Are people my focus?
Do I focus on action and stay out of the minds of characters as
　　much as possible?
Have I used humor and avoided seeming too intense?
Are the stories inclusive?
Do they reflect a range of experience?
Do they serve good moral behavior?
Are they and their language appropriate for the pulpit?
Is mission identified?
Is an important issue identified?
Do I avoid using any details of violence?
Am I aware of the emotional or spiritual impact of the stories
　　I have used?

Do I remember to tell no more than one story about myself in this sermon?

Do I demonstrate suitable pastoral sensitivity in relating stories?

Have I been sure to empathize with the worst person I mention?

Do I communicate my own vulnerability before God's Word?

Do I speak from the perspective of faith even when I acknowledge doubt?

Does this page appeal to logos, pathos and ethos?

SECTION IV
PAGE THREE: THURSDAY

CHAPTER EIGHT

God's Action in the Bible

Lack of focus on God is common to many contemporary and ancient sermons. Yet in some ways the problem is unique to our time; never before in the history of preaching has preaching the Bible meant what it means today. Preachers through the ages were not constrained to preach a complete unit of Scripture taken in its context with some view to its historical setting. Primarily they preached doctrine and pulled verses from anywhere in the Bible to support or often proof-text what they were saying. However, because they preached doctrine they had less reason to leave God out of sermons altogether. They were freer to talk about God as the author of the Bible. They were also not constrained by time—they could preach for well over an hour, for there were few competing social interests or attractions, and thus they might visit God's grace several times in a sermon. Moreover, they enjoyed an authority that is rarely found today, which meant they could entrust the message of the gospel to abstract propositional discourse and summons to obedience, and they often did. Still, they were not necessarily much better at preaching grace than we are since they focused minimally on the biblical text and did not look for God's action in the world.

Readers might respond, "If this is a problem with sermons of all ages, maybe the problem lies in your approach." This is possible. However, the challenges facing the church in our era are as great as any the church has faced since the Reformation. We need a new approach to preaching, one that centers on God, one capable of fostering responsible lives filled with hope and a renewal of faith. Whatever approach we take needs to be based in sound theological reason and practice, not fad, whim, intuition, or the latest interesting literary-critical approach, sociological analysis, or theological trend. Most current preaching is deficient in its representation of God and God's action in our world. God has revealed Godself in Scripture, has intervened in history in Jesus Christ, and remains active in the world in the Holy Spirit, yet many of us who are pastors, ministers, or priests aim our homiletical cameras in the other direction, at human activity.

The Need for Page Three

Page Three is a new page for many biblical preachers to contemplate. Page One, exposition, and Page Two, application, are so familiar to most preachers they are like a field that has been ploughed, planted, and harvested many times. We know the land in its slopes and furrows, yet we may not notice that the plants we grow are mostly from the seeds of trouble Moreover, the harvest we gather and place on the backs of our congregation during the sermon makes their steps more labored as they leave church—and this too we may not have noticed. Too often we explore the depth of human trouble and cast members on their own resources and abilities to make the necessary changes without identifying the help that God offers.

Normally, when a child does something wrong, what good parent first kisses and hugs the child and then scolds? There is commonly an order to be followed: from instruction to affirmation, from correction to embrace. The same is true when God deals with God's children. At minimum, there is a theological movement from brokenness and trouble to restoration and grace. The Bible has several ways of depicting this divine movement: from expulsion from Eden in Genesis to the New Jerusalem in Revelation; from Exodus to the Promised Land; from crucifixion to resurrection; and from Good Friday to Easter. In the sermon we mark this movement by moving to Page Three.

Other people have used different terms to discuss this important movement.[1] Frederick Buechner puts it this way in his now nearly classic reflection on preaching, *Telling the Truth: The Gospel as Tragedy, Comedy and Fairy Tale:* he imagines a hotel scene in which Henry Ward Beecher cuts himself shaving while meditating on his accused sin of adultery, prior to giving the first Lyman Beecher Lecture at Yale in 1872:

The Gospel is bad news before it is good news. It is the news that man is a sinner, to use the old word, that he is evil in the imagination of his heart, that when he looks in the mirror all in a lather what he sees is at least eight parts chicken, phony, slob. That is the tragedy. But it is also the news that he is loved anyway, cherished, forgiven, bleeding to be sure, but also bled for. That is the comedy. And yet, so what? So what if even in his sin the slob is loved and forgiven when the very mark and substance of his sin and of his slobbery is that he keeps turning down the love and forgiveness because he either doesn't believe them or doesn't want them or just doesn't give a damn? In answer, the news of the Gospel is that extraordinary things happen to him, just as in fairy tales extraordinary things happen. . . . Zacchaeus climbs up a sycamore tree a crook and climbs down a saint. Paul sets out a hatchet man for the Pharisees and comes back a fool for Christ. It is impossible for anybody to leave behind the darkness of the world he carries on his back like a snail, but for God, all things are possible. That is the fairy tale. All together they are the truth.[2]

Page Three opens theological terrain that for many preachers has had restricted access for the simple reason that few preachers were taught how to preach grace. On this page we proclaim God's amazing nurture and saving acts without further putting the burden of action on the congregation. We proclaim God's faithful and redeeming love without hesitation, reserve, or condition. This is not a way of removing the listener's duty to act, of ignoring God's demands, or of erasing the trouble that has been established biblically and theologically on Pages One and Two. Rather, it is a way of putting our trouble in perspective before the cross of Christ who has taken our place, entered suffering, and gone into death for us, and thereby accomplished something so decisive that all life is changed by it. The possibility of trouble having the determining word over us humans is ended. Our old way of being, with its freedoms that led to death, is replaced by the death of One who gives us our freedom for life.

Page Three As a Turn to God

Page Three marks the negation of the world's powers before God and it puts God before listeners in unconditional, self-giving, restoring, and liberating power. Preaching is awesome in that it is the means whereby God chooses to be placed into and before the world in redemptive love. Preachers who have difficulty distinguishing between theological trouble and grace may recall our rule: At the simplest level, trouble puts the burden of responsibility on people to act; whereas grace puts the burden on God in Christ, who has already acted decisively on our behalf.

When we speak of grace in the sermon, we primarily think Christocentrically and of God as Redeemer, who in freedom restores us to unmerited communion in covenant love. Although as humans we broke our covenant with God, God renewed it in Christ. What was needed God has done in an ongoing relationship that overcomes human sin. The purpose is not merely that we humans may be right with God, but that we may be right with one another and with the created order, that we may be gathered and upheld in this present moment through communion in the Body of Christ, empowered by the Holy Spirit. This radical kind of self-giving interrelationship with God, others, and creation is what it means to be human.

We rarely hear God's unconditional love proclaimed, though it should not be unusual; but many preachers are locked into preaching judgment. Other preachers speak thematically or topically without reference to the Bible or to God and thus have no foundation from which to move to grace. On Page Three, we return to the biblical text and turn to God. We shift attention from human trouble to God's activity by turning to our theme sentence. God's action is the focus of this page and the unifying theme of the entire sermon, what Pages One and Two were leading toward. By now the congregation should have experienced the relevance of the theme and the need for help beyond themselves. God's action stands over against human troubles, our sin and brokenness, and the divine imperatives.

What authority do we have for speaking for God? Our primary source is naturally the Bible, the same source that initially allowed us to speak of the human predicament. God chose to be revealed in history to the biblical witnesses and God chooses to be known today through the Scriptures and the church. Many of the doctrines or traditional teachings of the church imply grace, for instance, the doctrine of justification "by grace through faith apart from works prescribed by the law" (Romans 3:28). The doctrine of the church implies grace, for through the community of faith, and by the power of the Holy Spirit, individuals receive liberation from bondage to sin and death: a new world of justice, peace, love and mercy is begun. The doctrine of Christian hope in its individual, corporate, and cosmic dimensions similarly implies grace. All Christian doctrines have a grace dimension; even the doctrine of sin requires that we speak of how sin is overcome in Christ Jesus.

Typical Preaching Practice

When individual preachers are asked whether they preach grace, typically they will answer that they do. Yet many of these same preachers, if heard in actual practice, in fact keep putting the burden on the congregation and speak little, if at all, of what God is doing to lighten the burden.

Take a collection of sermons off the library shelf and read it to see how many sermons speak about God's action in the biblical text and our world. Not all sermons have a Page Three. If they have it, we can easily find it: God, in one of the Persons of the Trinity, will be the subject of sentences. God's gracious actions on behalf of humanity will be the focus.

For example, a recent fine eight-volume series of collected sermons entitled *The Library of Distinctive Sermons,*[3] edited by Gary W. Klingsporn, wishes to help preachers connect with their congregations. Volume One contains sermons from twenty American preachers, some well-known, and is remarkable because of its range of denominational representation, from Bible Fellowship to Episcopalian. Each of these sermons has its own excellence. For our purposes, though, six of the twenty sermons do not mention God acting on behalf of people; they cast listeners entirely on their own ability to change. Such preaching is anthropocentric, focusing on people, or may make mention of faith and God only in relationship to human responsibility. And such "you-do-it" preaching, often characterized by the words must, should, and have to, is found in every theological camp and every denomination.

Seven of the twenty sermons have brief passing comments referring to God's actions, usually only a portion of a paragraph. The remaining seven focus on God's actions in several paragraphs, still often only one-tenth of the total sermon. Only one sermon devotes half of its length to God's action on behalf of God's people. Of course sermon length is not the only criterion; placement of the material on grace also matters. Often several paragraphs can be preparing for just one powerful sentence of grace. Overall, however, a sermon should build on the grace, explore it, amplify it, and demonstrate how God continues to act in our own lives in a similar manner. Thus sermon length is significant and provides part of our encouragement here for individual pages of roughly equal length.

There is another problem: all seven of the sermons with some good news are on texts that have obvious grace or positive thrusts, such as Jesus appearing to the disciples on the road to Emmaeus, or the lost being found. In other words, the sermons preach grace only when the text is readily perceived as grace. One could argue that this is both natural and appropriate. God's Word is a living Word: it is Jesus Christ speaking in the moment through the power of the Holy Spirit. Exegetical responsibility demands that we render the text as we find it.

On the other hand, hermeneutics is not a theologically neutral activity. The church has known this from the beginning of *the rule of faith:* the biblical text means what the church says it means. In other words, the authority to interpret rested with those who were most qualified in the eyes of the church. Prior to Constantine the most faithful practitioners of the faith, generally, the confessors were the ones best suited to read and interpret the text to the community. With time, this authority gradually shifted to the hierarchy. While this was a positive means of preserving the faith in the early church, in our own time the narrowness of this perspective has become evident. Hermeneutical awareness of how experience affects interpretation prepared the way for African American, feminist, and liberationist theologians in our own time. Perspective is important in all acts of interpretation. What the church said a text meant can no longer be entrusted to a privileged party or confined to just one party's line. No longer can any group or individual claim neutrality in handling a text.

By the same token, preachers who preach grace only when they find it in a text may not be merely neutral. They may be reflecting a frequent habit in the church's culture of not looking for grace, not looking for what God is doing. Or they may be reflecting their own lack of experience in identifying grace. In other words, grace may be present, but they may be so influenced by our culture that they do not see it and unintentionally may shut God out.

160

God's actions may be found in or behind nearly all biblical texts. Trouble and grace, dilemma and gift, judgment and forgiveness, threat and promise, divine claim and succor, command and blessing, are two sides of the same coin. The word that binds is the word that frees. The preacher is responsible for helping each emphasis to be heard. On every Sunday God mandates the fullness of the gospel to be heard.

Unfortunately, most sermons have minimal focus on God. Another excellent collection, *Best Sermons 7*,[4] edited by James W. Cox, demonstrates this lack of focus on God. Out of forty-one sermons, eighteen, or nearly half, have virtually no grace; ten have passing reference to grace; and thirteen have substantial grace, sometimes up to one-half their entire length. Once again, in nearly all cases where grace is preached, the text is obviously about grace (like the lost being found). By contrast, many texts that are obviously about grace, surprisingly, yield sermons on trouble.

It is as though many preachers have been taught excellent exegetical skills but not the use of theology in reading Scripture. If we have not been trained to see God in the biblical text or to name God acting in the world, we will find it hard to speak about God in ways accessible to congregations. Unless we can speak about God in concrete events, our conversation is just abstract and propositional. Most of us preachers approach preaching largely in intuitive ways: an idea comes and we run with it. We need a more ordered, time-efficient, and effective approach that will also help our ability to preach God.

Collections of excellent sermons are presumably our best, most reliable indicator of what is going on in pulpits from sea to sea. If God is being given insufficient attention in our best sermons— judged by how little God is the focus—and if God's grace receives minimal attention, no wonder the church in many quarters is in trouble. An immediate question for the church is this: Can sermons be joyful and lead to lives of joyful service to others when God, who alone is the source of joy, is given so minimal a focus? Why do even evangelicals leave out the Evangel?

Typical Problems in Preaching Grace

If most contemporary sermons have so little focus on God and grace, then what are they focused on? What kinds of emphases are commonly being preached? What tends to dominate contemporary sermons? Eight common problems in preaching grace are identified as follows:

1. Preachers identify God's action in a sentence or paragraph, and then shift the focus back to human tasks, as though they are afraid to continue. For instance, "God has given so much to each of us" quickly becomes "When will we allow our lives to be transformed by God?" "God loves us" too quickly becomes "Believe in Jesus." We step on the flower of grace before it blooms. On Page Three, we should stay focused on God's love as seen in the text. We have already proclaimed human responsibility; anything more than the briefest of reminders beyond Page Two is unnecessary. We may trust that the Holy Spirit is active in the tension between trouble and grace in our preaching. Moreover, grace is the unmerited favor of God: even if humans fail to do what is required, that failure is not the last word. God can find a way around human resistance. Sustained and substantial God-focus is needed to develop authentic hope.

2. Preachers confuse imperatives with grace. No matter how good and important the imperative, it puts a burden on the listeners: "We need to recognize . . . ; Let the risen Christ come to you; You must turn to God; Claim Christ's Spirit in your life." We can put statements such as these on Page One or Two, where they belong. The same statements, if they appear on Page Three of a sermon draft, can be rephrased as declarations of grace: "God's truth is pursuing you; The risen Christ has come to you; God has turned to you; Christ's Spirit has permeated your life."

3. Preachers confuse nonaction verbs with grace. Statements such as, "God is present; God hears; God cares," etc. are good as far as they go but they are not much better than Bette Midler's song verse, "From a distance God is watching." On their own, such words are not much help if listeners are in trouble and need God to do something. God is no mere spectator, onlooker, sightseer, or voyeur. God cares enough to do something, to become involved, to get messed up in human affairs, to work for good, to bring forth transformation, to be vulnerable, to suffer, even to die on a cross.

4. Preachers stop short of the fullest expression of grace. We often imply grace but do not make it explicit. For example, if we ask people to imagine what it is like to be without a home, we may stop short of claiming God as the one who seeks homes for all. Or we assume that God's invitation has been received: but even an open door can be ignored or rejected because of human sin. We should envision God overcoming human resistance by not using statements like: "God invites us to be children of light; God calls us to be transformed; or God wants us to. . . ." Instead, such statements can be revised and strengthened: "In your baptism, God made you a child of light; God is working a mighty transformation in your life and the life of this community; God not only wants us to do this, God has already begun it and is empowering us in this moment . . ." In a similar manner, Jesus' words "Come to me, all you that are weary . . ." (Matthew 11:28) now become, in light of the cross, "I come to you who are weary."

5. Preachers fail to establish a tension between trouble and grace and emphasize one or the other, or switch rapidly back and forth. A tension between the two is essential, for neither one can stand as an adequate statement of the faith on its own. Further, each allows the other to be heard more clearly: trouble can be explored in greater depth if the preacher has an equally strong countering word of hope to add. For example, a preacher can develop tension between faith, hope, and charity as human responsibilities, on one hand—and, on the other hand, as gifts God gives through the power of the Holy Spirit.

6. Preachers delay the introduction of grace in a sermon, holding it back as if it were the punch line of an amusing story that will be ruined if used too soon. Grace commonly appears only in one, perhaps the last, paragraph of the sermon.[5] Preachers do not demonstrate that grace arises out of the biblical text, and do not develop its impact on individual lives. Grace that is quickly dispensed is soon forgotten.

7. Preachers mistake trouble and grace for problem and solution. The gospel is not a bandage or a fix-it. The gospel is primarily a relationship of faith and trust in God who is revealed in Jesus Christ and comes to us in the power of the Holy Spirit in the midst of joy and sorrow. Everything is not made "all better" according to our plans; yet, in faith we claim that every-

thing is made new through the liberating and transforming power of the sovereign God. Most events in everyday life contain ambiguity because sin exists and signs of God's activity are rarely unequivocal. The best stories of grace reflect this ambiguity and offer no simple solutions but, instead, offer God in the midst of the perplexities of life.

8. Preachers employ sermon forms that work against grace, such as: a single exposition/application; a lecture/essay format that stresses information rather than communication and offers ideas of God but no encounter with God or pointers to where such an encounter might be expected; and a single narrative format that has the preacher playing a role that may impede speaking God's grace directly into the lives of the congregation.

A Practical Example

I had a student in introductory homiletics class who could find no grace in her text. Moreover, her husband, who had been a preacher for twenty years, could find no grace. He had not been taught about grace. Philip Yancey speaks of his own experience:

> I attended a Bible college. Years later, when I was sitting next to the president of that school on an airplane, he asked me to assess my education. "Some good, some bad," I replied. I met many godly people there. In fact, I met God there. Who can place a value on that? And yet I later realized that in four years I learned almost nothing about grace. It may be the most important word in the Bible, the heart of the gospel. How could I have missed it?
>
> I related our conversation in a subsequent chapel address and, in doing so, offended the faculty. Some suggested I not be invited back to speak. One gentle soul wrote to ask whether I should have phrased things differently. Shouldn't I have said that as a student I lacked the receptors to receive the grace that was all around me? Because I respect and love this man, I thought long and hard about his question. Ultimately, however, I concluded that I had experienced as much ungrace on the campus of a Bible college as I had anywhere else in life.[6]

This plight is common. Many preachers have never been instructed to discern grace in the biblical text or encouraged to speak of God's gracious acts. They were helped with translation and exegesis, but their biblical studies left out an important theology of the Word and thus they never learned a hermeneutic of grace. Presumably, if we are unable to find grace in the biblical text, we will also have difficulty seeing or naming God's actions in the world.

My student's text was 1 Corinthians 8:1-13, Paul's instructions concerning food offered to idols. A cursory glance at the passage might confirm her suspicions: Paul tells the Corinthians to refrain from eating food sacrificed to idols since weaker Christians might be led astray. However, she had not asked "What is God doing in or behind this text?" In taking a closer look at the text, she discovered many hopeful possibilities in several verses and phrases: "love builds up" (v. 1); "anyone who loves God is known by him" (v. 2); "there is no God but one" (v. 4); "those weak believers for whom Christ died" (v. 11); "for us there is one God, the Father, from whom are all things and for whom we exist, and one Lord, Jesus Christ, through whom are all things and through whom we exist" (v. 6). Verse 8 mentions God in passing ("Food does not bring us closer to God"), yet its implication is clear: Christ brings us close to God.

In verse 6 alone, numerous possibilities for a sermon theme sentence arise: God is the only God; God made all things; God is the purpose of life. Jesus Christ is the only Lord; Christ is the agent of all things coming to be; Christ called us into life. Generally, we should rephrase the biblical words rather than use an actual verse in selecting a theme sentence: the emphasis on God will be clearer. Also we ought to choose the God statement that links with the overall thrust of the biblical text, which in this case might be "God is the purpose of life" because this is the truth that the Corinthians are forgetting.

In preaching grace we focus primarily on God as Redeemer who has chosen to be bound in a covenant of love to an ongoing community of people, as in the Exodus story and the Christ event. The approach is dominantly Christocentric.[7]

Guidelines for Composing Page Three

Many things we said about the biblical text for Page One apply to Page Three. Our focus here is God's actions of grace in the biblical text. Our primary goal is not to speak about God abstractly, or to turn the biblical text into propositions about God; it is rather to render God's actions in as visual a way as possible through the events that the text itself represents.

Making a Movie: Visualizing Page Three

As preachers, we are not writing an essay, we are taking listeners into the world of the text. Make a movie; be visual. Do not spend a long time on description but focus on people in action, and allow description to keep coming through the action. Include all five senses. Do not go into the minds of characters, something that frequently happens if we try to become the character. This can be one of the problems with monologues, for unless they are done well, listeners end up on a boring tour of the character's mind and both action and sensory language are left behind. What is more, the character the preacher becomes can stand as a barrier to the congregation and an impediment to the gospel. What if the congregation does not like the character and have difficulty identifying with him or her, or if the character is not believable, or if in their time of need they long for the preacher to speak more directly of the good news, and it never comes?

Use imagination to ask questions of the text. Use historical-critical scholarship and research to answer these questions, the way movie directors rely on research to make the scene authentic to the times, geography, and customs. Put in interesting sights and information that listeners might not otherwise encounter, not as commentary apart from the movie, but as part of the presented life and action. Again, the purpose is to keep sustained congregational focus on the biblical text. David Buttrick explains the problem: "While in one-to-one conversation, we can say 'God is a mystery' in the wink of an eye; to form the same understanding in group consciousness—oriented, imaged, explained—may take three to four minutes! A congregation of a few hundred people will not grasp ideas quickly."[8] Until listeners can picture what we are saying in their own minds, communication is not fully effective. We might even try to allow listeners to experience the reality of God's action in the text almost as though they were present back then.

In making movies, we still try to minimize distortion of the biblical text. If the text mentions crowds, we show crowds, and an individual in the crowd. But we set foot on shaky ground if we start inventing characters not in the text. For example, a student preached on Jesus' entry to Jerusalem in Luke 19:28-47, and did a splendid job creating a movie of Jesus and the disciples coming from Bethany down though the Mount of Olives with details accurate to the setting. However, this student then named two people in the crowd, and provided an extensive conversation between them; thus for the listeners the focus of the text shifted from Jesus to these two people. If the characters had been unnamed and their conversation brief, the student would have avoided the problem. Moreover, in this student's version, the two people understood who Jesus really is, which is an incorrect representation of the crowd in the text.

We compose Page Three best when we first have the text vividly pictured in our own minds and then share a few essential details with the congregation to assist them in picturing the scene and action in their minds. When resources allow us to say that we have been there, stood on that ground, felt the trade winds blowing rain off the Mediterranean, watched old folks sitting near doorways, heard babies laugh and cry, played with the children, seen the grapes ripening on the vine, labored and talked with the workers in the fields, smelled bread cooking on a heated stone, drawn water from the well, dipped our fingers into the common eating bowls, and slept on a mat on the dirt floor—only then are we truly ready to begin composing this page. In 1906, Alfred E. Garvie instructed his lay-preacher students that they "should not conceive [their] message as doctrine, but perceive it as experience."[9] The same sage advice can be given about the biblical text: perceive it as experience—not that everything must be experiential or has to be a movie, but we must communicate well and provide concrete material that offers a sense of real life as it is lived, albeit two thousand years ago or more.

Composing Page Three

To begin composing Page Three, simply return to the biblical text. This move is natural and expected of a preacher. We can use a transition phrase, though it is not necessary (e.g., "But the good news is. . . ." or "God has a different perspective on these matters" or "We may think that God is remote but the truth is the opposite" or "Ruth in our Bible text knew something we need to know"). Often the theme sentence is all that we need to start Page Three.

The focus of Page Three is God's actions in the biblical text. Find as many ways to use and to restate the theme sentence as possible. The congregation cannot read and reread the sermon and must rely upon our repetition to discover the unifying principle of the page and to recognize its importance. Repeating and rephrasing the theme sentence is not enough, however; God must remain the subject of our sentences. Most students will state the theme sentence and quickly shift back to discuss human action. This takes the focus off God, however. But the sentences need not be discarded entirely in sermon composition. They can be recast, this time from God's perspective. For example, the sentence "Christians must visit the sick in the hospital," can be recast and made theologically stronger when we say, "God empowers us for visiting hospitals," or, "Because we have received Christ, we now can do what we may have thought we could not do—'I can do all things though him who strengthens me' " (Philippians 4:13). Numerous additional sentences can be added to keep appropriate attention on God.

Not all texts lend themselves readily to the concept of making a movie. Nonetheless, we should keep working at this movie-making ideal, because our normal essay-prose is a cool medium ill-suited for preaching because it places high demands on listeners and excludes many, not least the young. As a rough guideline, preachers might strive to have no more than one paragraph of mildly difficult theological prose before returning to concrete, sensory language; even that difficult paragraph can be made more sensory, or can be composed to include rhetorical devices that create interest, like a repeating phrase, or parallel sentence structure, or a series of comparison and contrast, or arrangement according to mounting importance.

When we imagine the human situation that Paul and others were addressing, and when we contemplate the actual people and their circumstances about whom Paul was writing, we render the biblical text more accessible to listeners. In a sermon on Romans 1, I might say:

When Paul wrote to the people of Corinth from Ephesus in the spring of 54 A.D., he had travel on his mind, specifically, a voyage to see them. He may have had a touch of spring fever. Sea travel had been shut down over the winter. Shipping was still risky, and it would be another month before boats could safely travel the open waters of the Aegean and Mediterranean, but many boats were already plying the coastal waters. Writing, as he was, from his room overlooking the harbor, he could see seagulls wheeling in the air, and on the distant western horizon of water, he imagined he could see the skies above Corinth, cloudless as well. . . .

Such comments of course are of a general nature and similar comments could be made about many epistles, as a way of helping their real-life situations come to the fore in preaching. In scripting a movie of a specific text, we should provide what factual evidence we have gleaned from commentaries, Bible dictionaries, atlases, and other sources. We owe it to our listeners to prove that the text is in fact about our theme. We prove it the way a movie director would prove it—through concrete evidence and action that can be visualized or heard. Remember that the purpose in making a movie in words is not to follow a temporary trend but to make a serious attempt at communicating effectively God's action to diverse listeners, including teenagers, in a high-technology media-saturated society.

A congregation should not have to take only the preacher's word concerning the interpretation of a text. When, as preachers, we show that an interpretation is authentic, grounded in the text itself, the congregation becomes a partner with us. Preachers achieve this partnership of trust by presenting specific details of the text. For instance, if we are preaching on Ruth and, in particular, on the claim that God acts on behalf of Ruth, we would show what text justifies this claim. Three pieces of information supporting a claim are usually sufficient: God united Ruth to Naomi's son; God became Ruth's God; God provided for them. By communicating the portion of the story that portrays and supports each of these understandings, we could make a reasonably strong case for the interpretation we are offering. The congregation may have forgotten or not understood the previously read text and need it projected as a movie in front of them again in the sermon, even if they have their Bibles open. We include material now that we did not develop on Page One and that we saved for this purpose so that Page Three is fresh.

The Theme Sentence

Page Three, like any page, is about only one focus or idea, in this case the focus is the theme sentence of the entire sermon *as it relates to the biblical text.* I have suggested that at the beginning of sermon composition, the preacher take four blank pages and write at the top of each one the focus sentence for that page, as a means of reminding the preacher what it is to say. Across the top of Page Three the preacher writes the theme sentence of the sermon. This is the only topic of Page Three. It is God's action in the biblical text, with reference to other biblical passages and theology as appropriate. Page Three is not mere repetition of the thought, as though a sentence parroted often enough will be accepted. Rather, we repeat the theme sentence against a backdrop of concrete language, stories, and deepening thought, perhaps dissecting the theme sentence and developing each component of its meaning as we make its case from the Bible.

The theme sentence might sound trite or superficial at first hearing, perhaps in the introduction or on Page One of the sermon. Now on Page Three, we must develop it into something that gives purpose and theological meaning to the ordinariness of life. Often the baldness of a theme sentence like, "God creates a new identity for Isaiah," is a strength for sermon composition because, as preachers, we find ourselves wanting to qualify or elaborate what we mean by "identity," to help us picture this event. Through this process, the theme sentence prompts the sermon to write itself.

The theme sentence focuses on God. More precisely, it focuses on grace in or behind the text. This is not enough to ensure that Page Three will in fact speak about God however. As preachers, we need to make God the subject of many of the sentences if God is to be the subject of the page. By the end of the sermon, the divine becomes perceived in the midst of the ordinary and people experience God where they thought God was absent. In the process, the preacher takes seriously questions that people have uttered during the prior week and brought to worship. General religious questions, transformed into theological ones, and are now answered: "Why does God seem absent?"; "Who does God want us to be?"; "Is God in control?"; "How may I find God?"

The main theme of the sermon must grow, move, and develop and in this sense there must be a plot to the sermon. If the sermon is cut short listeners should sense that something is missing. For example, Jeremiah A. Wright, Jr., developed a strong theological movement in four distinct pages: he moved from the silence of God (Page One—trouble in the text) to our frustration when God is silent (Page Two—trouble in our world) to God communicates in the silence (Page Three—grace in the text) and, concluded by letting silence trigger our anticipation of God (Page Four—grace in our world).[10] H. Grady Davis's *Design for Preaching*[11] was one of the first homiletical books to call for preaching to be organically structured as something "that grows," instead of statically structured as separate points in a logical argument.

Sermon Unity

On Page Three we continue to be attentive to overall sermon unity, in particular those elements designated by our sentence, The Tiny Dog Now Is Mine. Early in the week we chose one text upon which to preach. Other scriptural references that do not require in-depth explanation can be appropriate, providing that their connection is obvious and they are not so numerous as to be distracting. Now, on Page Three, a preacher might be intentional about bringing in one or two other texts that quickly serve to reinforce the theme sentence or the predominant image. For instance, in preaching on John 12:1-8, Mary anointing the feet of Jesus with costly perfume, I recalled the verse in 2 Corinthians 2:15, "For we are the aroma of Christ to God among those who are being saved and among those who are perishing". It is a difficult verse, and therefore I needed to read it twice in the sermon to help listeners to hear it, but it helped link a remote event in history with the ongoing life of faith, for we are the perfume of Christ in the world.

On Page Two we identified one need to which we are speaking, and we were enabled to do this by the one doctrine that we chose with help from the theme sentence. Pages Three and Four are logical places for the doctrine to inform directly what is said. Even doctrines have a plot—a point that is so easily lost on preachers who try to avoid propositions. Doctrines are rooted in, and should not be separated from, scriptural narrative; they begin somewhere, something happens, and they end somewhere. For instance, incarnation begins in persistent human sin and suffering, moves to God doing something about it in Christ, and ends in the resurrection and ascension, Christ's ministry no longer limited by time and place. Some of this plot might be found in the biblical text at hand and may be woven into its development.

Theology tells us what needs to be said and, sometimes, how to say it. For each sermon, we should read about the selected doctrine in a reliable theology textbook, of which the preacher's library should have several. Since doctrines have a basic argument or plot, we must decide what small portion of the doctrine can be effectively communicated in relation to the text and what practical need it meets in a listener's life. The congregation's need is not first of all "What knowledge do they need"' While knowledge may be important, at least from the church's perspective, the congregation's need concerns life as it is experienced and felt by the listener. On Pages Three and Four, in particular, it is best to restate the doctrine in fresh, simple, concise ways, especially through discussion of the character of God in development of textual action and life-like situations.

If the sermon has one dominant image or refrain, it should also appear early in the sermon and certainly on Page Three or Four, for by the end of the sermon, it should be wed to the theme sentence. If in the introduction the preacher zooms in on a yellow taxicab bringing home a loved one to the door, that taxi can serve as an image or metaphor for homecoming. If the camera keeps repeatedly focuses on different taxis throughout the sermon (perhaps even on one developed in the biblical text), the image of a taxi will become the dominant image in the sermon. It will form a chain that adds unity. If the theme sentence is "God brings us home," then each time in the week the listeners see a taxi, they will have an opportunity to recall this theme.

We have seen in this chapter that grace on Page Three brings a reversal or shift in the direction of the sermon. Instead of looking at things from the perspective of trouble, the sermon now presents what God is doing about that trouble. Sometimes the dominant image can reflect that shift. For instance, on Trinity Sunday I recently preached on John 16:12-15, part of Jesus' farewell discourse at the Last Supper. Jesus in effect corrects the disciples. They have plans for him that disregard God's plans for them. As a way of talking about the Trinity, the first half of the sermon spoke of our human attempts to put God in a box where we can control God. The second half shifted to speak of God not respecting our boxes, of God being on the loose. The same image is carried throughout but, on occasion, a preacher may allow the image to shift slightly in this manner to reflect the movement to grace.

Normally, the one mission of the sermon would not appear on Page Three: mission concerns congregational action and hence deals with our time, not biblical time. Still, we may develop in the biblical text something that anticipates the mission of contemporary listeners, as found, for instance, in the biblical characters' response to God's action. We now turn, in the next chapter, to see how preachers have handled Page Three in practical ways in their sermons.

CHAPTER NINE

Filming Grace in the Bible

Page Three is a metaphor for speaking about God's action in the biblical text. Many preachers end on Page Two and never get this far in their sermons. The following annotated samples demonstrate how preachers have focused on God's action in biblical texts. Of course any time we isolate grace in a text from trouble, in the manner we do here, we distort it, and much of its significance and power are lost. Nonetheless, such samples point to what is possible and may encourage further reading and analysis of sermons.

Develop the Theme Sentence

In composing a sermon, how does one move from judgment to grace, from Page Two to Page Three? One returns to the theme sentence, first mentioned on Page One, that focuses on God's action. Page Three is devoted to developing the theme sentence, thus it needs to become obvious here, and can only become obvious through repetition.

In the following sermon on Jesus healing the man at the pool of Bethzatha, in John 5:1-9, Hank Langknecht establishes his theme sentence early on Page Three, "Jesus just heals the man," and then he repeats it eight times—often enough for hearers to understand its centrality for what he is saying. This frequency was helpful in his oral delivery. Earlier, he had portrayed the man at the pool as someone yelling, "I want to be healed, I want to be healed," yet all the while "he's got his arms wrapped around a column, with Jesus pulling on his feet, trying to drag him into the water."

The end of Page Two moves smoothly to Page Three:

And if you think [the picture of the man hanging onto the column] is unrealistic . . . its not. Because it's just a picture of my own life, except that I don't have my arms wrapped around a column. I've got them wrapped around a half-gallon of Decadent Chocolate Fudge Crackle Ice Cream. . . . [End of Page Two]

But it doesn't matter. Jesus doesn't call the man's bluff. Jesus cuts through the whole game; and he just heals him. No repentance necessary, no jumping into the pool, no particular willingness on the man's part to be healed, the man doesn't even ask Jesus to heal him. Jesus just heals him. "Stand up, take your mat, and walk." And at once, the man was made well. Jesus just heals him.

Even though it's the Sabbath. Jesus just heals him. And of course, it turns out that my suspicion is true; a life of wholeness and health turns out to be a burden this guy just isn't prepared to handle. And so when some of the religious leaders start to put some pressure on him, he caves. He gives them Jesus's name, "That's the guy. Jesus." And the leaders, they start to watch Jesus.

But Jesus just goes on healing. Man born blind? Jesus doesn't ask him if he wants to see, doesn't require any repentance, no particular indication that the guy wants to be healed. Jesus just says, "Go, and Wash, and See!" Jesus just heals him. And the leaders keep watching.

Lazarus in the tomb? Jesus doesn't ask him if he wants to rise again, doesn't require any repentance from him, no particular indication that Lazarus wants to rise again. Jesus just says, "Lazarus, Come out!" Jesus just heals him.

And finally the leaders have seen enough, and the sickness that infects the politics of Jerusalem and Rome festers to the point where they can't take this anymore. And they do their worst. Has the world gone to pot? Sure, but Jesus doesn't ask, "Who wants to be healed?," doesn't require any repentance, no particular indication that the world wants to be healed. Jesus just says, "It is finished!"

Jesus just heals the world.[1]

Use One Dominant Image

On Page Three several items should be present that are represented by the memory device, "The Tiny Dog Now Is Mine." One text, one theme, and one doctrine are likely to be present simply because this is the page on which the theme sentence is developed and discussed. On Page Three we might pay special attention to one image. Every time we use concrete language, we should evoke images, or word-pictures, in the mind of the listener. A dominant image is one that we repeat and focus on, usually in several places within the sermon. This image needs particular attention here because, by the end of the sermon, listeners should experience it as wedded to the theme sentence, so that when they encounter the image during the week in daily life, they may think of God's action.

Shirley Prince preaches a sermon on God's restorative action based on Joel 1:4 and 2:25. Using humor and the device of God speaking to Joel, she communicates relevant exegetical and historical material, and reinforces the grace she develops. Although she mentions trouble in passing, God's actions of grace are always her emphasis; she accomplishes this primarily through the dominant image of recycling. This image is particularly effective if Pages One and Two deal with what God will discard, in which case the image itself undergoes something of a transformation in the course of the sermon (i.e., from something useless to something useful). We begin at the bottom of Page Two to observe her movement to Page Three at the end of the first paragraph:

> But we are the church, the body of Christ, and we're busy destroying each other and God says, "You need to be recycled. Don't worry, I'm not gonna let you destroy my planet any more than I'm gonna let you destroy my church." God said, "Upon this rock I'll build my church and the very gates of hell shall not prevail against it." [End of Page Two].
>
> God says, "I've got a recycling process that you don't know anything about." Among the prophets in the Old Testament, there was a man named Joel. God said, "Joel, I want you to tell 'em, tell 'em ahead of time, Joel, you tell 'em that you are a minor prophet, not that your messages aren't important, but tell 'em that you're a minor prophet because you got a shorter message. Its quick and to the point, tell 'em Joel. Oh, you don't need but three chapters, Joel, you tell 'em. You tell them that I've got a recycling process that they don't understand anything about. Joel, I just want you to tell 'em that the *Lord is coming back*. . . ."
>
> God said, "Joel, I want you to use the imagery of your own time. In an agrarian society, I want you to tell them that they depend upon the land for sustenance. They depend upon the fields for food. But you tell them that one day the locust is gonna come and take every-

thing away. . . . Let 'em know that the field will no longer produce, that the herds will die in the middle of the field. Even the strong olive tree will not be able to bear [fruit]. Joel, you need to tell 'em. You need to tell 'em that the Lord is coming back, but in the meantime, Joel, I want you to let 'em know that its not right now. I'm gonna put a comma in the middle of that sentence and say, 'The Lord is coming back, but you still have time.' So tell 'em, Joel, the Lord is coming back."

. . . God said, "Tell 'em Joel. Tell 'em about the devastation that's coming, tell 'em they still have time, tell 'em that I'm such a good God, such a merciful God that I'm no shorter than my word, that all they have to do is cry out and repent and turn around again. I know that they need to be recycled, Joel, so you tell 'em that the year the locust has eaten I will restore. . . ."[2]

Create the Experience

John M. Rottman creates the experience of being with Jesus when Bartimaeus calls him in Mark 10:46-52. Rottman does not merely assume that the congregation knows the story. He takes time to retell or reconstruct his biblical text in his sermon. Moreover, he adds small details (like the coins flying) that are realistic to the story and help make the movie. Note the smooth transition he makes from the end of Page Two to Page Three. Note also that he feels no need to stay in the movie mode for the entire page, but in the last paragraph moves into what David Buttrick might call preaching in the reflective mode,[3] as a commentator, as opposed to preaching in the mode of immediacy.[4]

But the reality of it is that many of us keep our deepest, darkest problems shut up inside, not even bothering to mention them to God or to anybody else. We pretend that things are all right, or at least that they are far better than they really are. [End of Page Two]

Not blind Bartimaeus, though. He's no pretender and maybe he can't be. See him out there shouting at the top of his lungs. "Yo! Jesus, Son of David, have mercy on me." And the more vigorously the crowd shouts him down, the more enthusiastically Bartimaeus shouts out. "Jesus, Son of David, have mercy on me."

And lo and behold, Jesus not only hears the shouting blind man, he stops and calls Bartimaeus over. And as Jesus calls, the crowd turns from hostile to helpful. "Hey, chin up." "Hey, it's your lucky day." "On your feet, buddy," says another. Bartimaeus flips off his cloak, coins flying. He hops to his feet and he's on his way to Jesus.

The quieted crowd watches. "What do you want me to do for you?," Jesus asks him. Bartimaeus doesn't mince words. Something inside him tells him that Jesus can cure what ails him. "Teacher," Bartimaeus said, "I want to see." On your way," Jesus replies, "your trust in me has healed you." And immediately, Bartimaeus' blind eyes worked. And he followed Jesus down the road. From his place in the crowd, Bartimaeus needed Jesus, and called out to him. Jesus heard Bartimaeus, called him, and healed his blind eyes.

Now its important to realize, I suppose, that Jesus didn't do everything for Bartimaeus that he could have done. Jesus didn't make Bartimaeus a wealthy man. He didn't arrange for him to marry a super model. He didn't give him superior sports talent and transform him into a national hero. He didn't turn this blind beggar into Wayne Gretzky. You see Jesus did not aim to set Bartimaeus on easy street, but to show him something about God. The importance of the healing is seen in what God did for Bartimaeus.[5]

Eugene Lowry develops grace subtly and effectively in preaching on the woman at the well, in John 4:3-19, by creating the experience of Jesus giving the woman water before naming it. God's action in the text is clearly the focus. Pages One and Two in such a sermon could easily focus on human inability to draw the water that people need.

Finally, the woman takes off and leaves the container next to the well.
She hasn't drawn the water—
which means she is in a big hurry to get out of there
or she plans on coming back.
You remember that Jesus had told her to go get her husband and come back.
Well, she goes—and very shortly comes back—and brings a whole group with her.
I'll bet it was not the upper crust of that town.
You may be sure it was a collection of all the outcasts of the village.
Jesus and his friends stay an extra two days to visit with these people about God, the Law, and life.
But then a strange thing happens—
or rather, it is strange that something does not happen.

You remember he said to return and he would give her that
drink that wells up to eternal life?
    Well, when she comes back with her friends,
      She never mentions the drink again.
        Nor does Jesus.
    Now, isn't that peculiar?
      That is what he had promised.
    Well, you see, she did not have to mention the drink again—
      because she had already been given the drink.
      I mean, She was a Samaritan, and he treated her like a
human being—
        that is to be given the drink that wells up to eternal life.
      She was a woman, and he accorded her dignity—
        that is to be given the drink.
      She was a Samaritan woman of bad reputation,
      and Jesus treated her with respect—
        that is to be given the drink that wells up to eternal life.
    She didn't have to mention the drink again—
      she had already received the drink.[6]

Employ Doctrine in Developing the Text

Texts like the Road to Emmaus (Luke 24:28-38) provide an obvious answer to the question, what is God doing in or behind this
text? Charles B. Bugg keeps attention on God's action when it
would be easy to shift the focus elsewhere, for instance, as in the
text itself to the reaction of the disciples to Christ's appearance.
Bugg uses the doctrine of the sacrament of the Lord's Supper to
develop his text, and expands it to provide a measure of sustained
theological focus. When the disciples return to Jerusalem, they
return with much the same kind of experience that listeners might
have returning home from the Table. Note that in discussing this
doctrine, he continues to use the concrete language of the Bible
rather than resorting to the abstract language we commonly use for
theology.

Or were [the disciples'] eyes opened because Jesus took charge of the
supper and served them? Luke is clear. The house may not belong to
the stranger, but the supper does. He "began to give it to them" (Luke
24:30*b*). The bread represented life, and when Jesus took it and gave
it to them, it may have been a reminder that this is the Lord who

holds all life in his hands. That was important to these disciples. With their leader dead, these men had no center, nothing to give life any real purpose. The divine dimension was dead, and life was little more than helter-skelter. The only benediction that we can give when there is nothing beyond us is: "Make the best of it." . . . No wonder these followers were gripped by despair. But in the room their eyes were opened by something. In the place to which they had invited the stranger, they were invited by him to the table. It was his table, his bread, his life; and knowing this, they could live again.

The fact is that we don't really know what opened these men's eyes and gave them new vitality. But something happened in the room around the table that revealed the stranger's identity and gave his followers new identity. At this point Luke's Gospel records a most remarkable thing: "They [the disciples] got up and returned at once to Jerusalem" (Luke 24:33). They didn't even spend the night in Emmaus! They went back to Jerusalem—the place of pain and perplexity—but they went back with a new presence and power.

What is it that keeps us going? What is it that moves us back into the midst of life, to live with a sense of hope? . . .[7]

Reconstruct the Text

We should never assume that our listeners know the text. We must reconstruct it for them on Pages One and Three and not seek to engage them in a game of Trivial Pursuits on the Bible. William D. Watley preaches on Joshua 1:1-5, in which God instructs Joshua. Watley uses imagination to expand the few verses of the divine speech so that God remains the focus of listeners' attention for several continuous minutes. He thereby brings the good news home: God renews the promises made to Moses. Watley improvises the words of God to Joshua. A long speech within a sermon is hard to sustain, and generally I advise students to have characters speak only infrequently and briefly; monologues too easily lose sensory language and become boring tours of the mind. Watley avoids that. Listeners hear God speaking to Joshua and to themselves. Clearly God is alive and well. Observe the progression in Watley's thought: he does not remain in the same place nor does he move too far from where he started, from the theme sentence, "God sends Joshua."

This same God spoke to Joshua, the second in command who would now become the first in command, to Joshua, Moses' lieutenant, and said: "Now look, son. I know that your heart is heavy. I know that you will feel keenly the loss of Moses, especially since the mantle of leadership has been placed upon your shoulders. But no matter how much you grieve, Moses is dead. And when you finish crying and throwing accolades upon him, he'll still be dead. Nothing is going to change that. So lift up your head and look around you. There's still a job to be done; there's still a charge to be kept; there's still a responsibility to be discharged. So get up from where you are and go on. The land that I promised your ancestors remains to be conquered; the wilderness has yet to be cleared; the cities still must be built. So arise, you and all your people, and go over the Jordan into the land of promise. Every place that the soles of your feet shall tread upon shall be yours. Every piece of land that your eyes shall rest upon from the rising of the sun to the going down of the same will be yours. No man shall be able to stand against you all the days of your life. So arise and go on.

"Now don't think its going to be easy. Sometimes you'll give your best, and your best won't seem good enough, and you'll begin to wonder if you really are called to this work, but just go on. Sometimes you'll go out of your way to help folk, and the very ones you've tried to help the most will be the first to talk about you when your back is turned, but just go on. Sometimes when you try to stand for the right, it will seem as if you are standing by yourself, but don't worry about it; just go on. Sometimes the opposition will seem too great. . . ."[8]

I preached the following Page Three in a sermon on Luke 4:14-23, in which Jesus preaches his first sermon in the synagogue in Nazareth. In preaching this story we must decide where to end it: after the congregational praise, or after the attempt to kill Jesus (i.e., are these two separate incidents or one?). Here I take the shorter version, even as next time I might follow the longer one. Making a movie of a text is much easier if we can place ourselves in it, if we can remember a similar kind of experience in our own lives, and present what we are saying in part from that perspective. The immediacy of the experience contributes to the vitality of the language we then employ.

There are times when God's timing does not seem to be so good, when we wonder if God knows what time it is. Just a bit too late to

181

save a girl from being wounded, or a boy from drowning, or a woman from a murderer, or a factory from going under, or a church from closing. [End of Page Two]

The prophet Isaiah knew God's timing. As surely as Isaiah knew his lips had been touched with a burning coal in his call from God, he knew a day would come whose heat would purify the unrighteous, and whose light would never fade. When the Scriptures were handed to Jesus in the Nazareth synagogue, he rose from his seat to read, as was the custom. The passage on the scroll was one of those Isaiah passages that anticipates the coming day of God. Anyone knows that the hardest place to preach is in your childhood congregation. While they may not be your best critics, they are certainly your hardest. The difference with a home town crowd is that it knows. Every word that you say is like a bud that bursts with colorful memories you wish were forgotten, memories of schoolday pranks and lax summer evenings when things other than the word of God were your calling. God, in God's great mercy, has already blotted these things out of the Book of Life, but these neighbors still carry them around. And of course the worst part is that you do not know what might trigger them, just a change in inflection in your voice might bring it on, you don't know, you simply see it happening. Here and there someone is watching a different channel, and you look in their eyes as you speak, and like looking into a camcorder viewfinder, you see the old videotape rolling. There is no worse crowd to speak to, because they don't have to listen: they can just sit and remember.

And yet when Jesus read they did listen. As was the custom, he raised his voice when he read in order to honor Scripture, so that when he sat down to preach, his preaching voice would not be louder. This is what he read: "The Spirit of the Lord is upon me, because he has anointed me to bring good news to the poor. He has sent me to proclaim release to the captives and recovery of sight to the blind, to let the oppressed go free, to proclaim the year of the Lord's favor." Everyone knew the passage. They had heard it many times before, like a favorite song on the radio. And yet as can sometimes be the case in excellent reading of Scripture, it was as though they were hearing it for the first time. Jesus returned the scroll to the attendant who had brought it to him, and sat down. And into the shawled silence he preached his first hometown sermon. And his townsfolk actually heard what he said. And what is more, on this occasion (at least at first), they agreed on what he said. They knew that every sermon should be built around one simple idea, one succinct sentence. The sermon-in-a-sentence that each of them heard Jesus preach was this: "Today this scripture has been fulfilled in your hearing." It was a good word. They knew from Isaiah that the word of God goes forth and accomplishes that which it speaks. To pronounce good news to the poor and release to the captives was to identify God's current action. Who could dispute it? It was their own story for when they were a captive people, they had been restored to their promised land. Where poor find comfort is God's work. They praised Jesus, every one of them saying, "Isn't it amazing! This is Joseph's son. The former carpenter. The one who left town not so long ago. I knew he would do well! I told you he would succeed!"

For thirty years Jesus waited to preach. He waited to know what he would preach. He waited. All of Israel waited. The whole world waited. Even the heavens waited. And time kept ticking by. But of that hour, only God knew. Like people stuck in a traffic jam, or at a New Year's celebration without a clock, there was really only one question in people's heart's, "What time is it?" When it seems late, that is the question we all ask. God's timing seemed off. And yet when Jesus preached in Nazareth, when he announced that today this Scripture is fulfilled in your hearing, he answered that one question in everyone's heart, "The time is now." In spite of appearances, it was exactly the right moment, for it was the moment that God ordained to fulfill the promises made to Israel.

Visualize the Scene Behind the Text

Epistles are among the easiest of texts to preach doctrinally because the doctrine is often so obvious, yet they are among the most difficult texts to preach in ways that will be vital and interesting to hearers. All preachers struggle to preach them effectively. John Richard Foulkes, Sr., preached Philemon, an epistle in which many preachers struggle to find grace. Note how Foulkes brings the text alive: he visualizes Paul meeting Onesimus as a runaway slave who originally belongs to Philemon. Paul sends him back home—for now he belongs to Christ—and Paul requests Philemon to honor the new relationship. The theme statement here could be, "Christ has claimed Onesimus as his own." Pages One and Two in such a sermon might deal with enslavement.

As Onesimus stood at Philemon's door with [Paul's] letter in his hand he must have considered the reason Paul had sent him back to Philemon. Paul must have met Onesimus as an inconspicuous person on a Roman street over one hundred miles from Philemon's house.

183

After having established a relationship with Onesimus, having been an instrument of bringing Onesimus to faith in Christ Jesus and having experienced Onesimus' care, he could have told Onesimus to keep on running. A rationale could have been developed to support Onesimus' not returning to Philemon because of the possible consequences of his escape and violation of Philemon. But Onesimus knew that Paul had introduced him to a new freedom—a freedom in Christ Jesus. This new freedom elevated Onesimus above his social/economic status and gave him a new basis for relationship. "On the basis of love" Philemon was no longer his slave master but his brother in Christ. . . .

Paul tells Philemon that he wants Philemon to receive Onesimus as if he were Paul. That slave standing in front of you, Philemon; that person that wronged you, Philemon; that person that you could legally kill, Philemon; receive him as if he were me and if he owes you anything, put it on my account. If you need to have the money back, I will repay it. If he is in trouble, I will stand for him.

God sent forth God's Son into the world that he might stand in our place for sin's sake.[9]

Edmund Steimle visualizes the scene behind his text. He uses the imagery of his epistle lesson, the imagery of awaking ("So let us not sleep, as others do, but let us keep awake. . . ." 1 Thessalonians 5:1-11), to present the good news. Note that he allows the contemporary scene to blend with his text in a manner that is often advisable if a movie is to be made and the background material for the text is sparse:

So God sends what someone has called his alarm clock, Jesus, crying, "Repent. for the Kingdom of God is at hand." To awaken from all kinds of sleep, the sleep of escape or the rebellious sleep of the unbeliever. "Awake, awake, put on your strength, O Zion."

And that can happen too, miraculously enough. For what is this process of waking up, the rubbing of the eyes, the orange juice and coffee, the planting of the feet on the floor to face a new day? It's a miracle. Like rising from the dead. A new day. None like it ever before, and none like it will ever follow. It's a daily act of God's creation. No matter that one day seems so much like another. It's not. Each day God summons you to get up to a new life. To be sure, the old problems are still there. But there is the miracle of another day to wrestle them, to accept them too as the gift of God.

184

So we are called to be awake to the same old problems: in your family, in the cities—the sickness and the death, the pollution, the poverty, and all the rest of it. But that's not all. There is also the possibility of laughter and beauty and joy: in the family, in the cities, in the world. Repent, to be sure, but only because the kingdom of God is at hand. The world—your little world as well as the big world of which your little world is a part—has not slipped from God's hands. . . .[10]

Make a Link to Christ Where Possible

Every Christian sermon does not have to speak about Christ. When we are preaching the Old Testament, our Bible professors will tell us, we should let the Old Testament speak on its own terms. Still, as a regular principle, our sermons should speak of Christ, and when we are preaching on the Old Testament we can allow the text to speak its own truth in its own context and then, once that is established, we can identify that same truth as it points to or as we find it reinforced in the New Testament. This sermon by Austin Farrer on the communion of saints is based on 2 Kings 6:16, "Fear not, for they that be with us are more than they that be with them" (KJV). In the first half of his sermon Farrer ponders why the glory of God shines so dimly in this world. Now he develops the good news in the story of Elisha and Elijah (preachers should always develop good news first from the text at hand) and moves to a strong parallel in the Gospels to reinforce the hope he finds.

> So (we read) the Lord opened the eyes of the young man, and he saw; and behold the mountain was full of horses and chariots of fire 'round about Elisha. These were the hosts of God, these were the holy angels made visible to that disciple's mind, so he might understand what Elisha had told him: they that be with us are more than they that be with them.
>
> . . . Elisha's disciple saw the regiments of angels, standing by to rescue his master; and they did not rescue him. The disciples of Jesus did not see any twelve legions of angels for their divine master refused to summon them: he would not be rescued, he went to his death. Yet by that very death Jesus opened the eyes of his disciples to see the angels, for whom in his greatest need he had refused to

pray. The women went to his sepulcher on the third day, and there the angels were, one at the head, one at the foot of the place where Jesus had lain. It was by dying that Jesus set open forever a door between earth and heaven: his sepulcher is a piece of heaven, a place of angels. Where Jesus lies sacrificed for us, heaven is opened, a great shaft of light falls from above, and the angels of God are seen ascending and descending upon the Son of Man.

For the act of love that makes the Son of God die for us brings all the angels down. . . .[11]

Preachers who have difficulty answering, What is God doing in or behind the text?, might try alternatives: Whose action in this text is like God's? What does this text tell me about God's love? Barbara Jurgensen seems to have asked one of these secondary questions to discover the good news in Ruth 1:1-19*a*, where too easily a preacher could be sidetracked by the characters in the story and forget about God. As a result, Jurgensen treats her text theologically and points listeners to God. Her theme sentence is God loves Ruth and Naomi. Were we to preach on this, the first half of the sermon might consider the apparent absence of God's love and the hardships of life. Jurgensen uses the whole story of Ruth, not just the portion read in church that Sunday. Observe the clever way she uses her exegetical studies in the last paragraph to tie the story to the Christ-event:

> The story [of Ruth and Naomi] does seem beautiful as we look back on it. It has inspired numerous works of poetry, music, and art. But to the people who actually *lived* it—the famine, the deaths, the widowhood—it was anything but idyllic.
>
> All Ruth and Naomi have left is the love of God for them. But that, of course, is enough. It is, in fact, everything. With it they are able to make their way back to Bethlehem, taking perhaps the same route the wise men from the East would take more than a thousand years later to pay homage to one who would be a direct descendant of Ruth and Naomi.
>
> The important part of this story is *where* Ruth and Naomi find the strength to pick up the pieces of their lives. Naomi has been greatly embittered by all she has had to go through. When they reach Bethlehem she tells her friends to call her "Mara," which means "bitter." "The Almighty has dealt very bitterly with me," she says. "I went away full, and the Lord has brought me back empty. Why call me

Naomi (which means "my delight") when the Lord has afflicted me and the Almighty has brought calamity upon me?"

But gradually Naomi's bitterness leaves, and the dark night of her soul gives way to dawn, so that when Ruth returns one day from the fields to tell her that she has been helped by a good man named Boaz, Naomi is able to say, "Blessed be he by the Lord, whose kindness has not forsaken the living or the dead!"

Love, after all, originates with God. "We love," John says, "because he first loved us." Even Ruth's love looks pale in comparison with the love that God has for us. Ruth could stay with her mother-in-law as long as she herself were living, but our Lord promises to stay with his people through all time and eternity.[12]

Often the good news we find in a text is determined in part by the circumstances in which we read the text. Paul Yung preached on the subject of "Who is My Neighbor?" in Young Nak Presbyterian Church in Los Angeles. It was the Sunday after the 1992 riots precipitated by the verdict acquitting the white police officers accused of the videotaped brutal beating of Rodney King. Many Korean businesses were destroyed. This is part of the good news Yung found in his text: Jesus comes, like the Good Samaritan, to us. Again we see a preacher make a link from the text being preached to the larger Christian story.

I want you to [take] notice here. The good Samaritan, when he came to this robbed man, did not say anything judgmental. This road from Jerusalem all the way down to Jericho was a notorious road. It was known for being a dangerous area. No one who knew the area would dare to pass by after the sun [had] set. And scholars tell us that the road had a nickname: the "blood road" or the "blood way." But this good Samaritan came to this man and didn't say, "Didn't you know that this is a dangerous area?" He just took care of him and did his best to bring the healing.

Just like that, our Lord Jesus Christ comes to us. He will not say, "Didn't you know that the kind of business that you had, that's where the most crimes are happening?" Not all Korean Americans lost their businesses because they did business in the crime area, the dangerous area. But the Lord didn't say anything about that. He simply came. Without rebuking, he provided the care and healing. That's our Lord![13]

Use Parallel Sentence Structure to Help Sustain Interest

Mark Trotter, in an intriguing sermon on Philippians 2:1-11, manages both to proclaim the good news and to exhort people to action. He pictures the quarreling Philippians, and in consecutive sentences uses the same device: a statement of what Christ did in contrast to what they do. It functions as Page Three because the grace in the passage is slightly louder than the trouble which is directed primarily at Paul's church, not the contemporary one. Yet, because of its muted grace, might this function as well on Page One?

> The church at Philippi was having a church fight. People were putting each other down, insulting each other, boasting about how they were better than each other. Paul's answer to petty fights was to hold them up to the greatest act in the history of the world, as if to say, Christ humbled himself to save the world, why can't you humble yourself enough to end an argument? Christ did not wait for you to come to him; he came to you, took on your flesh, lived your life; and you sit there smugly, self-righteously, waiting for the one who has offended you to come crawling for forgiveness. Christ humbled himself as a servant, but you refuse to humble yourself to the likes of these. And being found in human form, he became obedient unto death, even death upon the cross, that you may live. And you won't sacrifice your pride to say the word that will bring new life to the person who is dying to hear it from you.
>
> Paul had a way of writing like that. He takes the petty things that we do and reveals them for what they are by holding them up to the greatest thing that God has done.[14]

Avoid Weak Grace

Normally I prefer to use positive examples, yet the errors even experts make can instruct us. Preaching grace is difficult because we were not taught how to do it and for most of us it is a matter of trial and error, if we are even convinced of the need to preach it at all. Here we examine examples of two common problems. Preachers often *mix grace with trouble* in one location, instead of keeping trouble on Pages One and Two, and grace on Pages Three and

Four, and developing a tension between them. This sermon on Genesis 3:1-6 provides a typical mix: on the occasions when the focus momentarily seems to shift to God and what God does, it quickly returns to what humans must do. The practice is problematic because neither the trouble nor the grace comes fully into focus or is experienced.

> When Satan approaches us, he never comes dragging the chains that will enslave us. He . . . only promises we will fill all the desires of our hearts. That is how we are destroyed. That's the lesson: the temptations that destroy us strike at the heart of God, [Trouble] at God's integrity and God's goodness. [Grace] As we deny God's goodness, we reject his Word. When we reject his Word, we do so at our peril. [Trouble]
>
> Hear me well. I do not advocate some kind of tight religion. Christianity is not morality—toeing the line and keeping the rules. Christianity is a relationship with God who loves you so much that he gave you his child. God's every gift is good and perfect. He can never cast a shadow on your life by turning from his goodness. [Grace] The essence of sin lies in doubting God's goodness and then rejecting his Word. [Trouble] The garden belongs to you as a gift from his hand. [Grace] Enjoy it. Trust him. [Trouble][15]

A second typical difficulty arises when preachers focus on human ability, rather than God's action on Page Three, as is apparent in this sermon on Luke 8:41-56.

> When the woman touched Jesus, something happened to Jesus which was outside his control, and . . . the woman immediately healed herself. Her healing was not granted as a reward for her honesty in coming forward afterwards, nor was it dependent on the words of Jesus. She touched him, and in so doing, she brought about her own healing. She did not ask permission "Would it be OK with you, Jesus?" She knew what she needed and she took it. She literally helped herself. . . . Jesus doesn't reprimand. Rather he says something like "Good on you!" She took, and Jesus says "Well done."[16]

The above sentences do not have to be discarded—they simply can be reworked to make God the actor. For example, one might revise the first sentence to make God the subject: "When Jesus' garment touched her hand, something happened to the woman which was beyond her control." Or one could say, "The woman reached

189

out to Jesus because God told her to touch him." The text does not literally say this, yet from a theological perspective we could claim this as true. God is the author of all good, even in the biblical text.

Find Grace Even in Tough Texts

Often the grace in a text is not immediately obvious, and we must struggle to discern it. In such instances we become like Jacob wrestling at the Jabbok with the stranger, demanding a blessing. Barbara Brown Taylor preached a sermon on the parable of the laborers in the vineyard (Matthew 20:1-16) who were all paid equal amounts. What is the good news in this unfairness? To find out, she *shifts to focus on God* and discovers God's generosity. Notice how effective she is in moving her thought forward one small step at a time from one paragraph to the next. Her turning point and a portion of the grace she finds are as follows:

> It is entirely possible that, as far as God is concerned, we are halfway around the block, that there are all sorts of people ahead of us in line, people who are far more deserving of God's love than we are, people who have more stars in their crowns than we will ever have . . . [the end of Page Two].
>
> God is not fair, but depending on where you are in line that can sound like powerful good news, because if God is not fair then there is a chance that we will get paid even more than we are worth, that we will get more than we deserve, that we will make it through the doors even though we are last in line—not because of who we are but because of who God is.
>
> God is not fair; God is generous, and when we begrudge that generosity it is only because we have forgotten where we stand. On any given day of our lives, when the sun goes down and a cool breeze stirs the dusk, when the work is done and the steward heads toward the end of the line to hand out the pay, there is a very good chance that the cheers and backslapping, the laughter and gratitude with which he is greeted will turn out to be our own. . . .[17]

Fred B. Craddock preaches on John the Baptist's ministry in the wilderness in Mark 1:1-8. Good news is hard to find in John's unyielding words, but Craddock nonetheless manages to develop grace from them by *answering our question, "What is God doing in or behind this text?"*

> Persuasive. Did you ever hear [John the Baptist] preach? It's kind of frightening. Oh, not just the images he used. He did use some strong images. Ax at the root of the tree. God can raise up children of Abraham from these stones. The winnowing fork is in his hand. Wheat and chaff. Chaff is burned, save the wheat. Are you ready? Repent! (Pause.) . . . It's kind of, you know. . . . But that's not what was frightening about it. What's frightening about listening to John preach is that he puts you in the presence of God. And that's what everybody wants, and that's what everybody doesn't want. Because the light at the altar is different from every other light in the world. . . .[18]

Pavel Filipi preached on the "servant" in Isaiah 42:1-4, and he turned verse 4 ("He will not fail or be discouraged until he has administered judgment on the earth; and the coastlands wait for his law"), which might have seemed appropriate for Page One, into good news for Page Three. He is preaching in Prague, Czechoslovakia, on the first Sunday of Advent, 1989, when his country is in turmoil. Perhaps this radical situation contributed to his insight concerning the grace in his text, that God's judgment can be grace. When we are faced with a difficult text in which grace seems hard to find, we might *ask if there is anyone for whom the text might sound like good news.* Note that Pavel does not make a movie with his words, yet this is still an effective passage.

> "That he might produce judgment on the nations." When we talk about "judgment," we do not feel comfortable. Most people prefer to avoid judgments, and we think about the judgments of God with some uncertainty and anxiety. But the biblical witnesses speak differently. "Judge me, Lord," entreats the psalmist. For him, God's judgment is something desirable, something that needs to be demanded, for it is a judgment that puts an end to disorder and chaos. The Lord's judgment will put an end to the capriciousness of human judges and decision-makers and bring into the light justice, right, and God's covenant. The Lord's judgment means putting things right, not destroying them. It means normalization, returning to normality, abandoning the abnormal conditions in which we are living in our relations with God, with our neighbor, with nature. A few moments ago we heard these words, taken from another prophecy of Isaiah, about the one who it was promised would carry out God's judgment:

"He shall not judge by what his eyes see or decide by what his ears hear; but with righteousness he shall judge the poor and decide with equity for the meek of the earth." All this—including the lamb that lies down with the wolf—is what God's judgment will mean, what it will bring about. "No one shall do evil or harm any longer." This is the task with which God's servant [in the text] is entrusted: to put right the whole of God's creation, which has been damaged through human sin: to restore it to its normal state; to right injustice; to put an end to war; to destroy pride: to put a stop to the exploitation of the weak and the oppression of the powerless.

It is toward this, toward setting things right in this way, that our God is already working. It is for this that he is calling and arming his servant. Just imagine: He himself is taking on the responsibility of setting right everything that we have damaged through our selfishness, our desire for pleasure, our avarice, through our sin. Broken human relationships, enmity with God and humanity, life that has been devastated and nature that has been laid waste—all this, God has decided, should not remain like this. He is already working on it. He has already chosen and armed his servant. . . .[19]

In preaching the apocalypse in Luke 21:25-36, a very troubling passage because of its imagery of earthly destruction, I found it helpful to ask, *What difference does the cross, resurrection, and ascension make to Jesus' own words?* Does Christ not rule over even the worst that may face God's creation? By discovering good news, I did not need to downplay the seriousness of the signs in the text, as I might have been tempted to do were I unable to find any. I include a portion of Page Two to set the scene.

When we see the mighty signs of the end times, of which Jesus spoke, when we see portents of great suffering all around, it will be very hard indeed to speak of God's will: "And there will be strange events in the skies—signs in the sun, moon, and stars. And down here on earth the nations will be in turmoil, perplexed by the roaring seas and strange tides. The courage of many people will falter . . . " (NLT). We are not to ask when the end will come, for no one knows, not even Jesus in his earthly ministry, but only God. The description is sufficiently vague that it could be almost at any time. There were portents in the heavens at Jesus' crucifixion that could have marked the time. There was massive upheaval and destruction at the fall of the temple that helped identify the immediacy of the end for Mark's community church. There were other signs in Luke's time that Luke cautioned against believing. In fact, in every age there have been more than a few people who have been all too willing to throw in the towel, to hold their hands in despair, to give in to the negativity of the moment, to will the end, and to wish for death, their own or other's.

Right and wrong are not so hard to determine as good and evil, for evil masks itself as good. Evil grasps the heart of a child of God who is out of work and convinces her that life has no more meaning; evil makes giving in look good. [End of Page Two] We should not be giving in. We should be looking up. When things are so bad that we think life cannot get any worse and will not get any better, when we feel like there is no where to go, when evil tempts you into thinking that life has no meaning and has laid out the red carpet for us to the grave saying, "Come on," don't go. Look up, look out, get ready, raise your heads, stand straight, get on your tiptoes, because your redemption is drawing near. Your rescue is at hand. Your Savior has not deserted you. Christ is approaching. You will see him nearing on the clouds. He is the final word. His voice is calling, not just from the empty tomb, where death has already been defeated, meaninglessness consigned to hell, and life without love annihilated. His voice is also calling from the end of time, saying, "When it looks like there is no purpose, look again. All creation has a purpose. God works all things for good."

Don't give up, except to give up your worries and give them over to God. Don't give in, except to give in to the power of God's love to bring forth God's intentions for this world and in your life, in spite of all appearances and no matter what anyone may say. Just give out, give out the love of God, reach out to those who are anxious, be the hand of God in helping those in need. If you don't have much love left, spend it and you will have more. If you are fresh out of prayers, just be quiet before God, which is what God would probably like more of the time anyways, and another prayer will be given to you. If you are running low on courage, more is coming your way. If you have nothing left, thank God, good news! For Jesus says that when we think it is the end, look up, "because your redemption is drawing near."

It has always been the case that life does not end when we come to the end of our own resources: life begins. Life begins when we run out of resources because then we start to put our faith where it belongs, in God, in God's strength, and God's purpose. And so it should be no surprise that when Jesus pictures the end of time, an hour no one knows, when everything seems falling apart, it is also time to trust in God's eternal purpose, for God's love, shown so clearly for us in the One on the cross, will be written high on all the clouds so no one can miss it, saying God's love is the end, God's purposes will reign, therefore, have no fear. God's love is as certain as leaves in the spring, sun in summer, wind in the fall, and cold in winter. Have no fear.

Any text that points to the virtue of human action is likely to lead the preacher away from preaching God. This is the temptation with Luke 18:1-8 (the widow and the unjust judge). Mary Harris Todd skillfully avoided the difficulty by preaching on the need for persistence in the first half of her sermon; then she turned to develop the text from God's perspective. She discovers a fresh angle by *envisioning God as one of the people in the text,* in this case the widow. Note that Todd develops conversationally the doctrine of God's nature with visual and multisensory, concrete language rather than the abstract language we usually associate with doctrine:

Again and again, the widow went around to the judge's chambers and knocked on the door. And for a long, long time he refused to help. She kept on until her knuckles bled. It was discouraging. I'll bet she did come near to giving up at least once. It is tempting to give up when it seems as though you're not making any progress and your hands are bruised and bleeding from the effort. It's painful and hard to hang in there. I'm sure any of the folks I have just mentioned could tell you about times when it was like that for them.

After he told the parable, Jesus said, "Now will not God judge in favor of his own people who cry to him day and night for help? Will he be slow to help them?" How does God help people who have knocked on the door until their knuckles are bleeding?

Well, isn't *that* what *God himself* does all the time? "Behold, *I* stand at the door and knock," God says (Revelation 3:20, RSV). *God* prays without ceasing. *God* seeks and knocks and works for what is right all the time. God's Holy Spirit constantly prays and groans with "sighs too deep for words" (Romans 8:26, NRSV). Behold, *God* stands at the door and knocks.

God is not just sitting back twiddling his thumbs and leaving everything up to us until that great day comes when God's reign is complete, and the kingdom comes in all its fullness. God is knocking on the door, crying out for justice now! God is like that relentless widow who won't rest until justice is done. God keeps on confronting a world that is like the unjust judge who doesn't have any regard for God or others.

There God is, demanding justice in former Yugoslavia. . . .[20]

Texts like the story of Samson and Delilah (Judges 16:4-31) are tough to preach as good news. But if we *adopt the perspective of a member of an oppressed group,* as Jeremiah A. Wright, Jr., does in approaching his text as an African American, good news may be more apparent. He recognizes Samson as someone put in chains. He documents his good news interpretation, even going beyond his immediate text, and provides his listeners with at least three pieces of evidence to support his conclusion concerning the source of Samson's strength, all the while making a movie of the text. He puts his own interpretation into the words of Samson's prayer:

> But the thing that Delilah missed, and that his enemy missed, was the whole answer to what made him so strong. You see, they mistook the symbol of his strength for the source of his strength. They didn't listen to his whole answer. His hair was the symbol, not the source. Look at his whole answer. He said, "My hair has never been cut." That's a symbol. Why? "Because I have been dedicated to God as a Nazarite from the time I was born." Now that's the source of his strength. The last verse of chapter 13 says, "The Lord's power began to strengthen him." But the Hebrew says the *ruah,* the Spirit of the Lord, began to move him.
>
> In chapter 14, when a lion attacked (v. 6), it says again the *ruah,* the Spirit of the Lord, came upon him. In chapter 15, when he grabbed that jawbone of an ass, verse 14 says the *ruah,* the Spirit of the Lord, came mightily upon him. The source of his strength was God, and the *ruah,* the Spirit of God. So he prayed (16:28) after his hair, the symbol of his strength, began to grow back, "Lord, try me one more time. I know I let you down before, but try me just one more time. Give me my strength just this one more time." What he's asking for is God's Spirit, the *ruah,* God's strength, not his own.
>
> What makes us so strong? God's strength.[21]

Such power can be ours in preaching when we seek to proclaim both the trouble and the grace in a biblical text. Page Three (like Page Four which follows) then becomes an opportunity to speak of God with sustained and joyous focus.

A Checklist for Page Three

Is the material presented here exegetically sound?

Have I reconstructed the text, using some fresh material not used on Page One?

Is this page about one idea, i.e., the theme statement?

Does the theme statement focus on God?

Does it focus on God's action of grace in or behind the text?

Is the theme sentence short and memorable?

Do I repeat it often enough for hearers to recognize its importance?

Is God's action or God's nature the subject of the whole page?

Is this page mainly a movie?

What can hearers see on this page?

Have I employed other senses?

Did I film the text from a fresh angle?

Does the grace here connect to the earlier trouble?

Do I focus on people in action?

Do I avoid going into the characters' minds?

Have I created the event rather than reported it?

Have I allowed my one doctrine to inform my filming of the text?

If I am using a dominant image, is it present on this page?

Does this page appeal to logos, pathos and ethos?

SECTION V
PAGE FOUR: FRIDAY

CHAPTER TEN

God's Action in the World

Passive statements, like God watches, God sees, and God knows, are in the Bible; there God is also occasionally portrayed in non-personal objective images such as wind, water, cloud, rock, and fire, that nonetheless enrich our understanding. Preaching these modes of expression are important; yet, because they are passive, they simply cannot be our constant mainstay and should not be our first choice. God's action is our focus. On Page Four the focus is God's action in the contemporary world.

Claims about God's activity are difficult to make, for we need to point to signs of God that are usually ambiguous in the world. God never leaves us without these signs; and Jesus promised, "I am with you always, to the end of the age" (Matthew 28:20). Still, preachers have good reason to avoid making claims about God. We are sinners; right and wrong are often easier to discern than evil, the nature of which is to look good. To make a claim about God's action is risky. We might be wrong: we might claim too much about the wrong things, or claim too little about the right things, or miss God entirely. Even when we are close to the truth, the right nuancing of claims is essential, without which we may still go astray. By contrast, passive claims about God are safe: we risk little because they are general propositions and they require little evidence in experience—but they also do little to foster faith. Nonetheless, God will be known. Our postmodern age is in need of knowing God in the first instance, and of knowing about God in the second.

How Page Four Connects with the Other Pages

Page Four speaks about God in our world, and thus might seem to be a difficult sermon page to write. But we simply follow the promptings of the biblical text from Page Three that identified God's action in the biblical text, and now on Page Four we seek signs of that same action in the world around us. The God revealed in Scripture is the same God now and for all time. We can see what Page Four would look like in relation to the other pages. If we were to write one sentence across the top of four blank pages at the beginning of sermon composition, one for each page, we might end up with something like this on the call of Isaiah in Isaiah 6:1-13 (remember that normally we might start the entire sermon process by determining the theme sentence, Page Three):

Page One: trouble in the Bible	Page Two: trouble in our world
Isaiah was not good enough.	The world is not good enough.

Page Three: grace in the Bible	Page Four: grace in our world
God gives Isaiah a new identity.	God give us a new identity. (i.e., in Christ)

Or on the Prodigal Son in Luke 15:11-32 (suggestion: preach mainly on one son or the other; covering both in one sermon usually becomes cumbersome):

Page One: trouble in the Bible	Page Two: trouble in our world
The son was prodigal with his father's money.	We waste what we are given.

Page Three: grace in the Bible	Page Four: grace in our world
The father is prodigal in his love. [i.e., God gives love in prodigal fashion.]	God's love is enough.

Or on Romans 8:14-24:

Page One: trouble in the Bible	Page Two: trouble in our world
All creation groans with disunity. [e.g., Paul's churches]	The world is divided.

Page Three: grace in the Bible	**Page Four: grace in our world**
The Holy Spirit intercedes	The Holy Spirit intercedes
for the church.	for the world.
	(i.e., Christ is our unity)

Anytime we write a sermon we should be able quickly to sketch the four pages and test whether they are likely to have as much unity as we hope and anticipate.

Two Key Doctrines in Discerning God

The Bible offers guidelines to assist our task in the history of God dealing with God's people. Jesus Christ came into the world to accomplish what we were not able to accomplish for ourselves, so that we might know the nature of God and have the means of living as God intended. In looking at Jesus and his ministry we see what God is like. When Jesus preached about the inbreaking of the Realm of God, in his own person he was that inbreaking. He proclaimed and performed characteristic actions of God: saving, searching, restoring to life, bringing home, reconciling, forgiving, healing—and establishing justice, mercy, healing, peace, promise, joy, and righteousness. These are the signs we are looking for in preaching—signs of the inbreaking Realm of God. In encountering Christ through the Holy Spirit and in experiencing empowerment to acts of love, we continue to discover God acting. God is the author of all goodness, thus when we see good things and discern that they are authentic (i.e., that love is not what passes for love in the marketplace) we proclaim them as signs of God.

In addition to the doctrine of the Realm of God, we may also use the doctrine of the Trinity to help us discern God's activity in the world. God exists as the Trinity and this is the identity of God from the beginning. Theologian Daniel L. Migliore uses the social analogy of the Eastern church—God is lover, beloved, and their mutual love (i.e., the Person of the Holy Spirit). This analogy implies "a social ethics grounded in trinitarian theology." Thus one can look to "experiences of friendship, caring family relationships, and the inclusive community of free and equal persons as intimations of the eternal life of God" as a communion of persons.[1]

Often when preachers look for stories about God they look for stories of religious people. Such stories are good, but week by week they are hard to find and, if used exclusively, they keep God confined to the church. We want congregations to be able to identify God's activity anywhere in the world, and amongst all people, in the mundane as well as the spectacular. The whole world can be the source of our stories. Most important, the stories do not have to be explicitly religious as we receive them in order for us to tell them from a faith perspective.

Four Functions of Page Four

Page Four has four functions that are related to sermon structure and theological purpose: Applying grace from the Bible to the world now; sustaining focus on God's action in the world; balancing the trouble on Page Two with grace; and maintaining the tension between the two.

1. Page Four applies God's grace from the Bible times to now. It proclaims biblical truth today, however inadequate our words may be to express such truth. Just as Pages One and Two followed exposition/application of trouble, Pages Three and Four repeat that process from the perspective of God's loving action.

2. It provides a sustained focus on God's action in the world. This allows not just information about God's grace to be communicated but an experience of God's grace in the present moment—listeners are encountered by the resurrected Christ in the proclamation and reception of the Word and part of that proclamation is the ideas, images, and stories that we tell.

3. It provides a balance to Page Two and the trouble there. If Page Two presents mainly vertical trouble, listeners need vertical grace—i.e., forgiveness—on Page Four. If Page Two presents horizontal trouble and the fallenness, suffering, and brokenness of the world, Page Four needs to develop horizontal grace—i.e., it must point to God overturning the powers of this world and restoring what needs restoration. There is healing where there was illness, joy where there was sorrow, and hope where there was despair. Yet these are not mere pious platitudes to be mouthed; they are truths that demand

spiritual and theological discernment and affirmation in the world. Churchgoers seek evidence that worldly powers seeming to have the final say in fact do not. Obviously we should not speak of someone suffering homelessness on Page Two and offer that person forgiveness on Page Four. She or he requires a home and we must point to God at work against those powers and principalities that resist God's will. If we point to an innovative housing solution, we may be close to identifying God at work, perhaps not for that person, but for others in similar circumstances.

4. Page Four puts the world into appropriate juxtaposition or tension with grace. It returns listeners to the most powerful or emotive story or issue on Page Two and identifies what the good news might be for that troubled situation, in light of God's grace. If the situation is too recent or too close to be able yet to discern good news, Page Four presents a related story that has some resolution or clarity about God. Page Four does not erase Page Two, and does not suggest "happily ever after," but it sounds a strong alternative note of grace in the midst of passing life. As preachers, we provide people with a transformed vision of ordinary life that now has deep theological purpose and meaning. We are saying, in effect, the trouble is less than true, because this affirmation concerning God is true. In coming last in the sermon, grace sounds a stronger, eschatological note, the note of God's final victory.

Dangers in Claiming God's Action

There are, of course, dangers in naming God in the world. Inexperienced preachers occasionally associate God with something relatively trivial or trite, such as the smile from the grocer to the stranger. The association is not necessarily false, yet the smile could have meant something other than kindness. In any case, the act is not of sufficient significance to bear the weight of the gospel for public proclamation, for God is always more than something nice. In any case, as people of faith we are able to point to larger contemporary events in which listeners may glimpse in more evident ways God's self-giving or all-powerful nature.

Another danger is to "pile on" actions of God. For example, one student preacher named several actions on Page Four: God forgives us; God helps different people; God uses humans to bring transformation in others; God encircles people in love; Christ empowers others to respond in love; God gives hope in despair; and God is at work creating new communities. The sermon sounded at times trite, fluffy, romantic, and sentimental. Any one of these ideas is worthy of singular focus but it is hard to imagine the listeners can concentrate on all of them, especially when they are presented in a series. Thus the preacher needs to be focused on one theme sentence and connect it with a single doctrine and point to where people might see God doing this specific kind of action today.

Some preachers might portray God's action as though it were automatic and mechanical, part of the nature of the universe. For example, a preacher might say, "In the midst of all of this suffering, life wins out. Jesus died to provide new life for all." The danger here is twofold: (a) the preacher generalizes God's action into a principle about nature, as though God's victory over death in Jesus Christ has resulted in something like cruise control on a car that always kicks in when life becomes an uphill struggle. Instead, each action of God in the present is to be honored as personal and specific to a time and place, a gift of unmerited grace. (b) The preacher negates the cost of Jesus' accomplishment. Life does not simply "win out"; in death and resurrection, Jesus Christ defeats the power of death. God in Christ continues to battle suffering and injustice; though the incarnation, cross, and resurrection were unique events in time and history, Christ continues to be crucified today and the outcome has already been determined.

Preachers also make a mistake when they portray grace as God's future activity, by saying, "God could or God will. . . ." Instead, it is often better to put the claim in the past tense as something that God has already done or begun. Future-tense grace leaves us humans still deep in trouble, and the grace is conditional.

Another danger can arise when we portray nature as an unambiguous sign of God's grace. Of course, creation is an act of grace, as is God's ongoing sustenance and continuing act of creation. And all of us can perceive grace in nature. We are wise to remind people of the miracle of life on this planet, the wondrous harmonies and balances God has created in nature and in outer space. We should evoke awe and mystery. However, to point to a particular sunrise as a sign of grace can be excessively personal for the purposes of preaching: we tend to project onto nature our own emotional or spiritual state at the moment, forgetting that the person who has just heard that her husband has died may experience nature as mocking. We can still speak of the sunrise, of course, especially if we acknowledge the ambiguity of it as a sign.

Further, some preachers seek to minimize ambiguity when they tell stories about God. If our claims about God are to be convincing, though, and are to match people's actual experience, some ambiguity or ambivalence is essential. We invite people into the certainty of faith, not proof of faith. God's action in the present does not result in "happily ever after" outcomes. (Perhaps the closest we ever come to "happily ever after" are stories of someone permanently kicking a drug habit, or a family finally staying together, yet even these stories have difficulty, for sin and evil are daily realities.) The most compelling stories of God's action often include ambivalence: healing in the midst of illness; joy in the midst of trouble; hope in the midst of suffering; or riches in the midst of loss.

Finally, some preachers are reluctant to claim God's action because they do not know what will happen next. We are right to be fearful, for the story of the prophet Hananiah's condemnation in Jeremiah 28:12-17 stands before all who would utter a false word from God. How can we be sure even in faith that we are pointing to God? For instance, we might want to claim God's hand in bringing enemies together for Middle-East peace discussions, yet we find ourselves hesitant because the agreement may fall apart. But we do not have to wait for the final outcome to pronounce God's present activity. We claim God in this moment and if peace fails in the next, we then must identify the powers of evil with which God still contends. If we always wait for the final outcome, we may forget to name God. (Many churches forgot to name God with both the collapse of the Berlin wall and the end of apartheid.) We thereby give our people little reason to believe that God is involved in world affairs. By showing God's involvement on the world stage and in individual lives, Christians are better able to proclaim their faith to others.

Mission

The purpose of the sermon is to invite people into faith; the purpose of faith is service to the gospel of Jesus Christ. From faith

205

issues action; thus the sermon points listeners toward their active ministries in the world. From the outset of sermon preparation on Monday we struggled to identify one mission to which the sermon would move. Preachers may have begun to identify this mission on Page Two. Yet in talking about duties on Page Four, preachers are in danger of slipping back into language appropriate to Page Two: they may again be perceived to be accusing; or casting people on their own abilities and resources, with a result that diminishes grace or speaking of should, must, have to and called to. Preachers might go back over past sermons and circle the number of times these words appear on their last pages. However, preachers can speak about mission on Page Four in a manner that avoids this.

Concern for mission began on Page Two with the discussion of situations in our world that need help and suggestions of specific action that listeners might undertake. On Page Four, as the sermon draws to a close, we demonstrate that mission is in partnership with God and is linked with prophecy and dreaming dreams. We may conceive of mission here in terms of Calvin's third use of the law—not just as instruction on how to live in the Spirit but as excitement to obedience. Stephen Farris identifies this understanding of law as "neither hammer or mirror but rather much loved guide."[2] This use of the law can be understood in one way as grace, for even excitement to obedience is not something that we must feel as though it is yet another expenditure of energy to which we must rise, but is a gift provided by the Spirit in which we choose to participate. As Daniel Migliore says, we catch exciting glimpses of the nature of God—the communion of God in three Persons—whenever we encounter authentic community. Such excitement arises from being enlisted by God and empowered by the Holy Spirit to accomplish God's will of vulnerable, self-giving love for others. We depend on God to fulfill our calling. God is the actor bringing forth God's purposes in which we have an important part to play. Mission on Page Four is not a task but a privilege, honor, and opportunity.

Again, comments about mission in the sermon generally function as symbols or suggestion of what might be an appropriate response to God's love. Particularly on Page Four, mission suggestions should seem like helpful ideas to enable what listeners will want to do out of thankfulness for God's love. Here, to speak of mission is like suggesting what a child might buy for her mother for her birthday—it does not feel like a burden but a welcome opportunity to express love in a particular way.

The gospel transforms even our duties. Unpleasant tasks become, with God's power, new opportunities to experience life. For every situation to which we are called, Christ has entered already. Mission activities on Page Four are portrayed in light of the gospel as invitations to encounter Christ, to serve others, to have our faith strengthened, and to have our lives renewed by the Holy Spirit. Imperatives such as: must, should, have to, become indicatives, we may now, or, there is nothing that can prevent us. Conditional statements (if we will; when we) that creep into sermon composition can be moved to Page Two where they belong. When we find that we have expressed the Gospel in future tense, we can revise it to become more effective as past or present tense: instead of, "God can make a difference," we proclaim, "God has already made a difference in your baptism and will not cease to work until. . . ." When asked to reach beyond their own resources, God's resources for their ministry, the congregation discovers good news to carry with them to the world.

Theological Use of Stories

Preachers often have difficulty using stories from everyday life and daily events to speak of grace in their sermons. They can use three simple paradigms or basic theological motifs to help them discern a story's potential application for grace. Nearly all stories of grace fit one of these paradigms. First, stories on Page Four can be used as metaphors of *God's forgiveness*. Obviously as soon as we start thinking of God's forgiveness, we start thinking of important stories of individuals—perhaps alcoholics or drug addicts—who prayed for forgiveness and received it, or who were able to turn their lives around because they experienced God. However, the preacher can use the paradigm of God's forgiveness to help make less dramatic stories into theological ones. For example, a preacher can use any story about one person forgiving another, or of two people reconciling, or of someone being willing to trust again, as a simile or metaphor to demonstrate not just good behavior, but also to show what God's forgiveness is like; or to claim that God empowers all people—not just Christians—to acts that conform with God's intentions.

Second, stories can be told as metaphors, similes, or demonstrations of *God overturning the world,* making the impossible possible. God acts in this manner throughout history, and nowhere is this more clearly seen than in Jesus Christ in the events marked by Christmas, Easter, and Pentecost. J. R. R. Tolkien spoke of the "eucatastrophe" (literally: good turning upside down) of the gospel, the joyous opposite of a catastrophe, the surprising and delightful turn of events toward God: "it denies (in the face of much evidence, if you will) universal final defeat and in so far it is *evangelium,* giving a fleeting glimpse of Joy, Joy beyond the walls of the world, poignant as grief."[3] Stories of the oppressed finding justice, the sick finding healing, and the homeless finding homes have merit in their own right, yet they become an instrument to proclaim God when harnessed for theological purpose.

Finally, stories can be used to demonstrate *God acting through people* to further those same purposes of God's will. Of course God chooses to work in the lives of all people, but many people choose not to acknowledge God, just as many of us Christians may not want to acknowledge some of those through whom God chooses to work. Yet if as preachers we start to view the world in terms of this paradigm, all individual acts of authentic kindness become opportunities for praising God. Whenever we tell a story of anyone doing an act of authentic good, in faith we need to claim that action as God's.

Portraying Jesus as Savior

Many students run into difficulty on Page Four by portraying Jesus as our example instead of as our Savior. This is a typical sticking place for students who are struggling with how to preach grace. For example, one student spoke on Page Four of various activities of Jesus Christ, most of which placed the burden to act on the listeners: Jesus shows us what to do; Jesus calls us; Jesus lets us take our cross; Jesus reminds us what is right; and Jesus asks us to be witnesses. Of course there is nothing wrong with these statements in themselves. They simply belong on Page Two, not Four. When we portray Jesus as our example whom we must imitate, we are generally cast on our own inadequate abilities to accomplish the task set before us. Those who are most concerned for social justice will tend to commit this particular error, relegating Jesus to the role of Model and Exemplar, without recognizing him sufficiently as Savior.

Instead, on Page Four we should be portraying Jesus as our Savior, the one who equips and empowers us, and whose endeavors we join. This Savior is One who does the saving. Thus on Page Four we avoid bald statements of what we are able to do (i.e., we are able to open our hearts to God, or we are able to witness to Christ), and speak more modestly, or proclaim more loudly, what we are able to do in Christ, or with the power of the Holy Spirit, or with God's help.

The Sermon Conclusion

The sermon conclusion is very important and exceptionally difficult. It is the last thing people hear of the sermon. There is relatively little time for it, yet it must accomplish many things—without merely rehashing the entire sermon. We can name several things we might try to accomplish through the conclusion, if they have not been accomplished already. For example, it might: bring the sermon to a close that clearly is complete; point back toward the theme sentence and the doctrine; wed the theme sentence to the dominant image; point forward to the coming week; and inspire people to mission.

What gives unity to the four-page sermon? Primary unity arises from the one theme statement, the sentence of grace with God as the subject that is the specific theme of Page Three. Pages One and Two are linked to it, perhaps by a form of inversion—they explore the trouble or in a certain sense the ways the theme sentence might not *seem* to be true. Page Four portrays the significance of God's gracious action in the present. Even though each page is devoted to one single idea or subtheme, all of the ideas connect and feed the one theme sentence that provides the overarching source of unity. Thus, by the conclusion everyone should be clear that this sermon was about one idea, and only one idea. The conclusion need not be a summary of the argument of the sermon or a review of everything discussed, unless of course the sermon is very long and has a didactic purpose that would benefit from such a summary. Generally, if the congregation has not got the message by now it is too late. The conclusion is not a place to introduce new ideas *per se* that move the sermon in a new direction; it should draw the congregation back to the theme statement by some means.

Secondary forms of unity in the sermon derive from the theme statement and can also provide strategies for the conclusion. Six strategies are identified here:

1. Return to a story or use a new story. The preacher can return to the Bible or a contemporary story. A story can be a fitting conclusion if it embodies grace and has sufficient weight and power; that is, if it seems to sum up the thrust of the sermon. One additional concluding sentence that draws listener attention back to the theme statement will often secure both the preacher's point in telling the story and the thrust of the sermon. (The listeners may derive different understandings but preachers are responsible for communicating clearly what they themselves mean.) If the preacher used a story of trouble in the first half and if it has a good news ending, the conclusion is an appropriate time to return to it. This return to the grace of an earlier story almost always signals closure of the sermon to the listeners and so the preacher needs to be sure to end the sermon promptly thereafter.

2. Return to the doctrine. The preacher needs to establish the doctrine in relationship to the theme statement before the sermon's conclusion. By returning to it here in one way or another (i.e., through idea, story, or image), the theological underpinnings of the sermon are reinforced. Those who follow a lectionary may not recognize that the church year is organized around doctrines (e.g., in Advent, eschatology, the Second Coming, and the Incarnation); thus, by returning to the special occasion or the day, the preacher is often returning to the doctrine.

3. Return to the dominant image. A dominant image, again, is a picture drawn either from the biblical text (such as a staff, or an oil lamp, or a bent woman) or from some contemporary experience (such as a child swinging, or a flower on a windowsill, or a motorcycle). If we used a dominant image in the sermon, by now we should have wedded it to the theme statement. Even if this image appeared only in the introduction, returning to it now signals completion (obviously if the preacher has used it only in the introduction, it is not yet fully

210

wedded to the theme statement and needs to be). Every time listeners see that image in the coming week, we can hope it will be an occasion for them to think of God's action in their lives, or to speak of God to someone else. We may still need to reinforce that intimate connection in the sermon conclusion.

4. Return to congregational needs. At some time in the sermon, grace needs to be spoken directly into the lives and circumstances of listeners. In other words, the sermon should answer the listener's question, How does this apply to me? If we have not already done this on Page Four, now is the time. Declare, proclaim, confirm that God is already at work in the listeners' lives, bringing forth transformation according to the new life they have in Christ. Name circumstances where people may expect to find that God has already gone ahead of them. Encourage their reliance upon God's resources. Such an ending is a close parallel to a benediction at the end of a worship service: it is literally the speaking of goodness, the bestowal of blessing on the gathered community.

5. Return to mission. If mission has not yet been developed on Page Four, develop or suggest it now. Preachers might suggest one practical thing that the congregants can do this week, or point to some specific act that someone has done, or dream some possibility that in faith we claim that God wills. Individual mission, of course, must be determined by each person in relationship to Jesus Christ, yet people need help to discern how best to use and to give thanks for the gifts God has given them.

6. Move to the cross and resurrection. If the cross and resurrection have not yet been mentioned in the sermon—that is they have been assumed rather than explicitly proclaimed—the conclusion can point in that direction. Obviously if the preacher belongs to a liturgical tradition that celebrates the Lord's Supper following the sermon, the need for this might diminish. Similarly, if one belongs to a tradition in which there is an altar call, an invitation to come forward following the sermon, the focus of this is the cross and resurrection. A reference to the cross or some other central Christian symbol nonetheless serves as a further means for the preacher to ground what has been said in the heart of the faith—after all, the cross is both

the occasion and the content of Christian preaching. Preachers wisely look for increased opportunities to discuss it.

An effective sermon is not over when the preacher has finished speaking, or even when the worship service has ended; —it is completed in the reflections and lives of the people during the week. A sermon does not need to follow the four-page format, but if it does, it engenders hope, joy, and an appropriate sense of celebration; it proclaims what God has accomplished in Jesus Christ, fosters reliance upon God in the present, and opens new possibilities in individual and corporate lives to assist in God's purposes of justice, mercy, and love. The next chapter examines a variety of practical possibilities for Page Four and provides good models from existing sermons.

CHAPTER ELEVEN

Filming Grace in the World

The purpose of Page Four is to identify God at work in the world today. Its purpose is not to try to prove the existence of God, which cannot be done in any case, but to point to signs of God's presence. Thus, in addition to developing grace in our times, Page Four is composed with a view to providing good news possibilities for the situations of trouble on Page Two. Similarly, it is not the purpose of Page Four to discern God in the world merely by human wisdom or insight, as though this is a reliable means of discernment and separate from Scripture and tradition. Yet Page Four does affirm in bold and faithful ways that God's truth and reality are experienced in daily life and events now as in biblical times. Revealed truth is applied to the present in faith and in the knowledge of God's continuing nurture and love.

Develop Grace

Pages Three and Four should present the good news as forcefully as possible, in tension with the trouble of Pages One and Two. We can mention trouble on Pages Three and Four briefly by way of reminder, but we should not develop it—if we find any more than a couple of sentences of trouble we should cut them out or move them to earlier pages. In the following sermon, John Claypool tells a story about his grade school spelling bees, touches briefly on trouble, and moves strongly to grace. In his last sentence, he could make grace even stronger by removing the conditional "if . . . then" and by keeping God as the subject. (Excerpted from The Library of

Distinctive Sermons, © 1996, by Questar Direct, and reprinted by permission of Multnomah Publishers, Inc.)

> My friends, if life is like a spelling bee, there is no hope for any of us. We are not just persons of sorrow acquainted with grief; we are also persons of guilt acquainted with failure. If life is a spelling bee, there is no hope. None of us has spelled life correctly. But what if life is this incredible gift of One whose mercy is everlasting, One who wants us finally to become perfect, full-grown, complete—and that does not mean spotless, or never making mistakes? Then it means that we can learn to trust mercy more than anything else. Then we discover that it is not what we have done, but what God is still willing to do that is the very basis of life. And we discover that God is not so much interested in what we did in the past as in what we have learned from the past, and what we are going to do with those lessons in the future.
>
> If there is anything that is basic to a hopeful approach to life, it has got to be this incredible vision of mercy—that God's goodness is bigger than our badness. His willingness to forgive is greater than our power to sin. If you will start processing your memories from that hopeful, merciful perspective, if you will take everything that comes to mind and use it to learn rather than to condemn yourself, then, because of the grace of God, you can become a different person and the future can assume a shape lovelier than anything that used to be.[1]

Preachers who are unsure whether they can preach grace, or even whether they want to, might consider good funeral sermons, for they are nearly all grace. The reality of death at a funeral means that little time needs to be spent on Pages One and Two; the difference between preaching at a funeral and preaching on Sunday is that we must spend time establishing the death that has taken place or that should take place in ways of human behavior simply in order to be able to speak meaningfully of God's grace. Joanna Adams brings this message of hope on Page Four of a funeral sermon. Although the passage is short, there is an abundance of grace in it.

> Where is God in all this? Grieving with us, weeping for us, but more than that—drying tears, creating life out of death, [creating] hope out of despair, forgiving sin, restoring wholeness.
>
> God is so relentlessly committed to being the God of life that God can use even the worst that can happen, in ways we cannot fathom, for God's good purposes. The question is not *why* bad things hap-

pen, but: Can God be trusted when they do? Should we hope again? Can we live again, and if so, how?

The gospel is so exquisitely clear and simple at this point: "Abide in Christ," it says. "Stay close to me," Jesus says. "Bring your brokenness to me." Cut off from him, how could any live? But abiding in him, staying close to his body, the church, we can endure. . . .[2]

John M. Rottman told this story on himself when preaching on the necessity of watchfulness in Mark 13:32-37 ("But about that hour no one knows . . ."). By the end it has become a story about God's gracious action through a colleague—it also models human kindness. Biblical and contemporary stories, particularly in the grace section of the sermon, should not only model good Christian action but be perceived and understood by the congregation to model appropriate ways of life:

For several years I worked the night shift on the nursing staff in a psychiatric hospital. The shift ran from 11 PM to 7 AM and employees were cautioned against falling asleep at the cost of losing their jobs. But staying awake when everyone else was sleeping was often a real battle, especially after a long weekend of late nights and little sleep. Sometimes I would guzzle coffee and at other times splash myself with cold water. On those nights I lived in mortal fear of falling asleep only to be awakened by the supervisor's cold touch and to hear her announce that I would be looking for another job.

And then one night it happened. I had had an especially exhausting weekend and toward five in the morning, try as I might to stave it off, I fell asleep. Sometime later I felt a surge of panic as someone called my name and tapped me on the shoulder. "John, wake up." But as I turned to face the supervisor, I saw the face of the nurse who worked on the unit down the hall. "I saw the supervisor's car coming," she informed me. "I knew how sleepy you were earlier, so I came to make sure you were awake."

The good news of the gospel today is that in a similar way those of us who belong to Jesus Christ do not watch alone. . . . Our spiritual well being does not depend upon fearful, heroic watching. No, Jesus watches with us and for us. . . .[3]

Encourage Gender Balance

Most preachers are men and many published sermons fail to include stories about women, or stories told from a woman's perspective, or stories with women in nonstereotypical roles. Karen L. Bloomquist tells the following story as an analogy concerning God. Again we see a story functioning both as a model for loving action (in this case, good parenting) and making a claim about God. Her theme, taken from Colossians 1:21-28, is that God's presence is among us. She includes brief snippets of conversation as a means of making her story come alive and uses a female character to provide gender balance:

> We are like the child who had begged his mother for months for a playhouse. He told her again and again, "I want one just like Mary's that can be set on the table," as he indicated a breadbox size with his hands. Their home had an old shack in the back yard which had never held much interest for him. One day he noticed that his mother was busy pounding away on the old shack, but he paid little attention to what she was doing. "It must be for grown-ups," he thought. One day when he came home he wandered into the back yard, and there before his very eyes he saw not an old shack, but an attractive, spanking-new, life-sized playhouse. He could walk into it with his friends, they could play inside, look out the windows, and run from there out into the world. . . ."It's been there all along, but only now has it become a part of our life," he exclaimed. . . .
>
> . . . The mystery [of God's emerging presence] has been revealed, not up in heaven, but here on earth. It's been here all along, but had gone unrecognized. Now, in the revealing of Jesus the Christ, what was mysterious has been made clear, namely, that Christ is present wherever we find ourselves. . . .
>
> . . . God is like the mother of the small boy who came through with a gift far greater than the small table-top playhouse that itself would have satisfied. God overwhelms us with the gift of his own Son![4]

Many female images of God are in the Bible. They can be in our preaching too, not just from the Bible, but from life around us. John Claypool told of a military friend of his whose young son had made a clay ashtray for him at school, but dropped it at the Christmas pageant. Again we see a story functioning both as a model for human behavior and as a theological metaphor concerning God's restoring love while also providing gender balance. (Excerpted from The Library of Distinctive Sermons, © 1996, by Questar Direct, and reprinted by permission of Multnomah Publishers, Inc.)

My friend has a military background. It made him very uncomfortable, he told me, to see a male child of his crying in public. So what does he do? He walks over to the little fellow who is dissolved in tears and says like some Prussian general, "Don't cry son. Doesn't matter, doesn't really make any difference."

"Of course it matters!" his wife exclaimed, pushing him aside. . . .

My friend said that he watched in wonder as that feminine image of God did two incredible things. She reached into her purse and got her handkerchief and began to wipe the tears from the little boy's eyes and from her own face. Then she said with real strength, "Come on, son. Let's pick up the pieces and take them home, and see what we can make of what is left."[5]

Use Humor

Good and tasteful humor is an important part of preaching, and especially of Pages Three and Four—which is why Frederick Buechner went so far as to refer to grace, in part, as "comedy."[6] A preacher's own natural humor is best for the pulpit. Fred Craddock, one of the finest preachers of our time who is known for his humor, is quoted in this sermon excerpt from R. Wayne Stacy. In the story Craddock is surprised at the way God acts through him. (Excerpted from The Library of Distinctive Sermons, © 1996 by Questar Direct, and reprinted by permission of Multnomah Publishers, Inc.)

Fred Craddock, retired professor of preaching at Emory, tells a story about an incident that occurred when he was pastor of a small Christian church in east Tennessee and was visiting his hospitalized parishioners. As he happened to be passing the room of a woman patient, she called to him, "Uh, sir, are you a minister?"

"Yes, ma'am."

"Would you come in here by the bed and pray over me?"

"Yes ma'am; I'll be happy to. What would you like me to pray for?" Craddock asked as he entered the room.

She looked at him as if he'd lost his marbles and said rather curtly, "That I'll be healed, of course!"

And so Craddock went over by the bed, took her hand and began to pray that she be healed.

When he had finished praying, the woman began to stretch in the bed a bit. "You know, I feel kind of strange. In fact, I feel pretty good!" she said, throwing off the covers. She got out of bed, jumped up and down a little, and started shouting. "I'm healed! I'm healed! Thank you, pastor, thank you!"

When Craddock got back to his car later, he bowed his head and prayed, "Dear God, don't ever do that to me again!"[7]

The humor works here for several reasons: Craddock tells the story on himself; the story indicates the preacher is not taking himself too seriously; and the gospel, as good news, elicits humor. Humor does not work in the pulpit when: the preacher gives no warning that what is going to be said is light-hearted; the story is at someone else's expense; the humor is inappropriate for worship; the humor is of a cynical sort that has a sharp edge to it; what is said has no relationship to anything in the sermon and is said just to get a laugh.

Use a Rhetorical Device to Add Interest to a Doctrinal Passage

Ester Tse uses parallel sentence structure to sustain interest and to keep doctrinally focused. The cumulative effect, even in a short passage such as this, is powerful:

Is it not amazing to know that the love of our God is so inclusive and unconditional? Is it not wonderful to know that the grace of God has always been present since we were born? . . .

. . . Salvation in Christ includes both sexes, all colors, all races, all walks of life, and the whole Creation of God. The philosophers and theologians are not more saved than you and I, though they may think better. The moralists and the ethicists are not better off than us, though they may make better decisions. The romanticists, the sentimentalists, and even the mystics are not closer to God, though they are richer in feelings and emotions. . . .[8]

Toinette M. Eugene uses parallel sentence structure to build an emotional component in the conclusion of her sermon, and there is no question of the good news she is heralding.

Because the child of God has taken the form of a slave, because Jesus came into the world of a lowly birth, because he ate with sinners and reprobates, we can dream. Because he befriended the outcasts, championed the cause of the downtrodden, proclaimed the release of the captives, because he has set at liberty those who are oppressed, we are able to act boldly as he did. Because Jesus died the death of a criminal, and assumed the keys of the kingdom, we are set free from sin and called to be disciples. Because Jesus Christ lived, died, and yet lives for us, we can take up Elijah's mantle, and we can live out the courageous spirit of liberation that makes this dream a reality of peace and mercy and justice for our world. We have received God's most precious gift, Liberating Love. Pick it up, take it up, hold it high, and pass it on! [9]

Apply the Text Theologically to the Present

The Pharisee and the tax collector (Luke 18:10-14) is a tough text to preach. Too easily preachers identify with the humble tax collector and disdain the condemned Pharisee with the same self-righteousness that Jesus rebukes. Jurgen Moltmann focuses on the theme, "God justifies the humble." He applies that understanding to the contemporary situation, not in a simplistic or mechanical manner—as would be the case if we were to repeat, in as many ways as possible, God justifies us—but in a manner that reflects theological development and deepening thought (though Moltmann is not trying to build an argument). His first paragraph states the issue in a bald and striking manner; his second considers justification in the church; his third and fourth reflect tradition (Luther) and the Bible. When we study closely how others develop theological sections, we are better able to strengthen our own.

> Jesus' justifying judgment brings about a splendid inward and outward deliverance. God condemns the good person who[m] I want to be, but am not, and accepts the bad person who[m] I do not want to be, but am.
>
> In community with Jesus, people have continually discovered that God accepts our tax collector's soul and rejects our Pharisee's soul. In community with Jesus, "the friend of sinners and tax collectors," we see that we are loved—and how much we are loved—in the place where we do not want to be at all: in community with the people we despise. In community with Jesus, we discover that doors open—the door to the repressed self in our inmost heart, and the door to the repressed "other" who is at our side.
>
> "God, be merciful to me a sinner." That is the truth, the whole

truth, and nothing but the truth in us. No one can go beyond this. Happy is the person who enters into it, rests in it, and continually returns to it. "We are beggars, that's the truth," as Luther put it.

"This man went down to his house justified." That is the still greater truth of God about us. This is Jesus for us, Jesus beside us, and Jesus with us. Happy is the person who lives in this assurance. For "if God be for us, who can be against us?" . . .[10]

Ascribe to God the Authorship of Good Deeds

Many preachers are unable to point to God in the world because they were not instructed how to do this. Any number of stories we might tell in the grace section of a sermon do not function as grace simply because we leave the focus on the person doing the action, rather than ascribing the authorship of all goodness to God. A wonderful story about Mother Teresa's kind action to someone in the slums of Calcutta often functions as a judgment on listeners because their own actions by contrast could not compare. However, if we name God acting through her life—the same God who acts through us—then listeners can experience not a sense of failure, but of empowerment. This story, which I used in a sermon in 1996, originally came from the newspapers where it was not a religious story. It models ethical behavior and I develop it to speak about God.

> Yet how are we to know where God is? God is the author of all that is good. I was moved last Sunday when Monica Seles won the Molson Open, her second in two years. Her first had been last year in Toronto, when she came back to tennis for the first time since 1993 when she was stabbed by a German fan. It was a tremendous struggle for her to be with people again, much less to play once more. Last year when she got on the plane to leave Toronto, everyone on the plane stood and clapped. And this year, after winning her second Canadian Open, her Spanish opponent, Arantxa Sanchez Vicario, whom she had defeated, gave a speech to the crowd of 10,000. And then it was Monica's turn. But no words came. She was fighting with her old demons and fear of crowds. And then, in a wonderful gesture, her defeated opponent saw Monica struggling. She walked purposefully over to her on the podium and quietly whispered words of encouragement. It did the trick, and Monica began speaking with ease to those present. Who is it but God who

can bring a person from fear to trust, even lifting a crowd on a plane to its feet? And who is it but God who can give courage where there is doubt, and words of hope where there were none? Such is the nature of God, who can bring even the most downhearted to a place of promise.

Allow for Ambiguity

The gospel does not make everything "all better," but it does put things in appropriate perspective before a loving and redeeming God who rules over all. When we tell stories of God's action, we are telling stories from the perspective of faith, and ambiguity in the outcome should not be removed. In this sermon Edmund Steimle alludes to the ambiguity of much experience and he nonetheless proclaims God. He uses theological reflection and other biblical texts (as is appropriate) as the substance of his Page Four.

I have been able to discern an unmistakable clue to the nature of God at only one point: in this strange and admittedly absurd story of Jesus of Nazareth, the man for others, the one man who is truly human, the man who is what I know in my tangled heart I should be and was meant to be, whom God raised from the dead as if to say, "Amen. Let it be so. Find me here in apparent weakness and you shall get a glimpse of what my power really means."

And though the problem remains, at least one thing comes clear. The power of God is not primarily a resource to get us out of pain and suffering and death. Every temptation our Lord had to meet was in one way or another a temptation to escape suffering and death. Yet we continue to think of God's power almost exclusively in those terms. Of course it's understandable, and particularly when we are concerned about the suffering others have to endure. But the strange answer from the New Testament is not "I will save you from these things," but, "Lo, I am with you always, even unto the end of the age."

. . . If we begin with Christ and see Christ as God's promise to be with us no matter what, then we begin to know what faith—what trust in God's power—really means: no miracles to pop us out of our problems, any more than a miracle saved our Lord from the cross; but a Resurrection as God's Amen to Christ's way of serving others with the assurance that God's power is with us in whatever it may be that life throws up at us.[11]

Continue to Develop the Chosen Doctrine

On Page Four preachers should restate the specific doctrine that has been informing and shaping the sermon. Every doctrine has a grace component. Elizabeth Achtemeier concluded a sermon in strong doctrinal fashion by reflecting on the doctrine of the church:

> So let us return, then, to our original question. Just what was it that Jesus left behind him when he ascended into heaven? Was it just a little ragtag group of several dozen ordinary people? Oh no. He left behind him his church, empowered by his Holy Spirit to forgive and to love one another, as he had forgiven and loved even them; recipients of his resurrected life, against which the forces of death and sin have lost all their power; sustained by the certain hope that Christ comes again to bring his good kingdom on earth.
>
> Christ left behind him you and me—this little group gathered here this evening. He lived and suffered and died and rose again that we may be his extraordinary people. We are his witnesses; we are his proof; we are the evidence of his work. By being here and by being his church, we show forth his life and death and the power of his resurrection. And because that is true, good followers of Christ, we can never be content—O let us never be content—to be ordinary people again! Amen.[12]

John Killinger speaks to the doctrine of the Holy Spirit in this sermon on Psalm 1:1-3. He uses sensory language and vivid imagery of a Scrabble board to enliven his doctrinal instruction. His words are very loving, as is appropriate for grace, and they provide the way out of trouble he has portrayed. When we preach grace we must first imagine the words we ourselves need to hear, before we can imagine what others need. (Excerpted from The Library of Distinctive Sermons, © 1996, by Questar Direct, and reprinted by permission of Multnomah Publishers, Inc.)

> But when you're resting in the arms of God, when you have a sense of well-being clear to the bottom of your toes and you know the divine Spirit is there, holding you and rocking you, you can't be that way. You can't hate, you can't strike out, you can't even feel irritation. You're missing that if you're not living in prayer and meditation, not following the inward journey that leads to peace and fulfillment. . . .
>
> If I were talking to Pentecostals or Holiness People, they would understand. But we have pretty much relegated the Spirit to those

fringe elements of society, haven't we? We talk about God the Father and Christ the Son because we can do that safely without threatening the status quo. They are the stuff of tradition. But when we talk about God the Holy Spirit we are talking about that aspect of our spiritual experience that unsettles people, that throws a hat on our Scrabble boards and messes up all the pieces, that makes us uncomfortable until we say, "All right, Lord, I've had it! I'll do what you want me to do!"[13]

Charles H. Boyer uses the doctrine of the Realm of God, or alternatively, the doctrine of the church, as a foundation for ethical action. He shows skill in keeping his emphasis on God, though he speaks of human action. He also uses a remarkable array of images to sustain interest.

As such the church invites the revolution that the coming of the Kingdom would surely bring. The church demonstrates the reality of that which is only in God's future.

Not that our prayers or our work bring in the Kingdom. That task is God's and God's alone. Ours is a proximate, not an ultimate task. As liberation theologians put it, we have been given a project. We do not establish the Kingdom, but we live as if the Kingdom were already in our midst. We look in the Bible to see what God's will is. We pray for it. And then we reach into God's future and seize a chunk of it which we bring back into the present. We provide a demonstration project, a preview of things to come. We invade principalities and powers of this present age with a foretaste of the Kingdom. We plant the leaven of the Kingdom in the doughy lump of our society.

The church is a beachhead of the Kingdom, etched out on the inhospitable shores of this world. As citizens of this new order we proclaim, by the way we live, that God not only will win the final victory, but that the victory has already been accomplished in the Resurrection of Christ.[14]

Use Stories from the News

Roger Lovette told the following story from the news. Notice that he has not just taken a story word for word as it is found in the newspaper, but he has made a movie of it, and he follows good movie-making principles. He gives the setting and the time before he introduces us to the characters. He starts with the action already underway (i.e., the prison breakout has already occurred) instead of starting at the beginning (i.e., with the prison breakout). The story could model mission (i.e., the attitude listeners are to have to those they meet), even as it implies an analogy concerning God's motherly love.

Something similar happened in Mason, Tennessee, in 1984. One day Louise Degrafinfried was cleaning up her little house. There was a knock at the door, and she went to answer it. Standing before her was a terrible-looking man with a gun. "Open up," he whispered. She opened the door. He looked around to see if anyone was there while Mrs. Degrafinfried looked him over. He looked awful. Dirty. Hair matted. Smelly. He had escaped from the state prison and was on the run and very dangerous. She had heard about it on her television. After looking at him for a long time she said, "Are you hungry?" He looked at her as if she was crazy.

"What?"

"Are you hungry?" she asked again.

"Yeah, I am."

"Well," she said, "come on into the kitchen and sit down. I'm gonna fix you some bacon and eggs. Before I do though, I want you to get yourself down that hall to the bathroom and wash your face and hands. Wash good. You look terrible."

The escaped prisoner was dumbfounded. But he went on down the hall to the bathroom. Mrs. Degrafinfried got out the bacon and began to fry.

When he had finished washing up, he came back into the room, and she inspected him. "Well, you look a whole lot better." Then she told him to put his gun down, that it made her nervous. And so he put it down.

She began to talk to him as he ate. She told him about her little Baptist church and about Jesus and how he had come into her life and how it had made such a difference. She talked to him about how God loved everybody and didn't want any of his children breaking into anybody's houses and scaring the wits out of them. She asked him about his own family, and he told her that his father and mother were both dead. He told her she reminded him of his grandmother who had died when he was eight. And she told him more about the Lord Jesus. And when he had finished his eggs and bacon, he did the strangest thing. He picked up the telephone receiver and called the police and gave himself up. The guards came and took him away. And as he was leaving, Mrs. Degrafinfried reached over and patted his cheek and said, "Now you be good, you hear?"[15]

Use Stories from Art and Culture

Raymond Bailey uses a brief yet powerful story from a play in this sermon. The passage is appropriate to Page Four because (a) it models moral behavior, and (b) it implies that God empowers the man to do what is right.

> In Sean O'Casey's play *Within the Gates,* there is a moving scene toward the end of the play as it reaches its climax. A bishop, as an indiscreet youth, fathered a child. Through the years he has done nothing but observe from afar as her life has been corrupted. Discovering that she is in serious crisis, he decides that he will care for her. The bishop responds, "It does not matter what people say or what people think. The only thing that matters is what God thinks. And what God says. What does it matter what men think a man to be if God thinks him to be a saint?"[16]

Jeremiah A. Wright makes substantial use of a painting and makes himself the butt of his story. In this sermon, he tells of preaching in Cuba in 1968 with a translator who knew nothing of Jesus Christ. He often spoke with her about Christ on the trip. In one sermon near the end of his trip, he told his congregation about a painting entitled "Checkmate," which his translator had also seen. He described the painting in detail: Mephistopheles has Faust's king in checkmate. Then he described an event with a tour group in the London gallery where it hangs:

> Nobody noticed when the group moved on, one person stayed right there in front of that painting and kept staring and pacing back and forth. I said that and my translator translated it. And the man in the museum was looking at the painting, and he kept looking at the painting. She translated that. As he paced back and forth, the group moved away and was two corridors away when all of a sudden, coming through those marble halls they heard this man hollering at the top of his lungs, "It's a lie! It's a lie! The king has another move!" And she translated that. Nobody knew that the man in the museum was the international chess champion from Russia. . . . And the same thing is true when it comes to the King of Kings, The King always has another move. . . .
>
> While I was preaching and as she was translating, I noticed that the group from North America . . . had stopped looking at me. They were watching her and waving handkerchiefs and saying, "Go ahead,

baby. Go ahead, baby." And I'm the one preaching the sermon. When I looked over at her, I realized (because I had studied Spanish for six years) that she wasn't translating one word I was saying. She had accepted the Lord Jesus Christ and was over there praising him. . . .

The King always has another move.[17]

Move Listeners to Action of Mission

One effect of God's grace is to open new possibilities in life. Mission on Page Four is not a matter of "should," "must," "have to," and "called to," but is a matter of excitement and a sense of empowerment in joining God in a great endeavor, as Gary W. Downing demonstrates when speaking of overcoming racial, cultural, and economic differences. To speak of mission is not to describe *what is* so much as it is to dream *what can be*—in other words, it is to prophesy. (Excerpted from The Library of Distinctive Sermons, © 1996, by Questar Direct, and reprinted by permission of Multnomah Publishers, Inc.)

> The outcome? We will be freed to treat everyone, including ourselves, as valued children in God's forever family. We can begin to develop relationships with strangers. We can invite people different from us into our homes, our church, our lives. We can actually love people who are different from us.
>
> Whether you have been following Jesus most of your life or are considering committing your life to Christ this morning, one of the tangible ways in which you can feel God's presence is finding that you are loving instead of fearing and hating people different from you.
>
> As members of Christ's family, we can affirm the differences that make us unique and special. But we will make no distinction when we meet people, sell property, hire workers, make loans, offer scholarships, elect political leaders, work for justice and peace, or worship and pray. . . .[18]

When preachers give the congregation one task to do in the coming week, it can be an important means of both grace and pastoral care, a concrete way of helping people to express their faith. The deed may be as small as reaching out to one lonely or needy person. Katie G. Cannon offers a suggestion of this sort. It does not feel like a burden, but an opportunity that listeners would be grateful to receive as a practical suggestion toward faithful living.

> There used to be a poster at Union Seminary in New York City that read, "If you had five minutes to live, who would you call and tell them you love them? Why wait until the last five minutes of your life?" I ask this now. Why wait until the last five minutes of our lives to express openly to people how much we love them? If we know a sister or a brother—wandering around lost unto herself or himself— who doesn't know which way to turn or where to go, who is bent on self-destruction and cut off from the joy of living because she or he has been cast out into the wilderness of life, then let us open ourselves to the Spirit of God so that we can help provide the spiritual water that sister or brother needs to come back home. Let us open ourselves to the grace of God and share the many blessings God has bestowed upon us. . . .[19]

Martin B. Copenhaver, preaching on Luke 14:12-14, told a marvelous story that is not only *about* mission, but it *inspires* mission, as good news should. The theme sentence of the sermon is "God loves to throw parties." In the Thanksgiving dinner he describes, clearly there is a foretaste of the Realm of God in the present. The reference to "Now Thank We All Our God" effectively acknowledges God's action in this event. (Excerpted from The Library of Distinctive Sermons, © 1996, by Questar Direct, and reprinted by permission of Multnomah Publishers, Inc.)

> For nine years I served a church in downtown Burlington, Vermont. We were aware that many in our church were alone for Thanksgiving, so one year we invited our members to come to a Thanksgiving dinner at the church. . . . We had more turkeys and cranberry relish and candied yams and pumpkin pie than we could possibly use. . . .
>
> The next year someone suggested that we invite the folks from the homeless shelter to join us for the Thanksgiving meal at our church. Others felt that this would be a disservice to the homeless poor, who might feel uncomfortable coming to a church and sitting with a bunch of middle-class folks for such a meal. They suggested instead that once again we take meals to the shelter. In the end, though, we decided to invite the residents of the shelter to join us at the church. We sent out invitations to the homeless shelter and posted a few notices around town. Fewer of our own church members showed up

that year, although of course they were invited, perhaps because they were the ones who felt uncomfortable about sharing Thanksgiving with such a motley collection of people.

But every seat was filled. College students, unable to get home for the holidays, showed up. The residents of the shelter came in great numbers. There were church members, some of whom were alone and others who brought their families. People who were dressed in special holiday clothes sat next to others who, because they lived on the streets, hadn't changed their clothes in days, if not weeks . . . .

. . . One young college student, stranded in town for the holidays, was asked to carve a turkey, something he probably never would have been asked to do if he had been at home. A woman who lives alone assumed the role of hostess at her table. One resident of the shelter . . . led us all in a rousing rendition of "Now Thank We All Our God."[20]

Make a Link to the Cross and Resurrection

A link to the cross and the resurrection is important in most sermons to remind the congregation of the resurrection that is at the heart of our faith that gives credence to any of our claims, that shapes our larger story, and that empowers our daily living. This link may be most important in sermons that are not followed by the Lord's Supper. If this link has not been made on Page Three, it can be made now; it does not need to be lengthy. The preacher can accomplish a direct link to the cross, or to other symbols of the faith, like the sacraments.

David W. Crocker, preaching on 1 Kings 18:20-39, moved from God blessing Elijah's sacrifice, to God's own sacrifice in Christ. He then told this powerful story that ends in a manner that exemplifies Christ's self-giving love. We must be careful to use such a story as a metaphor or simile of God's action in Christ, or as a demonstration of God acting now in a manner consistent with God's nature—and we need to avoid ever equating an individual's act of self-giving with the unique event of God's self-giving in the historical event of Jesus Christ, as though they are equal.

E.V. Hill is a well-known black preacher in Los Angeles. He tells of a personal crisis he and his family faced during the Watts riots years ago. Another pastor had already been killed, and word was that Hill would be next. He received a threatening phone call. When his wife asked who had called, he said, "Some things you don't need to know." Sensing danger, she pressed Dr. Hill to know. Finally, he relented, saying, "The caller said, 'Don't be surprised if you discover a bomb in your car.' "

The next morning he awoke to discover his car was gone from his driveway. In a few minutes he saw the car pull around the corner and into the driveway. His wife got out of the car and went into the house. Hill asked his wife, "Where have you been?" She said, "I decided that if somebody was going to be killed, I'd rather it be me." He says he never again asked his wife if she loved him.[21]

Stories on Page Four should correspond in some way to those on Page Two; the good news should help illumine those previous situations of trouble. In this sermon, I told a story on Page Two of someone who felt trapped by life and on Page Four I tell the following newspaper story of a trapped girl who is rescued. While we do not need to explain all of the implications of the second story for the first, the listener should be able to discern a connection in reflecting on the sermon. The cross and resurrection help make a story from daily life into a story that serves theological purpose.

On May 30, 1996, Amanda Sprague, a 13-year-old in Fergus, Ontario, was swept over a dam and pinned by the force of water against a concrete pillar. She was terrified when the police chief arrived. The water was up to her chin. "I have never seen a girl so scared. 'Don't leave me,' she pleaded holding onto my arm." He stood with her in the icy water, holding her head above water as she drifted in and out of consciousness, until they could save her, two hours later. A 330-pound fireman, the biggest man on the force, for just a few seconds put himself in front of the blast of water that was pinning her to the pillar. It was long enough to stop the blast on her and to save her. The police chief was asked why he had stayed and risked his own life in that icy water. He said he could not leave her because, "She asked me to stay." Later, in the hospital, when he saw her, he told her how much everyone in the rescue valued her life.

We know that he was empowered by God to do what he did, for God is the author of all true good. And we know it was God also, because that is what God did in Jesus Christ for each one of us, putting himself between us and the pinning power of sin forever. And sin will have no dominion over you.

Frederick Buechner made this brief yet effective link to the cross at the end of a sermon on Noah's ark:

> Noah looked like a fool in his faith, but he saved the world from drowning, and we must not forget the one whom Noah foreshadows and who also looked like a fool spread-eagled up there, cross-eyed with pain, but who also saved the world from drowning. We must not forget him because he saves the world still, and wherever the ark is, wherever we meet and touch in something like love, it is because he also is there. . . .[22]

Foster Celebration

When effective preachers preach grace, a tone of celebration is generated, as is appropriate, by the end of the sermon. This is of course one of the strengths of much African American preaching and is a key to strong preaching in any tradition. Richard O. Hoyer in a brief passage pictures Jesus being actually present in the preaching of the church. Short phrases add to a sense of celebration. The doctrine of the Word and Sacrament, which in careless hands can sound dry or boring, in fact contributes to the excitement of the prose:

> That's the glory of this church, this family of God to whom you belong, for it is here among us that God dwells and comes to us as Jesus promised: "Where two or three are gathered together in My name, there I am in the midst of them." Here He comes! In the Word and the sacraments He comes to tell us over and over again, and every time to hearts more joyously thrilled, that Jesus of Nazareth is the Son of God Himself, who came to this earth to save us, to pay for all the evil of all mankind once and for all, fully and freely by the blood of His cross. Here He comes to gather together all who would believe in Him as a hen gathers her chicks, that in Him we might be the children of God not just in name but in eternal fact.[23]

Harold F. Dicke preached a sermon whose conclusion anticipates the Sacrament of Communion. By reciting what listeners affirm in faith, he helps prepare them for what they will experience at the Table. The tone is upbeat, positive, and strongly rooted in tradition and faith.

But the words of Simeon are also very appropriate this morning for a very special reason. For in a few moments we will come before the altar of the Lord to receive the blessed Communion of His body and blood. Then, when we return to our pews, we will rise and sing: "Lord, now lettest Thou Thy servant depart in peace, according to Thy word; for mine eyes have seen Thy salvation, which Thou hast prepared before the face of all people, a light to lighten the Gentiles, and the glory of Thy people Israel." And how true those words will be when we sing them, for we will have just returned from this heavenly feast where we shall have seen the salvation of God, where we shall have joined in the closest communion with Christ that is possible this side of heaven, where we shall have experienced the love and forgiveness of God, and as a result of all this we shall be truly at peace. In this peace we shall depart from this place. In this peace we shall live now and throughout the days and years that lie ahead.[24]

Carlyle Fielding Stewart III turns circumstances of sin and brokenness into celebrations of God's love. He preaches on Matthew 10:34-39 ("Those who find their life will lose it, and those who lose their life for my sake will find it"); the connection of Page Four with the biblical text should never be lost.

Victory out of seeming defeat is one paradox of Christian spirituality people have difficulty comprehending.

But God with Christ instituted a new plan with a new man. Where the blind would see, the deaf would hear, the dumb would speak, the cast down would be lifted up, the lame would walk, and the demon possessed would be freed from their imprisonments. Where victory would be claimed over the forces of evil, destruction, and death! He who loses shall find. He who finds shall lose.

If you've gone through divorce, claim the victory. If you've experienced hardship from co-workers on your job, claim the victory! If you've been cast down, disappointed, disjointed, call in the anointed of God and claim the victory right now in the name of Jesus! Whatever your condition or predicament, you have the power to claim the victory by not allowing the cries of cynicism and despair to cloud your mental skies.

God's children never go down to defeat because they have an advocate, a savior, a counselor, a liberator! Victory through defeat is the watchword of faithful Christians. Just when the world is counting you out, Jesus is counting you in. Just when others say that you are finished, that's when Jesus says, "We're just getting started." Just when you thought there was no way out, you discover a way in, a way into his blessings, a way into his mercy, a way into his joy, a way into his promises, a way into God's son. We turn our defeats into victories and count it all joy.[25]

A Checklist for Page Four

In examining each of the four pages we have had an opportunity to sample portions of many sermons. We have still not heard what the four pages sound like when put together in sequence. Before we turn in the next chapter to one example, here is a checklist for Page Four.

Is this page about one idea?

Does it remain focused on God's action of grace in our world?

Does it sound and feel hopeful?

Is the doctrine clear?

Do I develop the doctrine?

Do I employ rhetorical devices to help keep doctrinal pag- gages interesting?

Do listeners see God and people in action?

Is the one need of the hearers met?

Can the most powerful story on Page Two be seen in a hope- ful light because of Page Four?

Has God been identified as the true author of good deeds that are mentioned?

Do I allow for appropriate ambiguity in claiming God's author- ship?

Has good news been offered to the worst person mentioned in this sermon?

Is the mission clear?

Is mission here presented as grace and invitation instead of as trouble?

Are listeners encouraged to think globally and act locally?

Is the connection with the larger Christian story clear?

Can a link be made to the cross and resurrection?

Is this page predominantly a movie?

Does the theme sentence appear in the conclusion?

Does the dominant image appear in the conclusion?

Does the conclusion wed the theme sentence and the domi- nant image (if this has not already occurred)?

Does this page appeal to logos, pathos and ethos?

SECTION VI
VARIETIES OF SERMONS

CHAPTER TWELVE

Imagining a Complete Sermon

The four pages of a sermon identify four theological and creative tasks for faithful biblical preaching. They can be arranged in different orders, and some are frequently left out, producing different models of varying strengths and effectiveness. When we use a four-page sermon, in the order we have discussed, we have a reliable model for preaching good news. Good theology and imagination are a powerful combination in sermons. When assigned to write such a sermon, the preacher may feel overwhelmed and possibly lose the sense of joy of preaching. However, if instead of thinking of one big task we conceive of four smaller, individual, yet related, assignments spread over four days, the task more readily becomes one that we feel we can accomplish. The preacher can again experience a sense of the privilege and joy of preaching.

If we have a strong theological model for preaching, such as the four-page sermon, we can raise our expectations of the results of preaching. After all, if the sermons of the nations were to proclaim God joyfully; if they were to name sin and brokenness without flinching and were to put trouble into perspective before God; if people were to leave church expecting to encounter and rely on God; who knows what might happen? With God, all things are possible.

We have seen sermons that model each of the four pages but we have not yet had before us an example of a four-page sermon to experience the whole. I delivered the following sermon as part of a convocation at Wesley Theological Seminary in Washington, D.C., in April 1997. William (Bobby) McClain, of Wesley Seminary, and Jana Childers, of San Francisco Seminary, and I were each asked to lecture and to preach on Pentecost, some weeks ahead of the actual celebration, so as to help prepare attending clergy for Pentecost in their own churches. The assigned texts were Acts 2:1-21 and John 15:26–16:15, and I chose as my theme sentence something fairly obvious: God pours out the Holy Spirit in power.

"Too Much of a Good Thing"

[Introduction]

Ever since Dean Douglas Meeks first contacted me, many pages ago in my date book, my sense of anticipation and excitement had been growing about this event—until a few days ago when I turned my date book page to April and I saw the schedule we had agreed upon. Jana was going to preach first. And then Bobby. And then me. It dawned on me slowly. Third. I'm going to be third. I'm not going to have anything to say. I will be like those students who preach third in preaching class. Every nuance of the text has already been milked, every commentary combed, every insight from word studies has been cited. And then another dawning: this is the third Pentecost service some of you will have attended. Driving in this morning did I hear the radio station counting 38 shopping days until Pentecost? Easter is barely over. You weren't in the right frame of mind even for the first Pentecost service, and I am preaching the third. This could be too much of a good thing.

[Page One: *Trouble in the Bible*]

Three times you have been walking in the early morning along these narrow cobbled streets of Old Jerusalem, past children playing and sleeping dogs, Roman soldiers on horseback and adults coming back from the market. It is windy today in ancient Jerusalem and dark clouds cruise by overhead. Again you come to the same rich person's house, able to seat 120. Other followers of Jesus are already singing hymns as you wash your feet in the atrium and find a seat on the wooden bench across the cool marble floor. The singing is simple, however, without lilt or passion for they have still not received the Holy Spirit. Peter and Mary Magdalene and others stand and remember Jesus, his sayings, his stories, his deeds. They speak with muted expression. They note that it has been ten days of waiting. Nothing. Outside, the clouds are rumbling like a freight train. Suddenly the clouds part. Blue sky. Sunlight fills the room and everything is blowing. Women clasp their shawls. Men pull their cloaks. Something like the sun's fire seems to be dancing on each person's face, as you would get in a room at the beach when the sun's reflected light dances and flickers. And Jesus' followers all start talking at once in each other's language. It is not babble—it is more like sweet music come down from heaven to hear your own native language spoken by all.

And that's why we can be there and make sense of it, because we hear English, Spanish, modern Korean and other languages spoken, and they didn't even exist then. Do you come from the deep South? Because for you they aren't speaking with a rapid northern clip, everyone is speaking with a southern drawl, which creates a little bit of a problem since the sentences you hear take longer to say than the same sentences in northern rattle. I'm from Canada and they are saying "out" and "about" and "schedule" the way John Wesley intended, and they are putting "eh?" at the end of every sentence, eh? It's like joy whooshed into that room, deep peace, abiding love. But I needn't be telling you this because you have been here before this week. You can have too much of a good thing.

Too much of a good thing. Especially if you are on the outside looking in. Especially if you are one of the Jerusalem neighbors who gathered to find out what all the commotion was about. It is a quiet neighborhood, normally. Especially in the morning. No matter what hour, if people are having a party and you are not invited, if you are an onlooker, if it looks like people are having a good time and you are having a bad day, it is not always a positive experience.

[*Page Two*: *Trouble in our world*]

Hartford Baptist church in Detroit is pastored by Charles G. Adams. He is called the Harvard whooper because he went to Harvard and his whooping isn't like any other African American's. (Harvard University can do that: there are some of us who have been in university so long that even the vaguest memory of a whoop is beyond recall.) Hartford Baptist has six choirs of sixty. They have soloists that make CD diskettes sound like AM radio. Those choirs have that two-step that gets the whole front of the church rocking with the music. And Adams himself catches fire in the pulpit. "The new right," he once preached, "is nothing but the old wrong." After church the people are all fired up, welcoming and speaking about their faith. You go once to Hartford Baptist and you come away all fired up yourself; you go twice and you are reliving the experience. But you go three times and you are starting to think about how your own church does not measure up. In some of our churches back home the choir is so still we've installed an emergency 911 line in the pulpit. One choir director has the choir members smile every fifteen minutes, whether they are singing or not, just to see if they are okay. Lord knows, some of our preaching is more sad, bad, and mad than glad; folks sitting in the pews have to take out their cellular phones to call home during the sermon just to feel better.

Why is it that some churches seem to have so much of the Holy Spirit and some so little? If God really has poured out God's Spirit upon all flesh, why doesn't my son or your daughter even go to church, much less prophesy? I suspect it is a lot easier to love a child who prophesies than one who has lost his or her way, than one who is hooked on drugs, or one who has nothing good to say. Why are United Methodist church schools down in attendance more than 50 percent since 1964? Oh, if God really has poured out God's Spirit on all flesh, why is it that some people have good marriages, while others break up; why do some people have jobs while others don't even have the education to find a job; why are some nations so wealthy while entire peoples worry through starving nights whether food will come? You can have too much of a good thing. More than your share. Three times visiting the first Pentecost can leave us sorely troubled by the inequities and iniquities of life. We may not want to join the party. We may prefer to be among the gathering crowd outside, casting our lot with those who have not, dismissing the celebrations as early drunkenness and potent wine.

[*Page Three:* Grace in the Bible]

Surely we are not the first to note the inequities and iniquities of life. God noted them well, and noted also that we were no match, no match for sin, in coming in Christ. Jesus knew our weakness and laid down his life, because we were no match for the trouble in us and around us. The Jerusalem Christians knew their own utter helplessness after the Ascension. They turned the pages of their Daytimers ten times. Still no appearance of Jesus. At the end of every day they would write in the square for the date, "No Jesus today. Still no power of ministry." Ten long days that but for God's eternal mercy, could have been ten years or ten centuries or ten millenniums. Without Jesus, they could do nothing. They just sat around Jerusalem. They lived only on a promise and a prayer. Jesus had promised to send the Holy Spirit to them. In that long period of spiritual drought, there was little but grief and common memory that bound them one to another—not in strength but rather more like limp celery stalks. They meditated on the wonderful names of the Holy Spirit Jesus promised: the Advocate, the Comforter, the Counselor, the Enabler, the Encourager, the Helper. But what is in a name? Who knew what was going to happen that morning?

But why am I telling you this? You sat in that room with Peter and Mary and those 120 people when the Spirit came. You saw what happened. They did not sit still on their benches for long when the Holy Spirit, with the sound of an earthquake, came upon them. They did not just pause, like they would in California, check it out, and go on rollerblading and chewing gum. You don't do that. You don't have God's holy flame resting on your neighbor's forehead and continue talking as though nothing is happening, chatting about lineups at the laundromat and socks that disappear in the wash. You don't experience the cleansing fire of God's love in your heart and just sit there clipping your fingernails. You don't experience a church being born, neighbors being bonded to neighbors, couples being reconciled, teens finding purpose, prisoners being set free, the lame being healed, the blind seeing, the deaf hearing, addicts giving up their additions, the rich sharing their wealth, the religious leaders repenting, you don't smell the perfume of Christ, even just a whiff, without getting up and saying, "Hallelujah!"

No. They had to get up, they had to push those benches to the side, they had to move, they had to get out of doors where only the blue heavens could contain their excitement, and they couldn't help but witness to their startled neighbors. This was the power of God they had been longing for, that all may be one. Not just for them but for their neighbors and all people, that all may be one. The Helper, the Enabler, the Comforter had come. The power of God's ministry was coursing through their veins, and so many people were waiting to receive God's love. Drunk? No. Not the way onlookers thought. Not with new wine. But perhaps drunk with the wine of the New Covenant. Wine shed for them and for everyone. Drunk with visions of all God wanted to accomplish on earth through the Body of Christ. Drunk with possibility and hope.

[Page Four: *Grace in our world]*

Too much of a good thing? Too much of a good thing? Too much of a good thing ever to be exhausted. Too much of a good thing not to have overcome the world's sin. Too much of a good thing for us ever to feel orphaned, as though we did not have one of the biggest families on earth. Too much of a good thing to stop dreaming of what God wants to accomplish. Too much of a good thing for justice not to be done. Too much of a good thing for racism or sexism or individualism to survive for long. Too much of a good thing for us to worry about whether the church will survive. For God will survive, the Body of Christ will survive, God's purposes will survive when all else has passed away. Too much of a good thing for us to ever feel powerless, save in the vulnerability of Jesus Christ, in laying down his life for another.

I don't imagine that it was all partying. You get a church taking shape, and there are bound to be more than a few people whipping out their date books, trying to plan some meetings. Someone was probably already worrying about having bishops. Someone else was wondering how she was going to explain that 1 + 1 + 1 = 1 not 3. Fortunately there was a week until the Sunday of Trinity to figure it out. Still, overall it was too much of a good thing to let worries take over.

Some of you may know the Methodist bishop in Florida who was approached recently by a woman in his congregation. "I want to make some blankets for the five men who sleep outside the church," she said. The bishop responded, "Is this something that would be easy for you to do?" "Oh yes," she said. The bishop replied, "I was just wondering because I think that when God calls us to do something, it is something that stretches us, and we receive from it. Why don't you make blankets for all the homeless people in the city?" The woman was challenged by his comment and organized several people and together they made over 2000 blankets. Too much of the Holy Spirit just to make 5 blankets.

A student of mine went out to The Vineyard Church in Toronto that has become known as the laughing church. People there break out in laughter, and sometimes laughter goes rippling like waves on water through the crowd, thousands each night. They call it the Toronto Blessing. People even bark like dogs or roar like lions. Some say it is like Azuza Street in San Francisco where contemporary Pentecostals find their roots. Others are less positive. "I went looking for a special blessing," this student said, "and the blessing I received surprised me." He surprised himself when he did not go forward for the blessing when others went forward. He suddenly realized, "Whether I received a blessing there did not matter. I realized I receive a blessing even in our pokey little church each time our scratchy little choir stands up and gives us what they have. Every time old Mrs. Raymond collects the offering, who has been there faithfully through the deaths in her family, it is a blessing."

He is right. A blessing is a blessing because it is from the Holy Spirit—wherever two or more are gathered in Jesus' name. When it is from the Holy Spirit, there is no such thing as a little blessing. You may already have as much as you need for your life of service to others. And you may have as much of the Holy Spirit as you want, depending on your need. If you are going to visit someone in hospital or prison, or if you want to start a housing project for the poor, drink deep. The Holy Spirit is given freely, for the asking. Too much of a good thing ever to run out. Too much of a good thing for us ever to stop praising.

Review Questions to Ask of This and Other Sermons

1. Are each of the four pages present? Where do you divide them?
2. What was the theme sentence?
3. What doctrine was employed?
4. What practical need is addressed?
5. Was there a dominant image and/or refrain? If so, what was it?
6. Is the trouble in the biblical text clearly identified? What is it? Did it develop or intensify?
7. What trouble is identified in our time? What contemporary or congregational need is named? Is analysis provided? Is deeper understanding fostered?
8. Is God's activity clearly depicted on Page Three? Is the theme sentence introduced early on Page Three, and in the sermon, and repeated and/or restated in various ways? Is God (in one of the three Persons) the subject of many of the sentences? Does the focus remain on God or does it shift back to human activities?

9. Is God's action named in our world? Is God given credit as the author of all good? Does grace develop and avoid sounding trite?

10. What was the toughest situation named in the sermon (i.e., on Page Two)? By the end of the sermon, can that situation be seen in a new light because of the gospel?

11. Was a movie made on each page? What people did the listener meet on each page? What scenes or images do you recall?

12. Was there a good balance of images (using concrete, multisensory words), stories, and ideas?

13. Did each page seem to be about one idea that was plain from the beginning of it, and did this idea serve the theme sentence?

14. What humor was used?

15. Did the sermon lead to a sense of celebration?

16. What is the listener to do? To what mission did the sermon lead? Did mission on Page Four feel like a burden or did it feel like grace?

17. Was there a link to the cross and resurrection or to another central symbol of the faith?

CHAPTER THIRTEEN

Reshuffling and Varying the Four Pages

At the beginning of our sermon journey together, I said that I am most concerned with offering theological tools with which we as preachers can analyze our own sermons and those of others, in order that we may improve our preaching. Homiletics has lacked such tools. Homileticians help us to create sermons, yet when we arrive with toolboxes in hand, ready to take sermons apart to appreciate and evaluate them—as we must do in homiletics—many of our toolboxes are relatively limited.

For example, in our sermon toolbox we may literally have a pair of scissors and glue that we use to cut and rearrange a sermon. We may have a metaphorical plumb line with which to test conformity to this or that theological or political ideal; or a tape measure with which to measure the distance the exegesis has moved from what we thought was the center of the text; or a smoke alarm to signal when the thoughts become too abstract; or a whistle to blow when language is inappropriate or insensitive; or chalk to trace the preacher's path in the sermon, to see if everything connects; or a thermometer with which to measure the personal warmth of the stories or the preacher; or a metronome and tuning forks to measure the preacher's rhythm and pitch; perhaps even a checkered flag to signal when the sermon should end. We may be able to name yet other tools in our sermon-fix-it box, tools that allow us to discuss sermon form and the preacher's use of biblical texts, stories and doctrine, introductions and conclusions, or deduction and induction.

For the most part, the tools that we have, while useful and important, leave us still some distance from the the point at which we are able to discuss sermons effectively in terms of the purposes and goals of preaching—they simply do not take us far enough theologically to make our discussions as substantive, satisfying, or instructive as they can be.

The four pages are a small but important step in this direction. A preacher does not have to be aware of our four pages for us to use them to discuss her or his sermon. The four pages designate four functions that are basic to preaching: discussion of trouble in the Bible and today, and discussion of God's gracious actions in the Bible and today. We should be able to read a sermon and readily determine what pages a preacher employs, the proportion of time given to each and, whether they were too short or too long, what the sequence was, which pages contained repetition and what was the effect of this repetition, which pages needed more emphasis, and so forth. In so doing, we ought to be able to articulate why a sermon was particularly effective, or why one portion of a sermon was better than another, or to isolate what was missing theologically from the sermon, or to conceive how a sermon might be reordered. By naming theological functions appropriate to proclamation, we can focus better on the purpose of preaching, and we can begin to compare and assess sermons using different forms from diverse traditions.

The four-page sermon we have been examining, with Pages One to Four in consecutive order, is only one model of sermon. On a practical level of sermon composition, our model has several strengths: it is relatively simple; it divides the task into four discrete, manageable assignments spread over four days; it helps prevent imagery from becoming excessive or stories from going astray; and it encourages preachers to be more creative and effective as communicators through conceiving of the individual pages as episodes in a movie; furthermore, it is versatile, because when the pages are shuffled it provides a multitude of other models.

From a theological perspective, our model also has additional strengths to recommend it as a basic norm: its emphasis starting with the Bible; its focus on human brokenness and sin; its equally or even stronger focus on God and God's action of grace; its fostering faith and hope through reliance upon God; its use of systematic or constructive theology through one doctrine arising from one theme sentence; its address of human need and the contemporary world; its guidelines that prevent doctrine from becoming turgid discourse; and its framework and movement serves as a basis for effective pulpit theology. There is an emotional or spiritual dimension to the order to the four pages: trouble in the Bible naturally leads to deeper awareness of trouble in our time for listeners, just as grace in the Bible leads to a sense of even deeper grace close to home today.

Learning to use such a model for preaching is important, yet many of the strengths of this model can be preserved even with other sequences of the pages. We are right to be attentive to other ways to preach.

When we depart from using all four pages, or rearrange the order, or blend, or repeat this page or that, we should do so knowing the risks, but nonetheless in confidence—because we have good theological or practical reasons for so doing and we have ensured that good communication will not suffer. Some possible rearrangements can help us to predict what is likely to work before we venture in a given direction. A student once commented that she thought she probably had most of the four pages in her regular preaching—just in a different order—and she was not sure what order she used. We are always most effective in preaching if we know exactly which page we are on, and what the purpose and function of that page is. If we know what we risk losing if we move this way or that, we can be intentional about compensating for it in any alternative structure.

In my own experience, two homiletical guidelines are like secure handrails on the steep homiletical paths. The first is this: sermons best can foster faith if we preach grace. Clearly God can speak a word of grace even through the harshest trouble, and the two are really just different sides of the same coin. The Word that binds is the Word that frees. Nonetheless, we are to assist the Holy Spirit in proclamation. Clearly, churches that preach only trouble can grow, although why they do is unclear. Some people may not distinguish between living by law and living by faith; others may not feel that they are deserving of grace, or may experience grace in other parts of the worship service or church life; others may welcome the sense that they are in control by being left to their own resources and abilities. Still, we preachers have the privilege of assisting God who uses preaching to foster faith and to encourage people to dedicate their lives to Christ.

The second handrail for me is this: I have not heard a hopeful or joyful sermon that devoted its second half to trouble. Perhaps it is possible, for with God all things are possible, and Christ can turn even water into wine. But I am unclear that listeners can leave church with more hope and faith than when they came in, if the last half of the sermon casts them on the insufficiency or their own resources. Here, again, the distinction is important between mission that casts listeners on their own resources (Page Two), and mission that is glad and willing service of the other in the power of the Holy Spirit (Page Four). The latter, I believe, is appropriately conceived as grace.

The four pages can be used to discuss the deep structure of other sermon models or forms, including expository, exegetical, doctrinal, point-form, deductive, inductive, and narrative sermons. Numerous variations are possible, and they may be considered in three dimensions: the order of pages, the relative duration of each of the pages, and the number of points in the sermon as a whole.

Variations in the Order of Pages

If we examine sermons through the ages, we can find some that are entirely Page One, others that are several Page Ones, hopping from text to text, and others that combine, drop, blend, and repeat different pages in all possible ways. Expository sermons, which might have one long exposition of the Scripture and an application, generally contain Pages One and Two or, alternatively, Three and Four. Exegetical sermons, which go often verse by verse through Scripture, explaining and applying each verse to contemporary life, might have twice as many pages as the number of verses (i.e., a Page One and Two, or a Page Three and Four, per verse). A three-point sermon might have three pages, if it does not deal with the Bible, or six pages, if each point starts in the biblical text. A single narrative sermon might stay on one page or move from Page One to Page Three, if it is about the Bible, or from Page Two to Page Four, if it is about our world.

While our model has four separate theological functions, with one function per page, some sermons may use these four functions in an arrangement of six or ten pages or more—we might need to be mathematicians to calculate the number of possible sequences. To discuss meaningfully the variations, I will limit conversation here to those possibilities that preserve the order of trouble and grace. I recommend experimenting primarily with five variations in page order:

1. Blend Pages One and Two and/or Three and Four: A common variation on the four-page format may blend the biblical and contemporary times. In any sermon some bleeding between pages is natural in the form of brief asides and other references. Actual blending of pages is another matter and may be useful when the historical situation of the biblical text is largely unknown, and/or when a text sounds contemporary (like a proverb). I heard a student preach an excellent sermon on the Prodigal Son, using this approach: she retold the biblical text through reflections on the childhood relationship of her younger brother and herself to their aunt. Gradually it became clear to listeners that the biblical text was being retold: when the student was speaking of her childhood she was in fact on Page One or Three, and when she was speaking of now, she was on Page Two or Four. But essentially the Bible and the present were blended. One danger of this approach is that we will use it too often and we will bypass essential historical-critical insights concerning biblical texts. A second danger is that the Bible will remain invisible and might be perceived to be irrelevant for preaching.

2. Follow the order Two-One-Three-Four: The introduction, if there is one that deals with the contemporary world, is prior to Page One, for Page One deals only with the Bible. Reversal of Pages One and Two means that we start with a substantial discussion of trouble in our world (which is similar to an extended introduction) and then we move to similar trouble in the biblical text. Essentially, then, we discuss the Bible only once—in the two pages in the middle (One and Three)—first trouble and then grace. In one version of this, Page Four examines two or three situations incorporating doctrine and mission, identifying God's action in our world. In another version Page Four could be a long concluding story, either the second half of an opening story, or a new one that counters the opening, bringing good news to troubled circumstances. This creates a pleasing, slow pace (contemporary story—biblical text—contemporary story) and is excellent for shorter ser-

mons, or for preaching when children are present. The structure is simple (it sounds like only three pages since One and Three are together) and its material is often easy to remember, both for the preacher and the listeners.

Again we should be aware of risks—not to discourage creative venture but to make such ventures less vulnerable to potential weakness. As soon as we put Pages One and Three together, we are in danger of treating the text only once, simply from the perspective of trouble, and we may need to remind ourselves to have a clear turning point. Two full pages on the Bible may seem unnecessarily long to listeners, and preachers may need to shorten each. Something can be lost if week after week the Bible does not appear to be the source that identifies trouble in our world, since Page Two comes first. Finally, when Page Two is first, the preacher may need to work harder to achieve sufficient depth in our world, in other words identifying or reaching a need felt in the congregation, for normally the Bible on Page One identifies the trouble and Page Two brings it home.

3. Follow the order One-Two-Four-Three: Reversal of the last two pages provides a sustained look at our situation in the center of the sermon. There the preacher might relate one long story or event that has both a trouble perspective and a grace perspective. Again, this can have a pleasing simplicity of pace and movement. The risk is that the good news seems to come from our situation rather than arising from the Bible; the Bible can be seen merely to confirm a truth already discovered in the world. In other words, we are in danger of drawing grace out of mid-air and making the Bible say what we want, rather than allowing the Word of God to speak. To counter this we will need to let the doctrine carry much of the weight of the good news. A further possible danger is that listeners may experience treatment of the Bible on the last page as an emotional or spiritual let-down from the previous page, particularly if the event related there had a powerful emotional or spiritual component, made all the greater by its contemporary immediacy. Thus we would need to be sure to present the Bible in a way that seems as vital and present as contemporary events.

4. Follow the order Two-Four-Three: This format finds trouble and grace in our situation and then goes to the Bible to rein-

force what the preacher has already said about God's activity. It is dominated by our situation (i.e., Pages Two and Four), which could be in part a discussion of an issue or a teaching of a doctrine. The preacher's treatment of the Bible may be brief but pointed, confirming a truth found in tradition or faith experience. To work best, the events recited on Page Two should closely parallel the events in the Bible that would have been on the missing Page One. Or the preacher may use theology to provide the turning point between trouble and grace. This approach could be seen as a form of "proof-texting," making the Bible say what we want it to say; attention to the Bible may be too brief to underscore its importance.

5. Follow the order One-Three-Four: This is a heavily biblical approach that stays with the Bible through trouble and grace (Pages One and Three), and then applies the grace in the text to our times. It can work best if the preacher reads contemporary circumstances into the biblical times so that the listener, though listening to the biblical account, can make connections to today's world without effort. In other words, we might present Page One so that it sounds like contemporary life although it is from the Bible. Since Page Two is dropped, we run the risk of never examining our situation for trouble; thus, in handling the Bible on Page One we need to reach appropriate emotional and spiritual depth. Otherwise, listeners can be left wondering what the biblical trouble has to do with them.

Variations in the Relative Length of the Pages

A second way in which preachers find variety is in varying the length of the pages. The four pages refer to theological and creative functions each roughly a quarter of the entire sermon, yet a four-page sermon might vary from ten minutes or under in some traditions, to thirty minutes or more in others. Here is a rough guide: four typed single-spaced pages (using a twelve-point font), spoken or read at an appropriate normal pace, about five to six minutes per page depending upon culture, might take around twenty or twenty-five minutes.

Here we can consider the possibility of adding pages in either the first or second half of the sermon or in both halves. We might still keep the rough fifty-fifty (sixty-forty or forty-sixty) balance between trouble and grace, with grace coming last. For example, we might visit the biblical text twice and apply it twice in the first half of the sermon, each time developing a different aspect of the trouble, the second time at greater theological or human depth. Thus the first half of the sermon might have four shorter pages and the second half only its normal two (or the first half might have two pages and the second half four; or the whole sermon might be eight pages). Obviously there are countless other variations but they are too numerous to name and explore in detail.

One danger of shortening pages and increasing their number is the sermon may feel choppy and have little or no focus. For the preacher to move below roughly a two-minute focus on either the biblical text or the human situation is to risk sermon unity. Listeners are in danger of losing the thread of the sermon if the focus keeps shifting. A preacher needs time to move listeners to a place of depth. If, as preachers, we increase the number of shifts back and forth, between the biblical text and the human situation, we increase the work listeners have to do. Every time we shift the mental stage scenery to another culture and time we risk leaving listeners behind. By contrast, we can move too slowly, such as in sermons that are one long, single narrative in the biblical or present time, where the contemporary situation or the connection to the Bible may never become clear. In any case, sustaining a long narrative takes more skill and talent than most of us have. It may not even be a worthy goal, for if a member of the congregation is in dire need, that person may long for us to proclaim God simply and and with direct relevance.

Variations Using Point-Form

Point-form preaching has come under attack from many quarters for various reasons. Some critics say it places too much emphasis on the sermon as proposition or as information (in agreement with Hans Frei); or that it seems authoritarian, or rigid, or simplistic (reducing every Bible text to three predictable points); or that it is too male, or old-fashioned, or modern, not geared to the listening patterns of a postmodern television generation. But points may not be the problem: the problem may be how they have been used or overused. They can still play an effective role in helping to organize the sermon and in giving structural aids to listeners that help them hear and remember what is said. Perhaps in our time the point-form sermon should be conceived as an occasional model, perhaps even as a back-up. For example, if a sermon draft lacks unity and direction, and if the preacher has little time for revision, adding points can often clarify and strengthen the development of the ideas that are present.

The four-page sermon naturally lends itself to a point format, perhaps one or two points about trouble and one or two about God's action. For example, Joseph M. Stowell gives a preview sketch of his three-point sermon: he moves from trouble to grace to mission.

> First, some cultural and theological background will help us understand the roots of a care-less correctness that, like the Pharisees, may be the very reason that we care less for the lost. Then Christ introduces through the parables a divine correction of our misperceived correctness. Third, the stories provide a clear three-step pattern of applied compassion for the lost.[1]

The danger with point-form preaching is that listeners find them rather mechanical and unimaginative, especially if used week after week. Preachers can be so preoccupied with finding points or with making them rhyme (a frequent preaching practice) that more important considerations are lost, for instance, a balance between trouble and grace.

A Sermon in a Different Format

The following complete sermon by Hank Langknecht, a Lutheran (ELCA) pastor, represents a considerable departure from the number and order of pages as we have considered them, which is one reason for including it here. It is an excellent sermon that handles the final portion of the Bible (Revelation 22:12-21) in a clear and highly imaginative fashion. It reflects amply his own emphasis on grace; I say of him as a friend, colleague, and doctoral candidate in homiletics, that when God handed out theologies of grace,

251

Langknecht took double portions. The four pages provide a good means of analysing any sermon theologically. Preachers thereby have a means to understand how a sermon works, and thus how they might employ similar principles to achieve a similar effect in their own sermons. This sermon stands on its own; I will follow it with brief analytical comments:

> When I was here last—3 weeks ago—I told you that the Book of Revelation (in spite of all the things you might have heard about it); the Book of Revelation is not at all hard to understand. In fact, it can be summed up in two words: God Wins. Against death, against despair, against the devil: God Wins.
>
> In the reading this morning from the Book of Revelation we heard the very last verses of the book, the verses which include the climax of John's vision. The heavenly city has come down, and all the saints are standing around in white robes waving their palm, cheering and yelling and singing the "Hallelujah Chorus." The river of life is flowing through the middle of town and the fruit trees are in blossom on both sides. And there in the middle of everything is Jesus. And he says, "I am the Alpha and the Omega; I am Everything from A to Z; I am the First and the Last; I am the Beginning and the End; I am the Big Bang and the Final Crunch; I am the one Who Was, Who Is, and Who Is To Be."
>
> But that's only the build up to the climax. The real climax comes when Jesus—the slaughtered Lamb of God, who now sits victorious on the highest throne of heaven—the climax comes when Jesus says: "Come."
>
> "Come." Just like he has said it before: "Come unto me, all you who labor and I will give you rest." "Come!" Just like he has said before: "Let the children come to me . . . ." "Come . . . all you who are thirsty, come." "The strife is over, the battle is won. God won. So come." To say that the Book of Revelation is too deep or hard to understand is to say you've never read it. Tell me what is too deep and hard to understand about Jesus saying, "I am Everything from A to Z"? Tell me what is hard to understand about Jesus saying, "I have always been with you . . . and I will always be with you"? Tell me what is deep about Jesus saying, "Come!"? This is easy.
>
> But let's go over how it all gets put together: The universe belongs to God. Every thing, every process, every place, every time, and every body. That's easy, right? That means that the whole universe is within God's care and scope; nothing escapes God's attention. You already believe that, right? So that's easy. There is no place we could travel in the universe; no planet, sun, no solar system we could visit

where God wouldn't already be there. Isn't that right? And even if we travel inside. We can walk down memory lane (or in some cases we can walk down memory dark alley). We can go into the interior of our souls and selves, even into the darkest places, and everywhere we go inside, God is there. Isn't that right? That's easy. I mean, it's a great mystery how this can be, but it's easy to understand, right?

Jesus is Everything from A to Z. And so Jesus is every letter in between. Jesus is B for Beauty; C for Cancer cured or coped with; D for Dying and rising again; E for Ecstasy. Jesus is H for Heaven; J for Joy; L for Lonely; M for Maybe the Toronto Blue Jays will get above .500; Jesus is P for Paradise; Q for Quality; Jesus is even S for Satan defeated; U for Underworld under God's control. Jesus is Everything from A to Z, and so yes, even the devil—who thinks he is so independent—even the Devil is somewhere within God's care because there is no place that is beyond God's care. Because, as Jesus himself puts it: "I am the Alpha and the Omega, I am the First and the Last, I am the one Who Was, Who Is, and Who Is To Be."

And then Jesus says, "Come." And he says "Come" in two ways. He says "Come to me." And he says, "I am coming to you." The Book of Revelation climaxes with Jesus saying: "The whole thing is in my hands, so relax a little, and come, let me love you." And really, what could be easier to understand than that?

Here's a visual image for you. Think of it all as a choo-choo train. All of it. All of creation as a choo-choo train. It started back at the Beginning, of course. And it is rolling down the tracks toward the Ending. And everything and everybody is on board. The engineer of the train would be? Sure, God. The conductor would be? Sure, Jesus. The public address system would be? Sure, the Holy Spirit. The baggage car would be? Nothing special, just the baggage car. But everything and everyone in all of history and in all of the universe is on that train. And that train is passing through time and space toward its inevitable destination. And only the engineer knows where and when.

There are thousands of cars on the train. Cars for every time and every one in history. There are Christian cars, there are Jewish cars, there are Buddhist, Hindu, and Moslem cars, there is even an atheist car. There are even a couple of cars full of devils and demons; but don't tell them because they don't know they're on this trip. But they are, because all of God's creation is on this trip, headed for God's destination whether they like it or not. Whether they even know it or not. Because how could they not be? Jesus is Everything from A to Z, the Beginning and the End. What could be left off?

Now, there are some who believe that the only people on the train are those who "Belieeeeve in Jeeeesus." But that can't be. Because then Jesus would only be everything from A to B; B for believe. But he's not. He's everything from A to Z! Including D for disbelief.

And there are some who live in horrible shame because of who they are or what they've done. And they're worried they might not be on the train at all. But that can't be. Because then the train wouldn't have a C or a D; C for crisis, D for doubt. But Jesus is Everything from A to Z.

There are some people on the train who like to think that their car is the only one "on track." But that can't be. Because then Jesus would only be Everything from A to S. S for smug, self-righteous, and stupid. But he's not, he's everything from A to Z! Including U for Universal.

Jesus says, "I am Everything from A to Z." I mean, either he is or he isn't. Are you going to call him a liar by leaving some of the letters out, 'cause I'm not!?

There are some eccentric people on this train. You've got some who think that by running toward the back of the train they can stop the forward progress, stay where they are, and maybe even make their way to the caboose, and jump off. But we don't even know for sure if there is a caboose; and, besides, anyone walking toward the back of moving train is still moving what? Sure. Forward. And some of those who have tried to make it to the back have died trying. But they are still on the train. There are others who are so used to the motion of the train they don't even feel it anymore, they've never happened to meet the conductor (who is? Right, God), or heard the PA (which is? Right, the Holy Spirit). And so they figure that all this talk about a train is just a myth. But they are wrong. But even in their ignorance they are still on the train. And then there is us. The Christians. We're one of the groups of passengers who have a job. It's a great job, really. We are called to travel in the Hospitality Car. We represent the Railroad, of course. And our job is to make sure that, (1) everyone on the train is comfortable; (2) everyone on the train is well fed; and (3) we are to reassure anyone who seems worried or scared by telling them, "Relax, the engineer of this train knows where we are going, when we will get there, and how to make sure you get their safely. Have no fear."

The Kingdom Train is rolling . . . and it will never stop until it reaches a time and place that only God knows. In spite of incredible sorrow, in spite of difficult times, in spite of fear and disbelief, in spite of the devil himself, this train will reach its destination. That's all the Book of Revelation is trying to say.

"I am the Alpha and the Omega, the first and the last, the beginning and the end." So, Come. And let everyone who hears say, "Come." And let everyone who is thirsty come. Let anyone who wishes take the water of life as a gift. The one who testifies to these things says, "Surely I am coming soon." Amen. Come, Lord Jesus!

The grace of the Lord Jesus be with all the saints. Amen.[2]

Brief Analysis

Hank Langknecht has an excellent sense of the simplicity and clarity needed for pulpit communication, as is evident even in his clever two-word summary of the Book of Revelation, "God wins." In terms of my memory device, "The Tiny Dog Now Is Mine," his sermon suggests the following:

One Text: While the sermon focuses mainly on one verse ("I am the Alpha and the Omega . . ." v. 13), this verse appropriately is central to the text as a whole unit. The context of the passage is communicated (i.e., the vision of the new Jerusalem), as well as specific details from many other verses in the passage.

One Theme: Jesus is everything from A to Z.

One Doctrine: Eschatology; or, The lordship of Jesus.

One Need: Can Jesus be trusted in all things?

One Image: Jesus' image of the alphabet becomes the image of an alphabet train.

One Mission: Ensure that everyone on the train is comfortable, well fed, and reassured.

What pages does Langknecht use? When analyzing a sermon for pages, one looks for the overall pattern, which here is a movement from Page Three (ending with the paragraph before he mentions the train) to Page Four. A close analysis reveals a sentence here or there that belongs to another Page (for example, the few sentences dealing with the difficulties of understanding Revelation sound like Page Two), but the general sweep and sustained focus is what matters most. Any time a sermon begins with grace, the hearers are likely to resist what the preacher says. People normally need their objections addressed before they are willing to assent to a positive claim or statement; they need to be persuaded. Langknecht uses that principle of resistance to advantage here, for right from the beginning when he says, "God wins," the listener is likely to say, "Oh yeah?" He is counting on that resistance to help sustain the interest of his listeners. Although Pages One and Two are absent, they are at least present by implication, for he repeatedly speaks directly to that resistance. Trouble is represented every time he mentions the difficulty of Revelation, or places or things outside of God's care, or cancer, or Satan, or other faiths, or people of no faith, or those who are off the track, or the eccentrics, or those who do not even know they are on a train. In other words, although One and Two are absent, he has partially compensated for them; he has included some attention to trouble in structuring his material.

Langknecht easily could have developed a Page One, for instance around the words of Jesus that he is coming "to repay according to everyone's work" (v. 12), or around the plagues that would visit anyone who alters the witness of Revelation (vv. 18-19), and a Page Two naturally would have followed. But he did not develop the sermon in that way, nor does it suffer for the route he took. Rigidity about sermon form and function is rarely a good idea in preaching or in teaching preaching. Instead we should learn to recognize what we are doing; why we are doing it; what will be missing if this or that is absent or under-represented, and how do we compensate for what is minimal or missing so that the sermon does not suffer.

Preaching Well

Our purpose in discussing various models with the four pages of the preacher has been to encourage preachers to experiment while retaining good biblical and theological strategies. When congregations look for a minister, pastor, or priest, they continue to name as their number-one priority someone who can not just preach, but preach well. For the church to remain healthy, God's Word needs to retain its place as the center of the church's life, along with the sacraments. If the church wants something more, perhaps to experience a renewal and offer the world something it has not been offering as well as it should, it needs to put more focus on God. The church also needs to be able to reach youth and teens, and to speak about God in ways that people can understand and apply to their lives. Preaching is God's gift to God's people, and God wills that their entire lives, not just their minds, be brought into sharp focus before God's sovereign rule and redemptive grace.

In sermons it is so easy for us to put all of our emphasis and hope on mere human endeavor, for what we do is important. But what God has done and is doing in Jesus Christ and through the power of the Holy Spirit is more important. Over history, the church has tried many preaching emphases, with varying degrees of faithfulness. However, for the most part, the church has not tried to communicate the gospel as good news for we have assumed that even to question whether the gospel is the good news is redundant. We have not often asked: What theological, emotional, and spiritual components facilitate grace-filled proclamation? What can we do to encourage dependence on God? How can preaching be structured to invite people to faith, and thereby be seen to hold a promise for the renewal of the church in the future? What does the Holy Spirit require of us? Following are some additional suggestions for answering these questions.

Form a Positive Image of the Congregation

Of course, it is also easy for teachers of preaching, like myself, to put all of our emphasis on what preachers can do, as if it were all up to us. If as preachers we are prone to lose sight of God in our sermons, we are also likely to lose sight of God's role in sermon preparation. Too often, preparing a sermon can seem like a lonely, perhaps even painful, venture, like going to the dentist—something many try to put off as long as possible. I often ask students to try to name what image of the congregation they take with them into the pulpit. If they have a negative image, for example the image of a fox waiting to attack, I suggest that they consciously shift that image to something more suitable and encouraging, for instance, the image of people lying ill in hospital beds in need of care. By the same token, even experienced preachers may have negative unidentified images of the sermon process that they take with them into their studys. Such negative images need positive substitutes.

257

Use Prayer to Call on God as a Partner

A positive image that we can all claim for sermon preparation is the image of prayer and time alone in relationship with God. In 1967, Reuel Howe wrote a book entitled *Partners in Preaching* (New York, NY: The Seabury Press), in which he argued for working with the congregation as a partner. Our great need now may be to rediscover God as a partner in the preaching process. God calls us to preach and upholds us in it, graciously providing for our needs, one day at a time. When we are at our study desks, as at other times, God speaks to us by the power of the Holy Spirit through the Scriptures, through biblical commentaries and other sermon resources, through books on theology and newspapers and magazines, through the congregation and our own experiences, and through our prayerful reliance upon God to provide the wisdom and words we need to discern what to say. The reason is simple, God loves good preaching. And God loves giving good things to God's children.

Use the Homiletical Process

Just as God uses our education and various academic and other sermon resources, so too God uses our knowledge of the homiletical process to assist and strengthen our preaching. If in sermon preparation we only ask of God, "What would you have your people do?," we are attentive only to the trouble God wants us to address. However, if we also ask, What should I say you have done and are doing to help your people?, we will follow God through doors that lead to the strongest kinds of proclamation. These doors lead to contemplation of God's action in and behind the Bible text, and to discerning God's vital activity especially in the midst of the most troubling situations today. Such discernment is in itself a testimony to the Holy Spirit at work in and through our efforts, and can be a source of much nurture for the preacher. If there is to be preaching for the congregation on Sunday, God first encounters the preacher through the week.

Continue to Rely on God

Of course, even once the preacher has composed the sermon, reliance upon God continues. The preacher depends upon God for the boldness and courage to enter the pulpit and to dare to speak on behalf of God. God also provides what we need to proclaim the Word: the energy, the confidence, the faith, the grace to benefit from the talents God has given us. God provides the congregation, gathering God's servants as a community, and the Holy Spirit is active in their midst, receiving as worthy their praise and thanksgiving and quickening their reception of the proclaimed Word. And of course, God is not finished with the preacher or the congregation once the service is over, but continues to uphold them as they scatter to their tasks in the world.

Through all of these activities, God's primary message to God's children is "I love you" not "you have to." The "musts," "shoulds," and "have tos," are one part of God's loving and empowering communication. But the other part of God's message, that God longs for us to proclaim with joy and enthusiasm borne of the Spirit, is "I have done this for you." Every demand that rests upon us has been lightened for all time, such that it is not we who bear it, but Christ who bears it in us and for us. Every trouble that stands ahead of us, God in Christ has entered before us and destroyed its ultimate power. Every power and principality that seems to have the last say, has met its end in the finality and supremacy of God's love that trumpets from the empty tomb.

Conclusion

We have paid considerable attention to sermon structure. Sermons are like stained glass windows: people look at the colored glass and see the light, not at the lead cames holding together the glass. Listeners generally are so busy trying to understand what the preacher is saying, and are so involved with the direction and thrust of the sermon at its surface level, that few are aware of its deep structure. Most people listen to a sermon simply for a way of understanding how God relates to the joy and sorrow of their own and others' lives. While they do not notice sermon structure, per se, they do notice if they leave church with more joy, hope, and promise than they had when they came.

The preacher is probably the only one who will know that the sermon has a theological structure that assists the Holy Spirit in bringing forth hope. To know that the four pages of the sermon can assist the Spirit does not lessen the wonder that God uses our humble efforts for the salvation of the world. The privilege and opportunity of preaching is about communicating God's Word as fully as we are able, offering the best that we have, allowing the Holy Spirit to use us to strengthen people's faith for Christ's work in the world. But it is also about offering what little we have for God to multiply.

Sermon Checklist

Preachers and students may use the following as a summary of this book and as a checklist for their own sermons. Teachers of preaching, using this as a textbook for a preaching class, might use this list to design a marking sheet for elements of sermon composition, as I do, assigning ten marks to each of the categories. (I also circle problem areas below, and elaborate with written comments.) In advanced preaching classes, where the inclusion and arrangement of the pages might vary, one might assess each page or its equivalent, identifying, for instance, how well the preacher has compensated for a missing page and its theological functions.

1. Page One: Trouble in the text. Is this page clearly about one idea? Is it exegetically sound? Does it seem fresh? Does the trouble here relate to the grace on Page Three?
2. Page One: Is the introduction interesting? Does this page state or signal the sermon's theme (Page Three)? Is it focused on one text? Is this page mainly a movie?
3. Page Two: Trouble in our world. Is it about one idea? Is one doctrine evident? Is there a sense of deepening theological thought as the page progresses? Does this page clearly link with Page One?
4. Page Two: Is one need identified? Does it lead listeners to their own possible struggle/s? Does it reflect their worlds? Are people the focus? Are the stories inclusive? Do they reflect a range of experience? Is this page mainly a movie? Is mission identified?
5. Page Three: God's action of grace in/behind the text. Is this

page about one idea (i.e., the theme statement or the major concern of the text)? Does it focus on God? On grace? Is it memorable? Is it repeated?

6. Page Three: Is God's action or God's nature the subject of the whole page? Is the material presented here exegetically sound? Does it sufficiently differ from Page One? Is grace the focus? Is it a movie?

7. Page Four: God's action of grace in our world. Is this page about one idea (i.e., the major concern of the sermon)? Does it remain focused on grace? Is the doctrine clear? Do we see people in action?

8. Page Four: Is the one need of the hearers met? Is the doctrine clear? Is the mission clear? Is it grace? Are listeners encouraged to think globally and act locally? Is the connection with the larger Christian story clear? Is it a movie? Is the conclusion fitting?

9. Ethos: Does the preacher display pastoral sensitivity? vulnerability? faith? leadership? Does the preacher use humour? Is it natural? Does the preacher appeal to both logic (logos) and experience (pathos or emotion)? Is the preacher's use of language/stories appropriate?

10. Overall impression. Does the sermon have unity? Is the theme clear? Is the doctrine clear? If there is one dominant image, is it appropriately developed? By the end are the dominant image and the theme wedded? Are thoughts clearly expressed?

NOTES

Chapter One: Movies, Pages, and God

1. *The Practice of Preaching* (Nashville, TN: Abingdon Press, 1995), pp. 125-94. See also, John H. Hayes and Carl R. Holladay, *Biblical Exegesis: A Beginner's Handbook*, rev. ed. (Louisville, KY: Westminster/John Knox Press, 1983); Thomas G. Long, *The Witness of Preaching* (Louisville, KY: Westminster/John Knox Press, 1989), pp. 60-91.

2. Brevard S. Childs, *Biblical Theology of the Old and New Testaments: Theological Reflection on the Christian Bible* (Minneapolis, MN: Fortress Press, 1992).

3. A criticism of narrative homiletics, and one of the best interpretations of Hans Frei on narrative, is found in Charles L. Campbell, *Preaching Jesus Christ: New Directions for Homiletics in Hans Frei's Postliberal Theology* (Grand Rapids, MI & Cambridge, UK: William B. Eerdmans Publishing Company, 1997).

4. Lutherans, whose law-gospel dialectic at the heart of their theology frequently fosters fruitful discussion of grace, were often a little better than others at preaching it though they also fall short. See for example the many fine sermons in an anthology like *The Concordia Pulpit for 1968*, Vol. XXXIX (St. Louis, MO: Concordia Publishing House, 1967). Gerhard O. Forde criticizes his Lutheran colleagues for the gospel becoming attached to the end of the sermon where it "is not the end of the law . . . just the ratification of the law. . . ." *Theology Is for Proclamation* (Minneapolis, MN: Fortress Press, 1990), p. 151. Stephen Farris has made a helpful contribution to the discussion in his "Preaching Law as Gospel: Some Reflections from Psalm 119" in Papers of the Annual Meeting of the Academy of Homiletics (Toronto, ON, December 2-5, 1998), pp. 25-33.

5. I discovered years later a sermon by Frederick Buechner on a similar idea, "The Message of the Stars," *The Magnificent Defeat* (New York, NY: The Seabury Press, 1979), pp. 44-50.

6. Bron Smith, a cartoon appearing in *Leadership: A Practical Journal for Church Leaders* 9:4 (Fall 1998), p. 59.

Chapter Two: Ensuring Sermon Unity

1. On seeker churches and the Bible, see Robert G. Duffett, *A Relevant Word: Communicating the Gospel to Seekers* (Valley Forge, PA: Judson Press, 1995), pp. 47-72, 82-87.

2. See, for example, my *The Practice of Preaching* (Nashville, TN: Abingdon Press, 1995), pp. 125-94. Or, see Stephen Farris, *Preaching That Matters: The Bible and Our Lives* (Louisville, KY: Westminster John Knox Press, 1998), pp. 51-74.

3. Lucy Rose encourages conversations around the Word of God that help to refocus life, in *Sharing the Word: Preaching in the Roundtable Church* (Louisville, KY: Westminster John Knox Press, 1997), p. 93 and p. 133 n. 1; Eugene L. Lowry favors "evoking" the proclamation; and values "the eloquence of the provisional" in *The Sermon: Dancing the Edge of Mystery* (Nashville, TN: Abingdon Press, 1997), pp. 39-53, esp. p. 47 and p. 52.

4. Carol M. Norén favors preaching in which hearers gather "symbolically at the round table where there is no head and no foot," in *The Woman in the Pulpit* (Nashville, TN: Abingdon Press, 1991), p. 155; see also John McClure's "collaborative homiletic" in *The Roundtable Pulpit: Where Leadership and Preaching Meet* (Nashville, TN: Abingdon Press, 1995). Norén states that "religious truths are not the goals of the preacher. Instead, preaching is a profound act of human connection and intimacy," *The Woman in the Pulpit*, p. 130. Richard L. Eslinger takes a similar position, advocating that "our homilies will not trade in propositions addressed to rationalist minds," in his *Narrative and Imagination: Preaching the Worlds that Shape Us* (Minneapolis, MN: Fortress Press, 1995), p. 9.

5. Eugene L. Lowry, *The Sermon*, p. 47.

6. Lucy Lind Hogan, "Rethinking Persuasion," in *Papers for the Annual Meeting of the Academy of Homiletics* (Oakland, CA: December 4-6, 1997), pp. 143-51, esp. p. 145 and p. 151.

7. See Charles L. Campbell, *Preaching Jesus: New Directions for Homiletics in Hans Frei's Postliberal Theology* (Grand Rapids, MI and Cambridge, UK: William B. Eerdmans Publishing Co., 1997), pp. 10-12.

8. John Calvin, *Commentary on St. John* (Grand Rapids, MI: William B. Eerdmans Publishing Co., 1949) v. 5.39, p. 218.

9. Martin Luther, ". . . Answer to the Superchristian, Superspiritual, and Superlearned Book of Goat Emser of Leipzig," *Works of Martin Luther,* Vol. III (Philadelphia, PA: Muhlenberg Press, 1930), p. 350.

10. Thomas W. Gillespie, "Biblical Authority and Interpretation," in Donald K. McKim, *A Guide to Contemporary Hermeneutics: Major Trends in Biblical Interpretation* (Grand Rapids, MI: Wm. B. Eerdmans Publishing Co., 1986), pp. 218-19.

11. Richard L. Eslinger states in *Pitfalls in Preaching* (Grand Rapids, MI: William B. Eerdmans Publishing Company, 1996), "The earlier orthodoxy of interpretation sought to identify a text's themes or treated the text as a window to an ancient world. Now biblical interpreters examine a text for its literary form, for its movement and structure. The former 'static' model of seeking main ideas from a text has given way to a 'fluid' interest in a text's movement and intentionality (p. 27)." The alternative he advocates "is to see a scriptural text as a dynamic form of language, inviting the reader/hearer along in its journey through a succession of 'locations,' or 'scenes'. . . . The outline of the old topical preaching is giving way to the notion of homiletic plot" (pp. 29-30). Lucy Rose similarly is scornful of sermon themes in her *Sharing the Word*, p. 31 and p. 137 n. 13. She speaks instead of the sermon "wager" (p. 101) and of the listeners "discovering their own meanings (p. 113), but she never explains in practical terms how this will be or can be different from a theme sentence or organizing principle.

12. Charles L. Campbell, *Preaching Jesus*, p. 173.

13. Jack Rogers, *Presbyterian Creeds: a Guide to the Book of Confessions* (Philadelphia, PA: Westminster Press, 1985), p. 27.

14. Gerhard Ebeling, *Word and Faith*, trans. James W. Leitch (Philadelphia, PA: Fortress Press, 1963), p. 424.

15. O. C. Jones, Jr., "The Preacher's Dilemma," in J. Alfred Smith, Sr., ed., *Outstanding Black Sermons* (Valley Forge, PA: Judson Press, 1976), p. 47.

16. This chart is composed using examples from the table of contents in Shirley C. Guthrie, *Christian Doctrine,* rev. ed. (Louisville, KY: Westminster/John Knox Press, 1994), pp. v-viii.

17. Duane Litfin, "Riding The Wind of God," in Haddon W. Robinson, ed., *Biblical Sermons: How Twelve Preachers Apply the Principles of Haddon W. Robinson* (Grand Rapids, MI: Baker Book House, 1989), p. 99.

18. O. C. Jones, Jr., "The Preacher's Dilemma," p. 44.

19. This kind of linear linking is a form of what is called metonymy, a linear chain of thought that establishes repetition, essential movement, sequence, development, and direction in a sermon. For a detailed discussion of metonymy and its relevance to theology and preaching see my *The Practice of Preaching,* pp. 220-37.

Chapter Three: Introducing the Sermon

1. James O. Rose in an interview in Haddon W. Robinson, ed., *Biblical Sermons: How Twelve Preachers Apply the Principles of Haddon W. Robinson* (Grand Rapids, MI: Baker Book House, 1989), p. 67.

2. Barbara Lundblad, "Patch This Work," in *The Past Speaks to the Future: 50 Years of the Protestant Hour,* Nashville, TN: Abingdon Press, 1995, p. 168.

3. Haddon W. Robinson, "A Case in Temptation," in Haddon W. Robinson, ed., *Biblical Sermons,* pp. 15-16.

4. Robert S. McCracken, "It's the Human Touch That Counts," in Paul H. Sherry, ed., *The Riverside Preachers* (New York, NY: The Pilgrim Press, 1978), p. 68.

5. Robert P. Waznak, *Like Fresh Bread: Sunday Homilies in the Parish* (New York, NY/Mahweh, NJ: Paulist Press, 1993), p. 63.

6. Susanne Vanderlugt, "Epiphany 6, February 14, 1993" in *Seasons of Preaching: 160 Best Sermons From the Preaching Resource Word and Witness,* John Michael Rottman and Paul Scott Wilson, eds. (New Berlin, WI: Liturgical Publications, Inc., 1996), pp. 78-79.

7. Barth, "Jesus is Victor," in *A Chorus of Witnesses: Model Sermons for Today's Preacher,* Thomas G. Long and Cornelius Plantinga, Jr., eds. (Grand Rapids, MI: William B. Eerdmans Publishing Company, 1994), p. 74.

8. L. Brown, "The Storms are Raging," in Darryl M. Trimiew, in *Out of Mighty Waters: Sermons by African-American Disciples* (St. Louis Missouri: Chalice Press, 1994), p. 17.

9. Carlyle Fielding Stewart III, "Hostage Crisis," in his *Joy Songs, Trumpet Blasts, and Hallelujah Shouts* (Lima, OH: CSS Publishing Company, Inc., 1997), p. 49.

10. "On Catching the Wrong Bus," in Harry Emerson Fosdick, *Riverside Sermons* (New York, NY: Harper and Brothers, 1958), p. 38.

11. See *The Toronto Star,* Thursday, January 30, 1997, A3.

12. See *The New York Times,* Monday, Feb. 17, 1997, A 14.

13. O. Jackson, "Robbery Without a Weapon," in Darryl M. Trimiew, in *Out of Mighty Waters),* p. 107-8.

14. David Buttrick, *Homiletic: Moves and Structures* (Philadelphia, PA: Fortress Press, 1987), pp. 95-96.

15. Ibid., pp. 94.

16. Ibid., pp. 92-93.

Chapter Four: Trouble in the Bible

1. Bryan Chapell, *Christ-Centered Preaching: Redeeming the Expository Sermon* (Grand Rapids, MI: Baker Books, 1994), p. 42.

2. Ibid., p. 47.

3. Ibid., p. 43.

4. Jarislav Pelikan, *Jesus Through the Centuries: His Place in the History of Culture* (New York, NY: Harper & Row Publishers, 1985), p. 12. A detailed study of ancient Jewish preaching may be found in Ronald E. Osborne, *God's Folly: The Rise of Christian Preaching, Vol. 1 of Preaching and Preachers in Christian History* (St. Louis, MO: Chalice Books, 1998).

5. T.H.L. Parker, *Calvin's Preaching* (Louisville, KY: Westminster John Knox Press, 1992), p. 79 and p. 89.

6. Philip Melanchthon is one of the founders of this approach for the Reformation. In his lectures of 1551, he advocated reading Scripture through various doctrines or commonplaces *(loci communes)*. See Timothy J. Wengert, "Philip Melanchthon," in William H. Willimon and Richard Lischer, eds., *Concise Encyclopedia of Preaching* (Louisville, KY: Westminster John Knox Press, 1995), p. 329. Jean Claude later had a similar approach. See Ann I. Hoch, "Jean Claude," in William H. Willimon and Richard Lischer, eds., *Concise Encyclopedia of Preaching,* p. 80.

7. George Herbert, *The Temple and the Country Parson* (Boston: James B. Dow, 1842 [1652]), p. 299.

8. Ibid., p. 300.

9. Frederick Buechner, *Telling the Truth: The Gospel as Tragedy, Comedy and Fairy Tale* (San Francisco, CA: Harper & Row Publishers, 1977).

10. Eugene L. Lowry, *The Sermon: Dancing the Edge of Mystery* (Nashville, TN: Abingdon Press, 1997), pp. 74-85.

11. Richard Lischer, *A Theology of Preaching* (Nashville, TN: Abingdon Press, 1981), pp. 46-65. See more recently Gerhard O. Forde, *Theology is for Proclamation* (Minneapolis, MN: Fortress Press, 1990), esp. pp. 147-64.

12. Chapell, *Christ-Centered Preaching,* pp. 263-310.

13. Buechner, *Telling the Truth,* p. 7.

14. David Buttrick, *Homiletic: Moves and Structures* (Philadelphia, PA: Fortress Press, 1987), pp. 59-68.

15. Catherine Fouré, ed., *The Holy Land,* Knopf Guides, translated by Wendy Allatson and Helen Grubin (New York, NY: Random House, 1995).

Chapter Five: Filming Trouble in the Bible

1. Samuel D. Proctor, "The Recovery of Human Compassion," in Samuel D. Proctor and William D. Watley, *Sermons From the Black Pulpit* (Valley Forge, PA: Judson Press), pp. 11-12.

2. Ralph J. Wallace, "Promises, Promises, Promises!," in *The Past Speaks to the Future: 50 Years of The Protestant Hour* (Nashville, TN: Abingdon Press, 1995), p. 140-41.

3. Barbara Brown Taylor, "Gospel Medicine," in *Gospel Medicine* (Boston, MA: Cowley Publications, 1995), p. 4.

4. James O. Rose, "The Big Valley," in Haddon W. Robinson, ed., *Biblical Sermons: How Twelve Preachers Apply the Principles of Haddon W. Robinson* (Grand Rapids, MI: Baker Book House, 1989), pp. 54-55.

5. Duane A. Burnette, "Rock or Lock," in *The Concordia Pulpit* for 1968 (St. Louis, MO: Concordia Publishing House, 1967), p. 200.

6. Raymond Bailey, "Do You Want to be Healed?," in James W. Cox, ed., *Best Sermons 3* (San Francisco: Harper & Row, 1990), p. 3.

7. Barbara Brown Taylor, "Betrothed by God," in *Gospel Medicine,* p. 51.

8. Laurie Haller, "Jesus Christ—Do You Accept?," in James W. Cox, ed., *Best Sermons 3* (San Francisco, CA: Harper & Row, 1990), p. 45.

9. Haddon W. Robinson, "A Case in Temptation," in Haddon W. Robinson, ed., *Biblical Sermons,* pp. 17-18.

10. Nancy Hastings Sehested, "Let Pharaoh Go," in David Albert Farmer and Edwina Hunter, *And Blessed is She: Sermons by Women* (San Francisco, CA: Harper & Row, Publishers, 1990), pp. 213-14.

11. B. Copenhaver, "How to Throw a Party," in Gary W. Klingsporn, ed., *The Library of Distinctive Sermons,* vol. 2 (Sisters, OR: Questar Publishers, 1996), pp. 46-47.

12. Martin B. Copenhaver, "Building Barns, Postponing Life," in James W. Cox, ed., *Best Sermons 3,* pp. 256-57.

13. Gerd Theissen, Professor of New Testament in the University of Heidelberg, is the most outspoken advocate of rewriting the biblical text for preaching in his *The Sign Language of Faith,* trans. John Bowden, (London, UK: SCM Press Ltd., 1995).

14. Helmut Thielicke, "The Parable of the Rich Man and Lazarus," in his *The Waiting Father: Sermons on the Parables of Jesus,* trans. John W. Doberstein (New York, NY: Harper and Brothers, 1957), pp. 44-46.

15. Suzan D. Johnson, "God's Woman," in Ella Pearson Mitchell, ed., *Those Preachin' Women: Sermons by Black Women Preachers* (Valley Forge, PA: Judson Press, 1985), pp. 120-21.

16. Ernest T. Campbell, "The Case for Reparations," in Paul H. Sperry, ed., *The Riverside Preachers* (New York, NY: The Pilgrim Press), 1978, pp. 118-19.

Chapter Six: Trouble in the World

1. John Calvin, *Institutes of the Christian Religion,* trans. John Allen (Philadelphia, PA: Presbyterian Board of Christian Education, n.d. [1813]), Vol. 1, Bk. 34, p. 638.

2. Robert G. Duffett, *A Relevant Word: Communicating the Gospel* to Seekers (Valley Forge, PA: Judson Press, 1995), p. 80.

3. Herman G. Stuempfle, *Preaching Law and Gospel* (Philadelphia, PA: Fortress Press, 1978), pp. 26-31.

4. James A. Sanders, *God Has a Story Too* (Philadelphia, PA: Fortress Press, 1979), p. 15. He refers to transcendent social trouble when he speaks of a "hermeneutic of prophetic critique" (p. 15). He advocates "applying the text sociologically and politically to a situation today in which we are involved, just as the prophets in like manner applied the traditions they inherited to ancient Israel and ancient Judah, and as Jesus in large measure did in his day" (p. 18). This is one of two theological principles that Sanders says the preacher uses; the other is constitutive hermeneutics, which is Christocentric and concentrates on God as the Redeemer who is faithful to God's promises to God's chosen people. See my chapter eight, below.

5. Eugene H. Peterson, *A Long Obedience in the Same Direction: Discipleship in an Instant Society* (Downer's Grove, IL: InterVarsity Press, 1980), pp. 79-80.

6. Herman G. Stuempfle, *Preaching Law and Gospel* (Philadelphia, PA: Fortress Press, 1978), pp. 26-31.

7. Much of the material in this section on global awareness was originally published as a portion of my, "Preaching at the Beginning of a New Millennium: Learning from Our Predecessors," *Journal For Preachers,* 20:4 (Pentecost 1997), pp. 3-8, esp. pp. 6-8.

8. Gustavo Gutierrez, *Bartholemé de Las Casas* (Maryknoll, NY: Orbis Books, 1996).

9. Mary M. McGlone, "The King's Conscience," *Catholic World* (November–December 1994), p. 284.

10. See, for instance, Theodore W. Jennings, *Good News for the Poor: John Wesley's Evangelical Economics* (Nashville, TN: Abingdon Press, 1990).

11. David Buttrick, *A Captive Voice: The Liberation of Preaching* (Louisville, KY: Westminster John Knox Press, 1994), p. 8; and his, "On Doing Homiletics Today," in Richard L. Eslinger, ed., *Intersections: Post-Critical Studies in Preaching* (Grand Rapids, MI: Wm. B. Eerdmans Publishing Co., 1994), p. 94.

12. See John Killinger, *Preaching to a Church in Crisis: A Homiletic for the Last Days of the Mainline Church* (Lima, Ohio: CSS Publishing Co., 1995), pp. 19-23. See also Millard J. Erickson and James L. Heflin, *New Wine in Old Wineskins: Doctrinal Preaching in a Changing World* (Grand Rapids, MI: Baker Books, 1997), p. 47.

13. Only 26 percent of "conservative Protestant Christians" think that "ministers should stick to religion and not concern themselves with social, economic and political issues." This is down from 35 percent in 1975. By contrast, other Protestants and Roman Catholics range between 43 percent and 58 percent, considerably up from 1975. Reginald Bibby, "Project Can 95," reported in *The Toronto Star,* Sunday, December 8, 1996, A4.

14. Robin W. Lovin, "Justice," in Donald W. Musser & Joseph L. Price, eds., *A New Handbook of Christian Theology* (Nashville, TN: Abingdon Press, 1992), p. 267.

Chapter Seven: Filming Trouble in the World

1. Chevis F. Horne, "He is Going Before You," in James W. Cox, ed., *Best Sermons 4* (San Francisco, CA: Harper Collins, 1991), p. 94.

2. Ronald D. Sisk, "The Big One and the Not-So-Big One," in James W. Cox, ed., *Best Sermons 4,* p. 102.

3. Jeffrey L. Ruff, "Dirty Work," in James W. Cox, ed., *Best Sermons 4,* pp. 79-80.

4. Edmund Steimle, "Gifts and the Giver," in his *God the Stranger: Reflections About Resurrection* (Philadelphia, PA: Fortress Press, 1979), p. 65.

5. Barbara Brown Taylor, "The Headwaiter," in *The Past Speaks to the Future: 50 Years of The Protestant Hour* (Nashville, TN: Abingdon Press, 1995), pp. 155-56.

6. Elizabeth Achtemeier, "The Things That Make for Peace," in James W. Cox, ed., *Best Sermons 4,* pp. 135-56.

7. Eric C. Kutzli, "The Fourteenth Sunday after Pentecost, September 10, 1995," in John Michael Rottman and Paul Scott Wilson, eds., *Seasons of Preaching: 160 Best Sermons from the Preaching Resource Word & Witness* (New Berlin, WI: Liturgical Publications Inc., 1996), pp. 237-38.

8. Joanna Adams, "Near Your House," in James W. Cox, ed., *Best Sermons 2* (San Francisco, CA: Harper & Row, Publishers, 1988), pp. 343-44.

9. Richard Groves, "Is Sex Ever Safe?," in James W. Cox, ed., *Best Sermons 4,* p. 166.

10. Billy Sunday, "The Devil's Boomerangs (Hot Cakes off the Griddle)," in Clyde E. Fant and William M. Pinson, eds., *Twenty Centuries of Great Preaching,* vol. 7 (Waco, TX: Word Books, 1971), p. 254.

11. James Ayers, "Caught in the Act," in James W. Cox, ed., *Best Sermons 4,* pp. 156-57.

12. John N. Jonsson, "God Depicted in Scars and Beauty," in James W. Cox, ed., *Best Sermons 6* (San Francisco, CA: Harper Collins, 1993), p. 228, p. 229, and p. 230.

13. Sanford Ragins, "A Sermon at the End of the Summer University Institut Kirch un Judentum Berlin," in James W. Cox, ed., *Best Sermons 6*, p. 158.

14. Jonathan Massey, "God Is Concerned for the Oxen, Paul!," in James W. Cox, ed., *Best Sermons 5* (San Francisco, CA: Harper Collins, 1992), pp. 187-88.

15. Eugene H. Peterson, "Our Mouth Was Filled With Laughter," in his *A Long Obedience in the Same Direction: Discipleship in an Instant Society* (Downer's Grove, IL: InterVarsity Press, 1980), pp. 92-93.

16. Samuel D. Proctor, "The Recovery of Human Compassion," in Samuel D. Proctor and William D. Watley, *Sermons from the Black Pulpit* (Valley Forge, PA: Judson Press, 1984), pp. 14-15.

17. Brian L. Harbour, "Found Faithful: A Daily Commitment," in James W. Cox, ed., *Best Sermons 3* (San Francisco, CA: Harper & Row, 1990), pp. 96-97.

18. Sharon E. Williams, "Studying War Some More," in Ella Pearson Mitchell, ed., *Those Preachin' Women: Sermons by Black Women Preachers* (Valley Forge, PA: Judson Press, 1985), p. 78.

19. Gary A. Wilburn, "Living With AIDS," in James W. Cox, ed., *Best Sermons 5*, p. 230.

20. John Killinger, "The 'Aye' of the Storm," in Gary W. Klingsporn, ed., *The Library of Distinctive Sermons*, vol. 2, (Sisters, OR: Questar Publishers, 1996), p. 294.

21. J. Woodrow Hearn, "Help for Today and Every Day," in *The Past Speaks to the Future: 50 Years of The Protestant Hour*, p. 50.

22. Penelope Duckworth, James W. Cox, ed., *Best Sermons 3*, p. 125.

23. Gary W. Downing, "Mommy, Why Am I Different?" in Gary W. Klingsporn, ed., *The Library of Distinctive Sermons*, vol. 2, pp. 188-89.

24. Gardner C. Taylor, "His Own Clothes," in Milton E. Owens, Jr. Ed., *Outstanding Black Sermons*, vol. 3 (Valley Forge, PA: Judson Press, 1991 [1982]) p. 66.

Chapter 8: God's Action in the Bible

1. The most common are the troublesome terms law and gospel. There may be no escaping the difficulty of these terms, notably used by both Luther and Wesley for preaching, and their historical association with Old and New Testaments, respectively. The best current discussion of matters relating to them is Gerhard O. Forde, *Theology is for Proclamation* (Minneapolis, MN: Fortress Press, 1990).

2. Frederick Buechner, *Telling the Truth: The Gospel as Tragedy, Comedy and Fairy Tale* (San Francisco, CA: Harper & Row, 1977), pp. 7-8.

3. Gary W. Klingsporn, ed., *The Library of Distinctive Sermons* (Sisters, OR: Questar Publishers, 1996).

4. James W. Cox, ed., *Best Sermons 7* (San Francisco, CA: HarperCollins Publishers, 1994).

5. Eugene L. Lowry advocates a "sudden shift" to "resolution born of grace" at a point five-sixths into the sermon or "on the last line." See his *The Sermon: Dancing the Edge of Mystery* (Nashville, TN: Abingdon Press, 1997), p. 78. In taking this position, apparently he gives priority to dramatic surprise instead of to the theological urgency of listeners meeting God and discerning God in the world around them.

6. Philip Yancey, *What's So Amazing About Grace?* (Grand Rapids, MI: Zondervan Publishing House, 1997), pp. 14-15.

7. James A. Sanders, *God Has a Story Too* (Philadelphia, PA: Fortress Press, 1979), pp. 15-17. Sanders identifies this emphasis on grace as "constitutive hermeneutics" in contrast to the "prophetic hermeneutic" that disrupts (p. 18). He claims that by

holding these two hermeneutical approaches in tension we accomplish the tension that is in fact in the Bible (p. 16). For some reason when he preaches he almost always employs only prophetic hermeneutics (p. 18): "Very seldom am I invited to preach in situations where constitutive or supportive hermeneutics, stressing God's grace or absolute committment, would be pertinent (p. 19)."

8. David Buttrick, *Homiletic: Moves and Structures* (Philadelphia, PA: Fortress Press, 1987), p. 26.

9. A.E. Garvie, *A Guide to Preachers* (London: Hodder & Stoughton, 1906), p. 242.

10. Jeremiah A. Wright, Jr., "When God is Silent," in Jini Kilgore Ross, ed., *What Makes You Strong: Sermons of Joy and Strength from Jeremiah A. Wright, Jr.* (Valley Forge, PA: Judson Press, 1993), pp. 111-26.

11. H. Grady Davis, *Design for Preaching* (Philadelphia, PA: Fortress Press, 1958), pp. 15-16.

Chapter Nine: Filming Grace in the Bible

1. Hank Langknecht, an unpublished sermon first preached at Runnymede United Church, Toronto, on February 1, 1998.

2. Shirley Prince, "You Still Have Time," in Daryll M. Trimiew, ed., *Out of Mighty Waters: Sermons by African-American Disciples* (St. Louis, MO: Chalice Press, 1994), pp. 181-82.

3. David Buttrick, *Homiletic: Moves and Structures* (Philadelphia, PA: Fortress Press, 1987), pp. 363-404.

4. Ibid., pp. 333-63.

5. John M. Rottman, "Blind Bartimaeus," a sermon preached at Grace Christian Reformed Church in Scarborough, ON, on Sunday, October 25, 1998.

6. Eugene L. Lowry, "The Drink," in James W. Cox, ed., *Best Sermons 3* (San Francisco, CA: Harper and Row, Publishers), pp. 241-43.

7. Charles B. Bugg, "What Keeps Us Going?," in James W. Cox, ed., *Best Sermons 7* (San Francisco, CA: HarperCollins Publishers, 1994), pp. 238-39.

8. William D. Watley, "Go On," in Samuel D. Proctor and William D. Watley, *Sermons from the Black Pulpit* (Valley Forge, PA: Judson Press, 1984), p. 48.

9. John Richard Foulkes, Sr., "From Paternalism to Partnership," in Darryl M. Trimiew, ed., *Out Of Mighty Waters: Sermons by African-American Disciples* (St. Louis, MO: Chalice Press, 1994), pp. 161-62.

10. Edmund Steimle, "Asleep or Awake?" in his *God the Stranger: Reflections About Resurrection* (Philadelphia, PA: Fortress Press, 1979), pp. 32-33.

11. Austin Farrer, "Holy Angels," in Thomas G. Long and Cornelius Plantinga, *A Chorus of Witnesses: Model Sermons for Today's Preacher* (Grand Rapids, MI: Wm. B. Eerdmans Publishing Co., 1994), pp. 275-76.

12. Barbara Jurgensen, "The Lesson of History," in *Augsburg Sermons: Old Testament Lessons,* Series C (Minneapolis, MI: Augsburg Publishing House, 1979), pp. 240-41.

13. Paul Yung, "Who is My Neighbor?," in Ignacio Casteura, ed., *Dreams on Fire, Embers of Hope: From the Pulpits of Los Angeles After the Riots* (St. Louis, MO: Chalice Press, 1992), pp. 20-21.

14. Mark Trotter, "The Sure Sign of Status," in James W. Cox, ed., *Best Sermons 1* (San Francisco, CA: Harper and Row Publishers, 1988), p. 221.

15. Haddon W. Robinson, "A Case in Temptation," in Haddon W. Robinson, ed., *Biblical Sermons: How Twelve Preachers Apply the Principles of Haddon W. Robinson* (Grand Rapids, MI: Baker Book House, 1989), p. 22.

16. Hazel Addy, "The Woman With Bleeding," in Heather Walton and Susan

Durber, eds., *Silence in Heaven: A Book of Women's Preaching* (London, UK: SCM Press Ltd, 1994), p. 103.

17. Barbara Brown Taylor, "Beginning at the End," in her *Seeds of Heaven* (Cincinnati, OH: Forward Movement Publications, 1990), pp. 79-80. Republished in Thomas G. Long and Cornelius Plantinga, eds., *A Chorus of Witnesses: Model Sermons for Today's Preacher* (Grand Rapids, MI: Wm. B. Eerdmans Publishing Co., 1994), pp. 19-20.

18. Fred B. Craddock, "Have You Ever Heard John Preach?" in Thomas G. Long and Cornelius Plantinga, eds., *A Chorus of Witnesses*, p. 39.

19. Pavel Filipi, in James W. Cox, ed., *Best Sermons 4* (San Francisco, CA: Harper Collins, 1991), pp. 198-99.

20. Mary Harris Todd, "The Pleading Widow," in James W. Cox, ed., *Best Sermons 7* (San Francisco, CA: HarperCollins Publishers, 1994), pp. 261-62.

21. Jeremiah A. Wright, Jr., "What Makes You So Strong?" in Jini Kilgore Ross, ed., *What Makes You Strong: Sermons of Joy and Strength from Jeremiah A. Wright, Jr.* (Valley Forge, PA: Judson Press, 1993), p. 158.

Chapter Ten: God's Action in the World

1. Daniel L. Migliore, *Faith Seeking Understanding* (Grand Rapids, MI: William B. Eerdmans Publishing Company, 1991), p. 70.

2. Stephen Farris, "Preaching Law as Gospel: Some Reflections on and from Psalm 119," in Papers of the Annual Meeting of the Academy of Homiletics (Toronto, 1998), p. 34.

3. J. R. R. Tolkien, "On Fairy Stories," in C. S. Lewis, ed., *Essays Presented to Charles Williams* (Grand Rapids, MI: William B. Eerdmans Publishing Company, 1966), p. 81-84.

Chapter Eleven: Filming Grace in the World

1. John Claypool, "Next Time," in Gary W. Klingsporn, ed., *The Library of Distinctive Sermons*, vol. 2 (Sisters, OR: Questar Publishers, 1996), pp. 92-93.

2. Joanna Adams, "The Only Question," in Thomas G. Long and Cornelius Plantinga, Jr., *A Chorus of Witnesses: Model Sermons for Today's Preacher* (Grand Rapids, MI: William B. Eerdmans Publishing Company, 1994), pp. 269-70.

3. John Rottman, "Mark 13:32-37," in John Michael Rottman and Paul Scott Wilson, eds., *Seasons of Preaching: 160 Best Sermons from the Preaching Resource Word & Witness* (New Berlin, WI: Liturgical Publications Inc., 1996), pp. 24-25.

4. Karen L. Bloomquist, "Christ Present In Us," in *Augsburg Sermons: Epistles,* Series C (Minneapolis, MN: Augsburg Publishing House, 1976), pp. 210-11.

5. John Claypool, "Next Time," in Gary W. Klingsporn, ed., *The Library of Distinctive Sermons*, vol. 2 , p. 94.

6. Frederick Buechner, *Telling the Truth: the Gospel as Tragedy, Comedy, and Fairy Tale* (San Francisco, CA: Harper and Row Publishers, 1977), esp. p. 7 and pp. 49-72. His use of tragedy corresponds to Pages One and Two, and comedy and fairy tale taken together correspond to each of Pages Three and Four.

7. R. Wayne Stacy, "A Labor Not in Vain," in Gary W. Klingsporn, ed., *The Library of Distinctive Sermons*, vol. 2, pp. 30-31.

8. Ester Tse, "Celebrating Christ's Mission," in James W. Cox, ed., *Best Sermons 3* (San Francisco, CA: Harper & Row, 1990), p. 39.

9. Toinette M. Eugene, "Liberating Love," in David Albert Farmer and Edwina

Hunter, eds., *And Blessed is She: Sermons by Women* (San Francisco, CA: Harper & Row, 1990), p. 166.

10. Jurgen Moltmann, "The Pharisee and the Tax Collector," in Thomas G. Long and Cornelius Plantinga, eds., *A Chorus of Witnesses,* pp. 31-32.

11. Edmund Steimle, "The Perplexing Problem of Suffering and God's Power," in his *God the Stranger: Reflections About Resurrection* (Philadelphia, PA: Fortress Press, 1979), p. 22.

12. Elizabeth Achtemeier, "What's Left Behind," in David Albert Farmer and Edwina Hunter, eds., *And Blessed is She: Sermons by Women* (San Francisco, CA: Harper & Row, 1990), pp. 104-5.

13. John Killinger, "Finding Spiritual Meaning in a Spiritless World," in Gary W. Klingsporn, ed., *The Library of Distinctive Sermons,* vol. 1 (Sisters, OR: Questar Publishers, 1996), p. 111.

14. Charles H. Boyer, "Reaching Into the Future," in James W. Cox, ed., *Best Sermons 1* (San Francisco, CA: Harper & Row, 1988), p. 233.

15. Roger Lovette, "Midwives of Hope," in James W. Cox, ed., *Best Sermons 3,* pp. 12-13.

16. Raymond Bailey, "Do You Want to be Healed?," in James W. Cox, ed., *Best Sermons 3,* p. 8.

17. Jeremiah A. Wright, Jr., "When God is Silent," in Jini Kilgore Ross, ed., *What Makes You So Strong?: Sermons of Joy and Strength from Jeremiah A. Wright, Jr.* (Valley Forge, PA: Judson Press, 1993), pp. 125-26.

18. Gary W. Downing, "Mommy, Why Am I Different?," in Gary W. Klingsporn, ed., *The Library of Distinctive Sermons,* vol. 2, p. 189.

19. Katie G. Cannon, "On Remembering Who We Are," in Ella Pearson Mitchell, ed., *Those Preachin' Women: Sermons by Black Women Preachers* (Valley Forge, PA: Judson Press, 1985), p. 50.

20. Martin B. Copenhaver, "How to Throw a Party," in Gary W. Klingsporn, ed., *The Library of Distinctive Sermons,* vol. 2, pp. 48-49.

21. David W. Crocker, "King on the Mountain," in James W. Cox, ed., *Best Sermons 3* (San Francisco, CA: Harper & Row, 1990), p. 64.

22. Frederick Buechner, "A Sprig of Hope," in Thomas G. Long and Cornelius Plantinga, Jr., *A Chorus of Witnesses: Model Sermons for Today's Preacher,* pp. 232-33.

23. Richard O. Hoyer, "If Only," in *The Concordia Pulpit for 1968* (St. Louis, MO: Concordia Publishing House, 1967), p. 199.

24. Harold F. Dicke, "Depart in Peace," in *The Concordia Pulpit for 1968,* p. 28.

25. Carlyle Fielding Stewart III, "Paradoxes of the Christian Faith," in his, *Joy Songs, Trumpet Blasts, and Hallelujah Shouts: Sermons in the African-American Tradition* (Lima, OH: CSS Publishing Company, Inc., 1997), pp. 108-9.

Chapter Thirteen: Reshuffling and Varying the Four Pages

1. Joseph M. Stowell, "Who Cares?," in Haddon W. Robinson, *Biblical Sermons: How Twelve Preachers Apply the Principles of Biblical Preaching* (Grand Rapids, MI: Baker Book House, 1989), p. 155.

2. Hank Langknecht, an unpublished sermon preached at Runnymede United Church, Toronto, on May 24, 1998.

INDEX OF NAMES

INDEX OF BIBLE PASSAGES